Mindful Ministry

Mindful Ministry

Creative, Theological and
Practical Perspectives

Ross and Judith Thompson

scm press

Published in 2012 by SCM Press
Editorial office
Invicta House,
108-114 Golden Lane
London, EC1Y 0TG

SCM Press is an imprint of Hymns Ancient & Modern Ltd
(a registered charity)
13A Hellesdon Park Road
Norwich, NR6 5DR, UK

www.scmpress.co.uk

British Library Cataloguing in Publication data
A catalogue record for this book is available
from the British Library

978-0-334-04375-1
Kindle 978-0-334-04466-6

Originated by The Manila Typesetting Company
Printed and bound by
CPI Group, Croydon, Surrey

Contents

Acknowledgements

There are many people without whom this book could not have taken shape, not least Natalie Watson of SCM, who commissioned and encouraged it and remained patient when it took longer to write than we had expected. But most important of all are the people who have ministered to us as we ministered to them in seven different congregations (between us) in the course of 25 years in Bristol; as well as those in the lovely setting and community in which we now live.

To all of them, as well as to many ministers of different denominations whose ministry we have observed and admired, to former academic colleagues and students in Cardiff, and to colleagues in the British and Irish Association for Practical Theology (BIAPT) with whom we have thought about these things, we dedicate this book.

Finally, in offering our own reflections on ministry, we invite others to share their thoughts and any comments and feedback, at judith vthompson@aol.com or rosskathompson@aol.com

Ross and Judith Thompson

Introduction

A man found an eagle's egg and put it in the nest of a backyard hen. The eaglet hatched with the brood of chicks and grew up with them.

All his life the eagle did what the backyard chickens did, thinking he was a backyard chicken. He scratched the earth for worms and insects. He clucked and cackled. And he would thrash his wings and fly a few feet into the air like the chickens. After all, that is how a chicken is supposed to fly, isn't it?

Years passed and the eagle grew very old. One day he saw a magnificent bird far above him in the cloudless sky. It floated in graceful majesty among the powerful wind currents, with scarcely a beat of its strong golden wings.

The old eagle looked up in awe. 'Who's that?' he said to his neighbour.

'That's the eagle, the king of the birds,' said his neighbour. 'But don't give it another thought. You and I are different from him.'

So the eagle never gave it another thought. He died thinking he was a backyard chicken.

(de Mello 1982, pp. 120–1)

Anthony de Mello's deeply thought-provoking parable – which we hope chicken-lovers will forgive – can be interpreted in many ways. But for the purposes of this book let us say the golden eagle is Jesus Christ, who showed us what it is like to be a human being rather than consumer chickens compulsively pecking away at the goodies offered by our society on condition that we never aspire to be more than chickens. Ministry is essentially about waking ourselves and other people up to our true nature in Christ, and so rediscovering ministry itself: it is about ceasing to be consumer chickens and becoming instead spiritual golden eagles.

Mindfulness is primarily about waking up. Waking up to what you are doing – scratching around, perhaps, in that barnyard. Waking up to what you really are – a unique colour of the rainbow that is Christ. Waking up to the disparity and repenting, changing, undergoing *metanoia* or change of heart, doing things differently so that what you do expresses what you are and what you believe.

It follows that a contagious mindfulness is the essence of ministry. For quite a lot of its history, ministry has been closely linked with hierarchy. It has been about keeping the laity unaware of their true glory, unaware of their royal priesthood, content to be little barnyard chickens, if not miserable worms! But in this scenario the ministers and priests became no more than big barnyard chickens, higher up the pecking order. A widespread recognition of the truth behind Luther's 'priesthood of all believers' has, in recent years, helped to develop a style of ministry that is all about collaboration, working together. But there is still a danger that all this collaboration takes place in the barnyard, while the glory of our true nature in Christ sails in the heavens far above. There is also a danger that we are just levelling ministry out and dumbing it down: a matter of seeing our priest or minister as 'no better than us', rather than seeing ourselves as being as glorious as he or she, as the minister, the one who embodies the *charisma* – that word which seems to sparkle, and means 'gift' – of bearing Christ.

This book aims to affirm and encourage mindful ministry in this sense – ministry in which lay people and those ordained inter-illuminate and awaken the sparkle of Christ's *charismata* in one another. It does so by reflecting theologically on the different ministries to which people may be called, and which the ordained minister is called to weave together that they may reflect the glory of the rainbow which is Christ.

The chapters of this book consider mindfulness in relation to eight 'ministries', each of which relates to an area of spiritual gifting or charism, and focuses on an archetypically representative figure. Both in the presentation and in the content, we have aimed to achieve a lightness of touch which we hope is consistent with our aim of seeking to follow Christ and enabling others to follow him on the wind-currents of the Spirit.

The use of language and exemplification in this book frequently betrays its authors' roots in Anglican parish ministry, but it is intended to be of value for anyone involved or considering involvement in Christian ministry, formally or informally, parish, chaplaincy or 'fresh expression', stipendiary or not, lay or ordained, of any denomination. It is particularly hoped that it may prove refreshing and reinvigorating for those who have been in ministry for some years.

Exercises and questions to ponder are provided for those who may wish to use them to reflect on the issues raised either alone or with others: other readers will prefer a straightforward read.

The pattern of the chapters

The number of ways in which charism or ministry can happen in us or others is very varied, but we have found it helpful and reasonable to classify it in an eightfold pattern, though of course the pattern is not definitive. As noted below (pp. xiv–xv), the New Testament has several different lists of ministries, of different lengths. It is often the case that what this book treats in one chapter has distinct areas that could each have had its own chapter, or perhaps that what we cover in two could have been amalgamated into one. Inevitably and obviously, different areas and approaches to ministry shade off into one another, but to give this book structure, distinctions and divisions have to be made. One could argue about distinctions in the colours of the rainbow – for example that indigo should be included with blue to give just six colours of the rainbow rather than seven (something one of us has contended for since childhood!). How we divide the rainbow is arbitrary, but its variety of colours is not. Likewise how we divide the ministries is arbitrary, but awareness of the varied 'rainbow' of ministries is essential if ministry is to be mindful.

Each ministry can be linked also with biblical and theological resources for reflection, and certain kinds of skill that can be learnt, and particular ways of rooting it in mindful practice. It is such correspondences that we have discerned that determine the broad shape of each chapter.

The eight identified ministries, which together build up the body of Christ, are discussed in the chapters numbered as follows:

1 **The apostle:** Mindful Representing as the Christlike shape of ministry.
2 **The holy one:** Mindful Praying as the still centre of ministry.
3 **The pastor:** Mindful Serving as the hardworking body of ministry.
4 **The teacher:** Mindful Nurture as the wise soul of ministry.
5 **The leader:** Mindful Oversight as the overseeing mind of ministry.
6 **The go-between:** Mindful Collaboration, Conviviality and Communication as the interlinking and encouraging hands of ministry.
7 **The herald of Good News:** Mindful Evangelism as the swift, urgent feet of ministry.
8 **The liberator:** Mindful Subversion as the courageous heart of ministry.

The overall pattern of each chapter is intended to follow, roughly, the cycle of theological reflection (p. xix), moving from experience, through reflection in the light of tradition, scripture and other resources, to possible courses of action. The surface structure varies a little from chapter to chapter, but the deep structure is similar, and contains these elements:

1 **A profile** of an imaginary person in whom the ministry in question is exemplified and somewhat caricatured. The key characteristics of this ministry are also related, symbolically, to the characteristics of a particular creature. The profile and the symbol are intended to stimulate the imagination in relation to the ministry in question.
2 **A focusing exercise:** an imaginary situation which relates to real experiences of ministry, and invites reflection on how the particular ministry under consideration might engage mindfully with it.
3 **Models** taken from scripture, of people and situations which illuminate the exercise of this ministry. Scripture here is treated in an imaginative and multi-layererd way, using Ignatian-style exercises and traditional modes of spiritual exegesis.
4 **Theology** arising from inter-illumination between these models and the experience of ministry, uncovering the ground of that particular ministry in the life and mission of God.
5 A look at actual **practices** (including a number from the authors' experience – positive and negative) to see how this ministry might be exercised mindfully and skilfully.
6 **Questions** that invite further reflection.
7 **Further reading.**

Before exploring each of these aspects of ministry in more detail, and how it may be approached mindfully, the key concepts of ministry itself, and of mindfulness, as understood in this book, need to be considered.

Christian ministry: what and whose it is

Probably the most significant trend in thought about Christian ministry in the second half of the twentieth century was the move from the solitary professional minister to the collaborative ministry of all. We are heartily in sympathy with that move, and collaborative, every-member ministry is what we always sought when we were parish priests. It is certainly through ministries, not primarily through ministers, that the Holy Spirit brings the body of Christ to birth in the Church and beyond.

On the other hand, like many today, we realize that this approach, far from letting the individual priest or minister off the hook, or being a good way of dealing with clergy shortages, places unprecedented demands on the ordained minister as the one responsible for ensuring that peoples' ministries are enabled and active, and work together to live out the gospel we proclaim.

As Stephen Pickard puts it in his perceptive *Theological Foundations for Collaborative Ministry* (2009, p. 7):

Precisely because the collaborative venture involves a measure of self-forgetfulness and the desire to see others develop their gifts and potentialities, the way of collaboration is also a delicate and fragile mode of togetherness. Its strength is its weakness: trust can be betrayed, competition can appear in subtle ways, creativity can be denied or thwarted, an ethos can be weakened and disappear. The way of collaboration is the way of the cross through brokenness and glimpses of ministry raised together in Christ. The spirit of collaboration is nothing less than the Spirit of Love that connects and inclines every member of the body of Christ towards the other. This is the work of the perichoretic Spirit who gathers, directs and energizes the ministries that serve the gospel of God . . . A collaborative approach to ministry is, like the gospel itself, a treasure to be valued and cherished . . . deserving of an appropriate agonizing over, just like the gospel . . .

One of the most obvious and problematic areas for collaborative ministry is between clergy and laity. Tensions here have often been resolved by one dominating the other or one simply cutting itself adrift from the other . . . Yet it is curious how little attention has been paid to the question of the relation between the ministries, particularly the basic relation between ordained and the corporate ministry of the Church. It is no exaggeration to say that the lack of inner coherence among the ministries is a major cause of conflict and dissipation of energies within churches.

The sometimes painful vulnerability of collaborative ministry, and the risk of dissipation of energies, has led some to revert to a strong notion of leadership by the ordained. But leadership is a very ambivalent concept. It includes everything from what the conductor does with an orchestra to what Adolf Hitler did in Nazi Germany. Needless to say, one of these models has much more to say about an appropriate style for the Christian minister than the other! Though Chapter 5 emphasizes the important spiritual gifts of oversight and administration, the priority at this stage is to provide a theology of collaborative ministry that affirms *both* the ministry of the minister or priest, *and* the other ministries within the Church. This is exactly what Pickard does in his book, and the best way of explaining what our book understands by ministry is to outline some of his arguments and develop them a little further.

Pickard broadly welcomes collaborative ministry but voices the caution that it tends to leave us with a weakened understanding of ordained ministry in which ministers and priests begin to flounder, unclear as to their authority and role. He likens wholesale every-member ministry to a monophysite Christology in which divine and human are confused, blurred into a hybrid that is neither fully human nor fully divine. In the same way, ordained and lay ministries can blur into a collaboration where neither has a clear role. In reaction to this has come the recently rather fashionable, but as noted, rather ambivalent appeal to clergy 'leadership'.

The traditional Catholic view was Christo-centric. Christ appointed apostles who appointed bishops who gathered the Church around themselves. On this view ministers (bishops) make the Church. This stands opposed by Protestant and charismatic, Spirit-centred understandings whereby Christ is present through his Spirit in the gathered congregation, and it is this congregation that delegates specific tasks to its ministers. On this view, the Church makes its ministers. Ecumenical documents like the Anglican–Roman Catholic 'ARCIC' (1978) and the World Council of Churches' *Baptism, Eucharist and Ministry* (1982), have tended to try to combine these models, but in a rather awkward way, such that ordained ministry and the priesthood of all believers run on what Pickard describes as 'parallel tracks', distinct channels of the Holy Spirit that do not meet.

There is, however, another possibility, based on the kind of Trinitarian model Robin Greenwood has pioneered (1994). Like chicken and egg, lay and ordained ministries may be interdependent and emerge from one another within a Church in which the Trinity is operative. To help understand how, Pickard interestingly resorts to the scientific concept of emergence. Some scientists argue that life, and we ourselves, have emerged by evolution from the basic elements, not by some explicit controlling mechanism but by a natural process that nevertheless manages to generate higher-order realities like life and consciousness that cannot be reduced to the basic elements. So the body of Christ, animated by the Spirit, generates ministers and ministries without the need for some overall control mechanism.

In terms of Christology this would suggest that Christ was neither God and man running on 'parallel tracks', nor a fusion into a hybrid God–man, but a person comprised of divine and human in complete interrelation. As the Dutch theologian Edward Schillebeeckx pithily put it, 'Christ is God in a human way, and humankind in a divine way' (1963, p. 14). In the Church, lay and ordained ministries are neither on parallel tracks nor fused, but interdependent, so that as John Robinson put it, one 'expands automatically with the expansion of the other' (1963, p. 17, discussed by Pickard on p. 97). The laity find their ministry through the ordained priest and vice versa, so that as well as the 'priesthood of the laity' we need to insist on the 'laity of the priesthood' (Robinson, p. 18).

Crucial here is the striking notion that Pickard (pp. 144–7) draws from St Paul, who states not only that we are all members of the body of Christ, but that we are 'individually members one of another' (Romans 12.5). So it is not only the case that our ministries are for the building up of the body; more radically, they inhere in and belong to one another. They are not in any sense possessions of the minister herself, but rather, ministries that 'bring each other to be' (p. 148). Indeed, ministry cannot ever avoid being a two-way collaboration – between teacher and taught, between healer and healed, and so forth – in which the 'receiver' also gives, and the 'giver' also receives.

We might then say the ministries of the lay people find unity by inhering in a single human being, the ordained minister. And the ministry of the ordained finds a liberating diversity through inhering in the many layfolk. In other words, the ordained minister is not only a leader holding the many ministries together. Primarily it is by her being one person in whom all the various ministries are reflected – for whom the thwarting of someone's ministry is a matter of personal pain, and the enabling of one a personal joy – that the ministries of the Church may succeed in working together to build up the Church. And conversely it is the diversity of the multi-membered Church that enables the ordained minister to be more diverse and rich than she could be alone. (We would certainly attest that that is how it has been for us.)

New Testament roots: from ministries to ministers

This interesting new vista on the theological understanding of ministry needs developing further in terms of its practical implications, and the working out of this model. It is our hope that this book may serve to do just that. But it seems important, first of all, to look at those crucial passages in which the Pauline epistles describe the *charismata* or gifts, which are also called *pneumatika* (spiritual things), *diakonia* (acts of service or ministries) and *energēmata* (inward workings, or our term 'energy').

Table 1 lists, on the left, the charisms as described in the key passages from 1 Corinthians (one of Paul's earliest letters), Romans (a later epistle), and Ephesians (later still, and believed by many to be by another writer).

- **1 Corinthians 12** describes the spiritual gifts (using all the Greek terms just mentioned) as not being distributed randomly but to different people in the same way that functions are distributed to different parts of a human body. The gifts are therefore distributed freely but not randomly. In the latter part of the passage, Paul speaks of something more hierarchical ('first apostles, second prophets . . . ' and so forth). Moreover, he begins by speaking of ministers (apostles, prophets, teachers . . .) rather than ministries, though later he has slipped back into ministries (deeds of power, gifts of healing . . .). Finally, he makes it clear that the whole point of these *charismata* is to build up the one body of Christ, in which all have equal honour.
- **Romans 12** is describing the new life in the body of Christ, returning to the same analogy of the members of the one body, but saying further, as just noted, that we are members not just of the body but of one another. Minister and ministry language is mixed, but to each minister or ministry there corresponds a quality or activity: to prophecy, there corresponds faith, and so forth.
- **Ephesians 4** relates ministry to the ascended Christ. It is now, moreover, not ministries that are given but a hierarchy of ministers. It is not prophecy that is given to the Church, for example, but individual prophets. Ministry is *diakonia*, not *charisma*, and the gifts are *dōmata* – an ordinary word for a present, without the spiritual resonances of *charismata* and its association with *charis*, grace, and *chara*, joy. And the list is shorter – only five. We seem to be in a transition from the old charismatic model to the threefold ministry that would, with the Pastoral Epistles, become dominant in the Church.

The fifth column of the table sets the ministries described in the eight chapters of this book in relation to these New Testament lists of charisms. This is impossible to do definitively, of course, since those lists are very varied themselves. The various specific links suggested, which will be firmed up in the chapters that follow, are therefore provisional and far from unquestionable. The important point is that we believe that the primordial reality for the Church, so to speak, is a range of 'inward workings' or gifts of the Holy Spirit, definable in detail in

Table 1: Charisms and Ministries in the New Testament and Beyond

1 Corinthians 12.8–11 (ministries)	1 Corinthians 12.28 (ministers and ministries)	Romans 12.6–8 (ministries)	Ephesians 4.11 (ministers)	Chapters (ministries > ministers)	Source in Christ	Sacramental correlate
Faith	Apostle	?	Apostle	Representing: Apostle	Handing over, Dying and Rising	Baptism
Miracle-working	Miracles	Acts of Mercy	?	Praying: Holy One	Prayer and Miracles	(Silence?)
Healing	Healings, Helps	Giving, Serving	Pastor-teacher	Serving: Pastor	Healing	Anointing for Healing
Word of knowledge, Discernment	Teacher	Teaching		Nurturing: Teacher	Calling and teaching the Disciples	Confirmation
Word of Wisdom	Administration	Leadership	?	Oversight: Leader	Ascension/Sending Spirit	Ordination
Tongues and their interpretation	Tongues	?	?	Collaboration Go-between	Table friendship	Holy Communion (and Marriage?)
Prophecy	Prophet	Prophecy	Evangelist	Evangelism: Herald	Preaching to Crowds and Authorities	Ministry of Word
		Encouragement	Prophet	Subversion: Liberator	Solidarity with Outcast	Reconciliation

different ways, but always representing, between them, the wholeness of Jesus Christ in his earthly ministry, and so recreating and building up his continuing presence in his body, the Church. The final column speculates on relationships between the ministries and the sacramental acts in which they are signified and focused.

But it remains important to remember that the fundamental reality is that of the Trinity at work on earth. Ministers do not make the Church, or the sacraments. Nor does the Church as a whole make either. It is the free gift, the inward energy, the ministry, of the Holy Spirit which makes ministers, sacraments, and the Church.

The energies of the Holy Spirit are, of course, as Orthodox theology affirms, dispersed throughout creation; indeed without her energy, which blew on the water in the beginning (Genesis 1.1), there would be no creation. This opens up the possibility that charisms, too, are scattered abroad more widely than the Church. In the local pub, for instance, we may find as much or even more conviviality, guidance and so forth as in the Church (just as we may find as much or even more backbiting and struggle for power!). So the mindful minister will collaborate with ministries beyond as well as within the Church.

What is, however, special about the Church is the way the ministries are woven together into a body that explicitly expresses the ministry of Christ. Ministries that are con-fused and implicit – though in some cases stronger – elsewhere, become co-ordinated and explicit in the Church. But if we take up our question about whose ministry it is, the answer has to be, in terms of where it comes from, *God's*; and in terms of where it happens and who has a claim on it, *the whole world's*.

We noted the move, even within Paul's epistles, from talk about charisms or ministries to talk about ministers. It is crucial in a book about ministry to understand the rationale of this movement rightly. How does the one minister relate to the many ministries? Certainly not as the one who does them all. Nor, we suggest, as the one who manages them all, as it were running through all the ministries as on a checklist and seeing that those currently lacking are implemented. Nor should we see the minister as representing the divinity or the headship of Christ while the laity represent the subordinate body!

The situation is rather the reverse. In a sense it is the layfolk who in their diversity of gifts and ministries represent the divinity of the Son – his participation in the dance of the Trinity. And what we need the minister to represent is more like the human body of Christ, which holds together and reconciles all manner of human beings and offers them to the Father. That means an ordinary down-to-earth human being who holds all the people's ministries in her heart and mind, in her imagination and her person. This 'holding together' requires more than functional skills that can easily be acquired: it is 'ontological' – to use the jargon – not in the sense that is sometimes suggested, that the priest is a different order of being with a different order of gifts, but in the sense that has to do with *who the priest is* as a person, and especially in her relationships with others.

The minister will therefore need a feel for the ministries and their interrelation, and how they might be encouraged and brought forth where lacking, and moulded and guided where they are strongly present but in an over-dominating or distorted way. To use an image to which this book will return, her task will be like that of the conductor of an orchestra, giving people the cue for when to 'play' their ministry, when to play more forcefully and when to hold back so that other players can be heard. Like the good conductor, she will need an imaginative feel both for the piece as a whole and for the different parts and how they harmonize together in the whole. Or perhaps – since she, like the rest of the people, will have her own special gifts for ministry – she will be more like a lead violinist who helps lead the orchestra by her own playing.

This is therefore a book for anyone who exercises, or feels called to exercise, a certain ministry within the Church, and wishes to do so mindfully and not narcissistically. However, the main readership of the book will probably be those whom the Church calls ministers (or priests or pastors): that is, those whose task is to see that all the ministries (including their own) are released and supported within the Church, and work together, mindfully to serve the whole.

Mindfulness and ministry

But what do we mean by 'mindful'? The use of the English term, according to the *Oxford English Dictionary*, is recorded as early as 1530 and has generally been a synonym for 'aware', and 'focused'. We speak of being mindful of death, the environment, the poor and so forth, meaning acting with concern for such things or bearing them in mind, allowing them to influence our actions.

But as many will know, the term is a central concept of Buddhism, where it translates the Pali term *sata* and the Sanskrit *smrta*. Right mindfulness is one of the three aspects of meditation that form the last three parts of the Eightfold Way to Nirvana. In this context it means developing a controlled, focused awareness of the entire content of consciousness, including sensations, bodily movements, intentions, emotions and thoughts, your own negative or positive reactions to these things. By carefully separating these things out in your awareness you begin to be able to respond intelligently rather than be carried away by the force of your emotions and desires.

For instance, instead of just feeling a punch on your jaw and immediately reacting by punching back, or running away, if trained in mindfulness you will be able to focus on the sensation on your jaw and separate this from the feelings of fear or anger, so that you will be able to reflect on what the best response really is, and act with a response that expresses your whole thinking and feeling self rather than an immediate unthinking reaction.

In the Buddhist context mindfulness is spiritually important because it enables us to live in and from a place that is more spacious than our deluded ego. Though for Christians the dissolving of the self and its cravings is not the ultimate goal, still Christians need something like the spaciousness of mindfulness, and freedom from the clutter of compulsive reactions, to allow the light of Christ to illumine the deeper and wider spaces of our souls.

This is explored more fully in *Buddhist Christianity* (Thompson 2010). You don't have to believe what that book argues, or be a Buddhist or a Buddhist Christian, to gain from the book you are now reading. For mindfulness has begun to prove valuable in diverse areas – so much so that books and courses on mindfulness proliferate. In the treatment of mental states like depression or phobias, training in mindfulness has been able to help people separate their experience from their reaction to it. Instead of seeing a terrifying spider, the phobic patient sees the spider and the fear separately, and begins to control the latter even when the former is present. Instead of having a horrible day, the depressed patient lives through a day in which she experiences misery. The misery then ceases to be an inevitable quality of the day. It becomes something she can, with long and protracted training, choose to go along with or to resist.

Mindfulness in ministry represents something more fundamental than a new way of coping with mental or physical pain or distress: it offers, rather, an unencumbered and joyous inhabiting of God's Kingdom on earth in which all are invited to share, or, to use the metaphor of our opening parable, the means of floating gracefully on the wind-currents of the Spirit empowered by the majesty and beauty of the love of Christ himself – even in the midst of difficult or mundane tasks and events.

Mindfulness and theological reflection

Reflective practice may not, a first sight, seem to have a lot to do with such spiritual empowerment. However, what reflective practice amounts to is doing your job with a critical awareness of the relationship between what you are doing and the ideals and goals you are trying to achieve. If, therefore, those goals are nothing less than enabling yourself and those among whom you minister, together, to be a living embodiment of Christ, the aim and result both of mindfulness and theological reflection are similar. Reflective practice often employs a 'learning cycle' in which experience is brought into relation with your ideals in ways that suggest changes in both; and so leads to new action and new experience that can be processed anew in a similar way as the change begins to take effect. In Christian practice and ministry, the relevant kind of reflective practice involves what is these days called theological reflection (see Thompson 2008) in which experience and practice are brought into critical relation with the whole of the Christian tradition.

This concept and that of mindfulness in ministry are clearly related but not identical. When we consider mindfulness in ministry we are focusing on two main things. One is mindfulness in the sense just described: being aware of the totality of what is going on in your ministry. The other is theological reflectiveness, which means setting that totality in the context of your theological beliefs, asking questions like: does what I see myself doing express what I intend or hope for theologically? Or is it springing from somewhere else, or effecting or communicating something different? Or is it expressing an implicit theology that is actually an improvement on my previous declared beliefs, so that I need to attend to it and learn from it?

This is a simplification, of course, because ministry does not happen in a vacuum. There may be differences between the theology the minister believes he is expressing and what is communicated to the recipient or the wider Church or community. The important point is that, although practical mindfulness and theological reflectiveness are not the same thing, they are interdependent and mutually enriching. You cannot discern the theological ideas that are implicitly at work in your ministry unless you have trained yourself to be aware of and to separate out ideas and experiences and feelings, and learnt to look them in the eye: so mindfulness enables theological reflectiveness. But a theological reflectiveness may also enable you to see your experience in a new and more mindful light. The experience of ministry may force us to unlearn preconceived ideas, and begin to learn them anew through reflection on practice. For mindfulness and reflectiveness are not about having a clear *idea* of ministry, but a life that *embodies* good ministry. In the same way, the good tennis player, for example, is not the one with the clearest idea of the nature and rules of tennis, but the one who plays good tennis in practice.

A threefold tension (Figure 1)

Theological reflection can enable a clearer mindfulness about one's own ministry as part of the greater pattern of God's self-giving to and in the world. This means, of course, having some understanding of the world, and particularly the part of it in which you are called to minister. It involves a theological understanding, rooted in scripture and tradition and deepened by experience, of God's sustaining and redeeming activity in the world. And it also involves an understanding of the Church in the context in which you minister, and of your fellow ministers, both within your congregation and in the wider community.

Figure 1 maps out these contexts in simplified terms. The minister (ordained or lay) operates in a kind of threefold tension between herself, God and the Church. Mindfulness of this tension is what can make it creative rather than conflict-ridden and destructive. From **God** the minister will derive a sense of being called, and responding, perhaps hesitantly, perhaps wholeheartedly, in self-offering. But what she offers will be her **own nature**, which may or may not feel equipped for the call. In either case, she will seek to make herself more equipped by practising the skills and developing the gifts of ministry. The interaction between the divine call and energy and the minister's own responding nature is

Figure 1: The Threefold Dynamic of Mindful Ministry

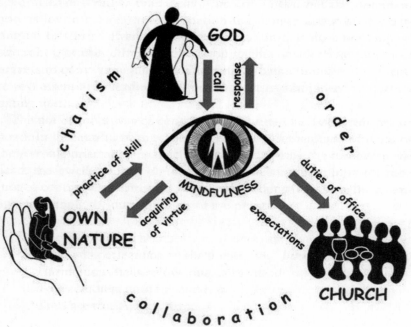

what produces charism, the spiritual gifts that form the person's particular contribution to the life of the Church and the world.

But it is **the Church** that actually validates the call with some form of ordination or authorization of ministry. With that goes the office of ministry which consists of certain duties of the minister toward the Church (and probably the wider community) and expectations of the Church (and wider community) of what the minister ought and ought not to do. These may be spelt out in a job description or contract; or it may be more implicit; or (most confusingly) explicit and implicit demands may be different, but coexist. These demands of office may or may not be in harmony with the minister's personal charism. In either case, the minister's mindfulness of these issues can enable collaboration between the individual's ministry and the other ministries within the Church.

However, things can go wrong in three ways, all of which we recognize from times in our own ministries (though in different proportions for each of us!).

If the minister prioritizes the divine call and response over all else, the result may be an arrogant self-righteous ministry unresponsive to needs and expectations of others. The result will be what we call **absent-minded ministry**: ministry that is all theory, working quite well at the ideas level but unrelated to what the minister actually does on the ground, or so related only in the minister's own head without communicating any meaning to others. I well remember a parishioner who criticized PCC meetings for being 'all talk and no do'. That was her way of saying the meetings were 'absent-minded'. Absent-mindedness is especially tempting early on in ministry, when you emerge from theological college full of bright ideas, and try to repress how hard it seems to relate all that theology to what a minister is expected to do.

If she prioritizes her own natural gifts, a self-indulgent ministry will result, with excellence in one or two areas but huge gaps. The result will be what we call **ego-minded ministry** that is about minding (in the sense of protecting and looking after the interests of) the ego, rather than being mindful of both self and other. At first sight this may look rather like the next possibility. For as the minister rushes around looking after people, or perfecting dazzling sermons or liturgy, she may seem very self-sacrificing. The danger is that it may all be done to gratify the needs of the carer rather than the cared for, the preacher or president rather than the congregation. And the give-away that distinguishes this alternative from the next will be the neglect of the other areas, where the minister feels vulnerable and incompetent, and therefore avoids.

If he prioritizes the Church and the demands and expectations of office at the expense of his nature and calling, the result will be what we call **mindless ministry**: ministry that is 'all do and no think', where the minister runs around like a headless chicken doing as many good things as he can, but without a sense of what he is doing it all for, beyond being an attempt to do what seems expected. Mindlessness is probably the main temptation of mid-life ministry, where the ideals of earlier times are fading and you are trying harder and harder simply to keep up with the tasks you have set yourself, or feel you have been set, crowding out the time to consider what might be worthwhile.

Practices of mindfulness

Few of us can have avoided these pitfalls at different times. This book offers no cure-all or counsel of perfection: but it is hoped that the reflections on the different ministries will in themselves offer mindful insights into aspects of ministry which you will wish to develop further. To help this come about, you may find that it helps to establish various practices, or what Buddhists call 'skilful means'. The first two listed are essential. The rest are offered as choices, depending on your spiritual tradition and personality.

Prayer

God knows us better than we know ourselves, so self-awareness comes through awareness of God's awareness of us, seeing ourselves as he sees us, with greater realism and compassion than we ourselves could ever achieve. Contemplation – resting in God – followed by petition for ourselves and others, is at the very heart of mindful ministry. In time, and perhaps with the help of some of the practices listed next, it becomes possible to 'pray without ceasing' (1 Thessalonians 5.17) even as we minister.

General self-care

This is obviously essential in ministry. A good craftsman looks after his tools; but in ministry you are your own 'tool', placed in the hands of God. Many have written about this subject of late (pre-eminently Kate Lichfield (2006)) so we will not repeat matters, but add mindfulness as something that both helps and is helped by good self-care: indeed, as something which cannot take place without it.

Meditation

This can enable mindfulness of what is going on in your body, mind and emotions. John Cowan (2004) provides a useful introduction to Christian use of Buddhist insight meditation.

Awareness of your body

Departures from mindfulness can often be detected on a bodily level, in a kind of shift in the centre from which you are perceiving the world. Absent-mindedness typically involves a retreat of awareness into the head, which can come to feel heavy and cocooned. In ego-mindedness you can become hijacked by feelings of fight or flight in the guts, which stiffen your body against the negative reactions you anticipate. Mindlessness may make you heart-focused so that you feel people 'tugging on your heartstrings' and are in danger of responding like a puppet to their demands. When you become aware of this kind of shift, it may be possible to relax your focus back to your whole self, body, mind and heart. (Some will find this kind of awareness particularly difficult, but it is suggested here as an option for those who wish.)

Awareness of your personality

Different personalities will find different kinds of ministry more easy or difficult, or more at the heart of or peripheral to their ideal. Some ministries will come naturally, while others will go against the grain or involve 'dancing with the shadow'. It is important to be aware of this, so as to be able to use your personality without being driven by it. There is a little more on this in the Conclusion.

Daily examen

Ignation-style reflection: looking back over each day and reflecting on the kinds of ministry you have offered and received, how it felt, whether you were uneasy about anything, and what particularly pleased you. Perhaps note one thing to be thankful for, and discern one to work on, each day.

Journaling

Extending these approaches into longer, theologically reflective commentary on your ministry.

Spiritual direction

Referring the fruits of all the above to a spiritual guide or soul-friend who can listen and help you discern and nurture your growth in mindfulness. The focus of spiritual direction is on your personal journey in God, rather than your ministry, and is, of course, quite different from the process of managerial-style ministry reviews.

Small groups

These are similar to those described at the end of Chapter 4, and consist perhaps of fellow ministers, or of a ministry team within the congregation, or just a group of like-minded people with whom you feel comfortable, who contract to work through their experiences of ministry in confidence. This could be done informally, perhaps with the help of a book such as this one, or with a facilitator – such as the clergy support groups in Bristol facilitated by Mary Travis (2008).

The burden is light – and shared

Mindful ministry sounds exacting, and both practical mindfulness and theological reflectiveness are certainly challenging disciplines. But they are also liberating and exciting – and the alternatives are much more draining. In the practice of mindful walking you generally get to the stage when you do not feel you are making any effort to walk; the walk is walking itself through you. In the same way, when ministry is mindful it is not full of effort, though of course it is not without effort either. But you could say that in mindful ministry, the ministry is ministering itself through the minister.

With mindful walking, you move from a stage of just walking mindlessly, through a concentrated-effort-full stage when you deliberately and at first rather awkwardly focus on the muscles in your legs and the feel of your feet on the ground, to an effort-free stage in which you are comfortably aware of the walking taking place through you. In the same way you can progress from a practically disengaged absent-mindedness, or a narcissistic ego-mindedness, or a theologically lazy mindlessness, through a process of initially difficult and rather awkward reflectiveness, to the goal of mindful ministry, which is an awareness of something being done in and through you for and with the other, and in and through the other for and with you. Ultimately it is a matter of simply opening oneself to the richness of what God can do in the ministering relationships. So mindfulness includes mindfulness of the joy and beauty of ministry. It also includes mindfulness of the pain and sweat – but by placing those in a wider and prayerful theological perspective, they can be something we come to affirm also.

Moreover, this ministry that can work through us is no straightjacket. We have ourselves read books and heard lectures on 'successful ministry' that have only left us feeling we were failures, because we could never see ourselves as becoming the kind of person that made 'the successful minister'. The skills and dispositions and virtues that seemed to be required were a million miles from our own. But this book – we hope – will not be that sort of book. We do not believe there is a kind of straightjacket that ministers have to fit in to. Rather, if your experience of ministry has made you, unwittingly, try to fit into a straightjacket, we hope this book may help to free you from it: for all ministers and all followers of Christ are called to share in the glorious liberty of the children of God, and to minister from their own uniqueness of being, not from some superimposed model or blueprint.

It is our contention that there is not one fixed thing which makes for 'mindful ministry' but a number of different ways in which ministry can happen through us. Some of those ways will happen quite readily through the kind of people we are, while others will happen if we make the effort to acquire new skills, and others again will never happen through us, but may well happen through someone we can recognize in our congregation as being much better able to do it, with training, than we ever will.

Looking back on our own ministry, as this book has required us to do, gave us a sense that the essence of ministry is easily missed while you are doing it. There was a beauty about many times in our lives as ministers that included the hard and painful and disastrous bits as much as the times when we felt we were doing well. Indeed, it seems to us that some of our own best ministry was done when we were really struggling with the task. It might have cheered and encouraged us, however, had we been dimly aware of some of the fruitfulness of our ministry in those harsh times. Part of what 'mindful ministry' is about is being able to step out of your own perspective and gain a sense that your ministry may be better – or worse – than it feels to you. And even when we were enjoying ministry, as we often did, because we were less than mindful we were often unable to attend to the joy and celebrate and use it as a motive and a source of guidance. We have become more mindful of our ministry in retrospect, and write this book in the hope of helping present and future ministers to be more mindful even as they minister.

The Apostle: Mindful Representing

The apostle's core concern is ensuring that everything that happens in his church furthers the true faith. He sees this as something revealed once for all in the incarnation of Jesus Christ, and passed on through the teaching and sacraments of the Church, which is thereby a continuation of the incarnation. It is his weighty responsibility, as the loyal servant of a God-given hierarchy, to ensure that this saving tradition is passed on to posterity by his own congregation. Buttoned up in his conservative clerical garb, the apostle is himself somewhat buttoned up and controlled, subordinating his humanity to his all-important role. He does not shout about his faith, however, but takes it for granted as his congregation do. He, his faith and his congregation are in every sense 'reserved'.

His church and its worship are full of undeciphered mysteries that nobody feels the need to explain, for they bear the accumulated weight of centuries of implicit faith, blending seamlessly into the folk religion and expectations of ordinary people. This works well in societies that likewise take the role of the priest and the Church for granted, but as expectations begin to shift, the apostle and his church may find it hard to adapt.

In terms of lay ministries, apostles will often like to be servers and acolytes. If they have numerical skills their focus on guarding what has been entrusted to them will make them good treasurers.

Focus: the school governor

Imagine you are a governor of the primary school in your town. At a meeting the headteacher is announcing a change in the RE curriculum, within the National Curriculum programme of study. He wants to shift the balance to a multi-faith basis with the emphasis on moral issues and learning about the ethical approaches of the different faiths as well as secular perspectives. This means inevitably that the Christian content will have to be reduced. In addition, he proposes that the traditional annual harvest festival parade, in which the children processed through the streets with their offerings to present them at the service in church, will be discontinued. True, it had become a part of local tradition which many – though by no means all – welcomed. But it sent out the wrong message about the allegiance of the school.

- Will you support these moves or argue against them?
- Either way, what arguments will you use?
- Would any of these factors make a difference, and which would be most important?
  - the status of the school: church voluntary controlled or aided, local authority, academy or independent? (These vary in terms of freedom to design their curriculum.)
  - whether the town is mainly white or multicultural?
  - whether you are the vicar or a lay member of your congregation?
  - the grassroots feelings in the town as a whole?
  - the feelings of the congregation?
  - your own personal view of the matter?

The faithful apostle

Whether you like it or not, as a minister you will not be able to avoid the task of representing. People see ordained ministers in particular, but also churchgoers in general, as representing the Christian Church and faith. Perceptions of the latter will be partly changed for better or worse by the things you say and do and are. This chapter explores the opportunities and pressures that result, and then considers the gifts and skills needed to be a mindful representative, apostle or ambassador of Christ. The opening example focuses the complexities of this task and the multiplicity of expectations people have regarding this role, which this chapter will attempt to tease out.

In the early Church, apostleship or representing was the most highly regarded of all ministries as it was uniquely traced back to direct commissioning by Christ. It appears first among the charisms in 1 Corinthians 12.28 and Ephesians 4.11. Interestingly, it is not listed in Romans 12 or in the earlier list in 1 Corinthians 12.8–10, though there we do find *pistis*, faith or faithfulness, which is arguably the chief gift required in an apostle. Strictly of course there were only ever twelve apostles – or thirteen if we accept Paul's claims to be one. But we are using this word in its original meaning, which was literally one *sent away* or *sent off* on some mission, dispatched on some service; by extension this meant a representative, messenger, envoy or ambassador. Paul uses the specific notion of ambassador twice (2 Corinthians 5.20 and Ephesians 6.20). The apostles were sent out to bring the gospel to the world. But, of course, the whole Church is apostolic in this sense, and the ordained minister has an apostolic role within the whole.

Two things characterize ambassadors or apostles. They are people commissioned or entrusted with a mission on behalf of a higher authority. An ambassador speaks with the authority of his country because that country has entrusted him with that role. The key requirement of an apostle is faith in the sense of faithfulness to what has been entrusted, being able to pass it on as it has been passed on to you. Catholic ecclesiology has tended to emphasize the way authority is handed down in an apostolic succession, from Christ to apostles, from apostles to bishops, and from bishops to those they ordain and confirm. In other faiths (for example, Tibetan Buddhism) there is often a 'lineage' that passes from teacher to disciple and is traceable back to the founder. The Catholic apostolic succession is different in that the bishop combines this teaching lineage with jurisdiction.

The ambassador can only represent his country by being true to his commission, and vice versa. Likewise the truly apostolic minister is the one who is concerned to be faithful both to the living tradition that has been entrusted to her (at baptism and perhaps ordination) and to become a 'high-fidelity' representative of the original, Jesus Christ, by engaging with him in a self-transforming way through study, reflection and prayer.

This chapter will focus first on the minister in the sense of commissioned bearer of the faith, and then on the apostle as representative of Christ. Exploration of the latter will lead naturally to the exploration of how priest and people 'inter-represent' each other, and how together as a priestly people they represent the wider world to God in Christ, notably in worship.

Handing on

Read **1 Corinthians 11.23–26**: the first account of the Last Supper.

Imagine yourself as one of the disciples. How do you feel about what you have been entrusted with?

Read **2 Kings 2.1, 7–15**: Elijah passes his spirit on to Elisha.

Imagine yourself as Elisha. How do you feel about what you have been entrusted with?

> • What similarities and differences do you note in these two stories?
> • What similarities and differences between your feelings as a disciple and as Elisha?

The priest and theologian, W. H. Vanstone, writes (1982) about the way Christ is 'handed on' and 'handed over' at his betrayal by Judas. Vanstone also notes that, though the words 'betrayal' and 'traitor' carry a heavy negative weight for us, the Greek word for 'betray', *prodidōmi*, is seldom used of Judas. The word that is used, *paradidōmi* and its derivatives, means simply 'handing over' and 'the one who hands over'. The word 'tradition' comes from the same root; it is what is handed over to us from our forebears.

It is instructive to look up these words in Strong's *Greek Concordance* (www.greek-dictionary.net) to gain an overview of the 177 verses in which *paradidōmi* occurs, and the 13 that refer to *paradosis*. This gives a sense of the importance of these words, and the way in which for the early Christians the tradition *was* the handing on of the God who in Christ had handed himself over to our hands. Vanstone notes the repetition of *paradidōmi* in the passage just discussed, which he renders:

> I received from the Lord that which I also *handed over* to you – that the Lord Jesus, on the night in which He was *handed over*, took bread and, having given thanks, broke it and said . . . (p. 14; our italics)

And the passage goes on to describe Jesus handing over to the disciples the sacrament of his body and his blood. Vanstone notes the startling way in which Paul claims to have received this 'from the Lord'. He is unlikely to be referring to a special receiving direct from Christ; rather, he is describing the handing over or tradition of the Church, which is regarded as a handing on of Christ which he in turn hands on.

This makes for a strong difference between the handing on of Jesus and Elijah's handing on of his spirit. What Elijah leaves, through his mantle, is *something* of himself, namely his prophetic *power*. But what Jesus hands on through his betrayal is his *whole* self, and his total *vulnerability*. As Vanstone argues, before, he was in control; now he is in the hands of others to do with him what they will. He becomes vulnerable to how we humans treat him; we can indeed pass him on to others, or we can betray him. 'In recent theological thinking', Vanstone concludes his book – and we might add, in recent thinking about ministry –

much has been made of man's role in sharing or even extending the creativity of God. Man has been seen, primarily, as 'fellow-worker with God' – as participator, albeit on a humble scale, in God's everlasting activity of remaking and redeeming the world. Perhaps this understanding of man's role needs to be balanced by the perception of man as 'fellow receiver with God' . . . He is one who, like God, is handed over to the world, to wait upon it, to receive its power of meaning: to be the one upon whom the world bears in all its variety and intensity of meaning: to receive upon his transforming consciousness no mere photographic imprint of the world but its wonder and terror, its vastness and delicacy, its beauty and squalor, its good and evil. (1982, pp. 114–15; The reader will forgive the gender-biased language of the 1980s)

So before he can be an active fellow-worker, the minister first needs to be a 'fellow receiver with God'. The minister is 'the one who hands over' the Christ that has been 'handed over' to her in the 'tradition' of the Church. She needs to ensure that she is not a betrayer of Christ. And she offers Christ, or betrays him, not only in what she is aware of doing and feeling, but even more, perhaps, in and through what she is not aware of in herself, but which others experience through her. What we say and do constitutes, as it were, the tip of the unspoken and often unknown iceberg of who we are. We all convey to others much more than we are aware of, through our demeanour, facial expression, tone of voice, the way our house and garden are organized, the whole realm of what we could call 'tacit' communication, of which more in Chapter 6.

But this challenge applies to the whole Church too. As the Christian ethicist Stanley Hauerwas has insisted again and again, Christians together are called to live together the life of the One who has been handed down to them. Christians thus form a living tradition in which the virtues of the Gospels are learnt through practice. This makes them, according to him, 'resident aliens' (1989) – thoroughly 'resident' in being immersed in the life of their local community, yet thoroughly 'alien' in the lifestyle that sets them apart from those who live by different traditions or no traditions at all. The role of the ordained minister is to oversee and maintain the totally immersed distinctiveness of this life by reference to the Christian tradition.

And that is a bold challenge we should not evade. It could, of course, lead to an anxious Christian perfectionism, or a striving for salvation by good works, or more likely, a hypocrisy in which we all pretend to be living better lives than we actually are. We want to ask, can we not hand Christ on even as the treacherous sinners we are? It was, after all, in a sinful act that Judas handed Jesus on.

Tradition or betrayal?

In the final episode of the first series of *Rev* (*Is The Answer Jesus, Sir?* – BBC2, first broadcast 2 August 2010) the inner-city vicar, Adam Smallbone, undergoes a crisis of loss of faith. To make matters worse, he is spurned by Ellie, the headmistress with whom he is infatuated, after pursuing her in a drunken and crazy manner at a Vicars and Tarts party. His wife Alex tells him to leave the party rather than go on making a fool of himself. On the way home, drunk and disorderly in his vicar's robes, he is pursued by two policemen. When they finally catch up with him, to his amazement he is not arrested but requested to attend the bedside of someone who has just died. He is reluctant, but finally persuaded, and the scene closes with him at the bedside alongside grief-stricken relatives, carrying out the rites appointed for the departed. Despite his doubts, he falls with grace – in more senses than one – into the ministerial role he has learned and into which he has grown.

Something similar is illustrated by the anonymous priest who is the hero of Graham Greene's novel *The Power and the Glory* (1991). The novel is set in Mexico in the 1930s, when the socialist government outlawed and suppressed the Church. The hero is a dissolute whisky-drinking priest who, among other misdemeanours, has secretly fathered a child. He escapes persecution by fleeing to a neighbouring province, but there he is approached by a man who asks him to return to hear a dying man's confession. The priest realizes this is a trap, but for him hearing confession is an absolute priestly duty. He sees no alternative but to return and attend to the dying man, whereupon he is arrested and shot.

The priest in the novel is far from Christlike; in many ways he is a hypocrite, living a life that is deeply at odds with the teaching of his Church. And yet in his ultimate loyalty he does succeed in representing the death of Christ. And he does pass the faith on. Though the authorities think they have conquered the Church and rid the province of its last priest, the novel ends with a boy who witnessed the bravery of the priest at the last, sensing something here worthy of his own loyalty, and offering himself secretly for the priesthood.

Hopefully, for you things have not turned out quite like this! Nevertheless in ministry there may well be times when you feel that what you are called upon to profess is greater than what you inwardly feel at the time, and what you *represent* for others exceeds what you are in yourself. If you are one of those who believe that the priest is called to represent Christ, this is in a sense bound always to be the case: the one you represent is always far greater and holier than you yourself are or ever could be.

A particularly poignant example of the tension between personal faith and what is demanded of us because of the tradition we represent is explored in Elie Wiesel's *The Trial of God* (Shocken, 1995). This play is set in a Ukrainian village that has been decimated by a pogrom in 1649. (It has since been made into a film, *God on Trial* (2008), set in a Nazi concentration camp; Wiesel was himself a Holocaust survivor, and the story is often related as an event that actually took place in such a setting, as one can well imagine it might have.) The survivors decide to organize a trial in which God is the defendant, accused of betraying his side of his covenant with his people. The 'jury' unanimously finds God guilty, whereupon those present are reminded that it is the time for evening prayer, in which all promptly join.

On the one hand the surviving remnant's belief in a loving God in covenant with his people has been shattered by events; in their minds and hearts they can no longer believe and trust. And yet in another sense they still keep the faith, remaining loyal to the tradition in which this idea of God has been handed down from generation to generation. Some might protest that the Jews would have been more honest, having condemned God, to abandon worship and lead a wholly atheistic life. Some Jews have taken this course. But would we want to say it was hypocritical to go on worshipping God in such circumstances? Or is there a deeper faith that consists in holding fast to one's tradition despite experiences which have made you question your belief? Certainly in Judaism the faith of the people is a corporate affair, much greater than personal belief, rooted in the people's covenant with God.

Likewise, would we want to declare it hypocritical for Adam to minister to the bereaved when he is struggling in his personal faith? Or is the loss of faith a relatively temporary and trivial thing when compared with the faith of the Church? Adam not only does good despite himself, it could be argued; but by allowing the tradition to speak through him in the liturgy, he was showing a faith deeper than his personal doubts.

Treasure in clay pots . . .

> Read **2 Corinthians 4.5–12**: treasure in clay pots.
>
> In your own case, what is the treasure? What is the pot?

The Book of Common Prayer calls the faithful to 'shine as lights before men [*sic*], that they may see your good works and glorify your Father in heaven'. But Paul, at least in this passage, says otherwise. According to Paul, the Christian proclaims not her own good works but Christ himself. She should not be drawing people's attention to wonderful virtues of her own; rather, she should have something in her that draws the focus beyond her to Christ.

In the passage quoted, Paul uses three powerful metaphors for this process. The first is creation. As it was out of darkness that God called forth the first light of creation, so it is out of the 'darkness' of the minister that the light of Christ will shine clearly. The last is redemption. And the metaphor here is extremely challenging. Ministers somehow carry in them the death of Jesus, so that life may be brought to those they serve. Sandwiched between these two theological metaphors is a much more homely one. According to the second metaphor that Paul uses, the Christian is like a clay pot in which the treasure of Christ lies. She is not called to be the treasure. Like a clay pot she is to be a humble thing made of earth, surrounding an empty space, which Christ can fill, for herself and others.

You might like to pause and ask if you can see Adam Smallbone, or Greene's whisky priest, in this light. Does light shine out of their darkness? Does life come through their struggles? Are they like clay pots full of treasure? What about Paul himself – a small man often full of anger, first against Christians, then against his rivals, fallible, vulnerable, often suffering, yet bearing the gospel treasure for others? What about that other early Christian leader, Peter? Or some of the Old Testament leaders: Jacob the swindler who wrestled with God and prevailed? Moses the murderer who was chosen to meet God on the mountain and carry down the foundations of the covenant? Ezra and Nehemiah, irascible and often narrow and self-righteous, but doing their best to reconstruct and pass on the treasures of the faith after the ravages of exile?

The Anglican priest-poet, George Herbert, seized upon the metaphor of the clay pot and reworked it in his poem 'The Priesthood'. But he focuses not on the treasure we carry but the way our ordinary 'clay' can be fashioned into an object of beauty by God's 'cunning hand/and force of fire' (cf Allan 1993).

. . . Or talents in the ground?

Read **Matthew 25.14–29**: the parable of the talents.

Reflect on this from the point of view of the slave who buried his talent.

8

This is part of a sequence of parables unique to Matthew's Gospel, sandwiched between the parable of the bridesmaids and the parable of the sheep and goats at the last judgement. It is often interpreted as urging us as individuals not to hide away the gifts we have received from God, but to put them to work and make them grow. Indeed, the word 'talent' used in the sense of gift or ability derives from this parable. This interpretation is not wrong, but the context – a series of parables immediately preceding the Passion narrative, all of them concerned with how we respond to Christ and the nature of the last judgement – ought to encourage us to look for more eschatological meanings. And the use of the familiar word *paradidōmi* in the very first verse, where the man 'hands over' his property to his slaves, ought to suggest a reading of this parable in terms of how we handle the *paradosis*, the tradition that Christ has handed over to us.

If we follow that reading through, the parable, in this context, makes a radical suggestion: that it will not be enough, on the last day, or in the ultimate perspective, for us to hand back to Christ the traditions he gave us intact and meticulously preserved exactly as they were given. That would be as if we had buried them in the ground. No, he expects us to have put the traditions to work and made them grow, so that on his return we will be able to hand back to him much more than he gave us. The gospel he gave us is not a 'deposit' we must simply maintain in its pristine state but (in this parable) a deposit in the bank, where we expect it to grow, or (as another parable puts it) a seed in the ground, that is to grow and bear fruit a hundredfold.

What is the 'bank' whereby the gospel grows in this sense? Surely the process of putting it to use in practice, and submitting the result to the process of theological reflection, where the gospel interacts with experience and through reflection and the power of the Spirit who leads us into all truth, we are taken forward into new understanding and action, and perhaps new insight into Jesus' teaching. So faithfulness here is about faithful reflection, sitting under the judgement of Christ regarding what we do with his teaching. Losing his teaching or exchanging it for something different and perhaps trendier will of course be unfaithful, but the parable warns us, perhaps, that simply to cling on to the teaching and preserve its pristine integrity, without allowing it to be honed and further developed through use and reflective practice, is equally unfaithful.

Of course, there are situations when doing the same thing faithfully again and again is important, even if there is no obvious reason for it. Or rather, perhaps, precisely because there is no utilitarian reason, doing the same thing can be a matter of sheer faithfulness to God. One of us, as a curate, was criticized by a member of the congregation for censing the Gospel the wrong way round – censing to the left before the right (or was it the other way round – being right–left challenged he finds it hard to recall!). At the time, though he conformed for the sake of peace, he felt that this was rather trivial: what did it matter! But looking back now I reflect that there are many things in a ceremonially oriented church – the order in which candles are lit, the various ways in which people and things are censed, who bows to whom when – that are important precisely because they are not (in utilitarian terms) important. Because they do not matter, such things can express a sheer attentiveness that points beyond them to God. A church in which one can sense this attentiveness to the 'right way' of preparing things before the service has a distinct feel, different from one in which things are done anyhow: something like polishing a mirror that it may reflect the beauty of God.

On the other hand, humans – especially religious ones – have a natural conservatism. How often have we heard changes to the service that have been carefully thought over, prepared and explained as being in line with authentic tradition, dismissed as 'change for change's sake'? People also have a natural tendency to proliferate rituals, and to give to things that have arisen historically for pragmatic reasons deep and important symbolic meanings. Such things may then become not a way to attentive stillness, but a burden that creates anxiety and distracts from worship, as described in this little story:

> When the guru sat down to worship each evening, the ashram cat would get in the way and distract the worshippers. So he ordered that the cat be tied during evening worship.
>
> Long after the guru died, the cat continued to be tied during evening worship. And when the cat eventually died, another cat was brought to the ashram so that it could be duly tied up during evening worship.
>
> Centuries later, learned treatises were written by the guru's disciples on the essential role of a cat in all properly conducted worship. (de Mello 1982, p. 79)

There is a time, then, to hold fast to tradition and a time to 'put it to work' and allow it to grow, or to become simpler (or both), the better to represent Christ. Discerning the difference is an extremely hard skill to learn, and probably all ministers make mistakes they come to regret, either holding on to tradition when they should have let go, or vice versa.

There is little in all this that theological training prepares you for. There is much that tells you what the tradition is – both the tradition of the Church as a whole, and one's own denomination; but little on the art of knowing when to hold fast to it and when to encourage change to happen. It is here that we need to move from 'tradition for tradition's sake' – being apostles who simply hand on what we have received – to apostles in the sense of representatives, attending mindfully to the Original we are trying to represent, and asking whether we would represent him better if some things changed.

Salt, light and flawed icons: representing Christ to the world

Read **Matthew 5.13–15**: salt and light.

These two sayings offer two different symbols of how we need to be faithful to the spirit of the beatitudes, even under persecution: salt and light.

Each image has things to say about faithful representing. Ponder the things that are the same and different in the way we are called to be faithful as salt and as light.

In many ways, both salt and light carry forward the thought of the parable of the talents. If we see our task simply as conserving the salt we have been given, we will probably want to heap it all together in one place where we can see it. But no, the point of salt is to spread it around so that it becomes invisible. Only then will it lend its savour to the food. This will not be so that the food will all turn to salt, but so that everything will taste more fully itself. Likewise, traditions are there not for us to keep to ourselves, but so that people will flourish. The salt and the gospel are there to bring change to the world.

In the same way, if we want to preserve the light that has been given us, we may want to hide it under some protecting shrine. But then it will cast no light (and will probably go out). No, the light needs to shine in a prominent place, and so that things in the world will be fully seen in their beauty.

There is a subtle difference, though. What salt needs to do in order to make things tasty is to keep its saltiness. If it loses that, it is worthless. The salt is like tradition: it needs to be spread around, not protected, but part of the ministry of the apostle is to ensure that it goes on tasting of the freedom and love that Christ has brought. But what light needs to do is to be seen. It needs to stand as a sign and means of shedding the light of Christ. It says more about the representing aspect of the ministry of the apostle, to which we turn in this second half of the chapter.

The focusing example at the start of the chapter brought to the fore the issues at stake in this apostolic ministry of representing. As a school governor, you may see yourself as representing a long tradition of faith that it is your duty to maintain against all odds; or Christian faith may be seen as a personal choice which our secular educational system should not be forcing on people. You may feel that long-standing local traditions should be cherished, and the feelings of the local community represented. And you may feel that this is more or less important than the feelings of the congregation you also represent. If you are the vicar, you may feel that your role as representative (of Christ, of Christian tradition, of the local community, of your congregation . . . ?) is part of your official duty, and must prevail over your own personal opinions. On the other hand, in a world where faith is often seen as extremist and proselytizing, you may feel that you represent Christ better by going against the strong views in your congregation, presenting Christianity as reasonable and accommodating, and seeing that a reduced but still friendly role at the school is to be preferred to antagonism. Whatever your understanding, however, you will have to be mindful of what you feel you represent in this situation, and how it will be seen by others.

The priest has been defined as 'a person who represents the person of Christ' (Allan 1993, p. 51). On the Catholic and Orthodox understanding, as Christ is the image or icon or visible representation of God, so the Church is the continuing representation of Christ, and the priest represents both Church and Christ. He is, in this theology, a kind of living icon. Orthodox theology particularly affirms this of the priest at the Eucharistic liturgy. The priest with his flowing beard and his glorious robes, and more profoundly, his offering of prayer to the Father, is a living icon of the risen and glorified Christ.

In these contexts, however, the way the apostle represents Christ to people is also the way Christ represents God to us and us to God. And this needs careful thinking through. We read that Christ is 'the image of the invisible God' (Colossians 1.15). Now the notion of an image of something invisible contains a paradox that should set us thinking hard. An image suggests a look-alike. When we say a girl is a 'spitting image' of her grandmother we are saying that she looks very like her. But you cannot look like something invisible. When Jesus is described as saying, 'if you have seen me you have seen the Father' (John 14.9) he cannot be meaning 'the Father looks just like me'. The Father, being invisible, does not look like anyone at all. What is being said is rather that Jesus is God in human form, or God translated into visible aspect, or God manifest as a human being, or the human embodiment of God. And to say that we too are in God's image is to say that we are manifestations or expressions of God, not look-alikes.

So the ministry of representation cannot mean being as similar as we can to Jesus Christ in all respects. There are many ways in which the apostolic minister cannot be like Jesus Christ: she cannot be a first-century Palestinian Jew, or without sin, or a member of the Trinity, one in being with the Father. But that does not mean she cannot represent Christ. For a representation needs to be different from, and in some respects unlike, the thing it represents. When this point is missed, many mistakes happen: for example, the exclusion of women from priestly ministry because they are not the same gender as Jesus or the apostles; and more generally, a perfectionism that leads ministers to seek to be more Christlike than they can possibly be.

For example, a painting of an oak represents the tree in certain respects: for instance the colours, and maybe the atmosphere it conjures up. But the painting is unlike the oak in many ways: it is flat and two-dimensional, it is inanimate and does not grow or reproduce, it is not a member of the species *Quercus robur*, and so forth . . . It represents the oak only insofar as the medium, paint on canvas, can do so. It is the same with an ambassador of the United Kingdom; he does not 'look like' the nation or represent it in everything he does, but only within the medium and conventions of diplomacy.

So likewise, to represent Christ is not to be an identical replica, but to represent Christ insofar as he can be expressed through the medium of the minister's own humanity. The priest needs to be mindful of when she is representing Christ; and when she is doing so, she needs to be mindful of what her words and actions will be telling of Christ. This is not a counsel of perfection. The priest is an ordinary and often sinful human being, but through that medium, as through the whisky priest and through the likes of Adam Smallbone, the likeness of Christ can shine. The priest can provide, frail as she is, an epiphany in which the human face of God in Christ is glimpsed.

An image that might sum up all these meanings is the flawed icon. Icons – unlike, for example, Renaissance and pre-Raphaelite art – make no attempt to make their object beautiful. There are no blond young men among the icons of Christ, and no sweet virgins among icons of the Mother of God. The icons' beauty lies in what they represent, not in what they are in themselves, which is wood and egg-based paint, often cracked and peeling or in some other way defective. The icon may be flawed, yet still it does its work of representing and embodying the holy ones. It does so through what it represents, and what is believed about it by the faithful. So it is with the minister as representative.

Inter-representing

This last remark suggests that the ability to represent Christ has as much to do with what the people believe about the minister as what she is in herself. But that in turn reminds us that apostolicity and representing are primarily the ministry of the whole Church. The sacramental sign by which we become representatives of Christ is not ordination but baptism.

This is abundantly clear when the full symbolism of baptism is used. The immersion (ideally) in water and rising again from the waters represents the dying and rising of Christ (Romans 6.1–4). The anointing with chrism on the forehead with the sign of the cross makes the baptized another anointed one, another Christ. The white baptismal robe (probably implied in Galatians 3.27) signifies being clothed with the purity of Christ. And the newly baptized are sent out with a lit candle to shine with the light of Christ. All this suggests that it is the ministry of every Christian to represent Christ in his dying and rising, in his anointing by the Spirit, in his purity and in his message to the world.

The Introduction suggested that it was the layfolk in their variety of ministries who represented the person of Christ, reflecting the perichoretic dance of the Trinity in their shared life. And that the priest, in his person, represents the down-to-earth humanity of Christ, the flawed human nature that Christ has gathered to himself. However, no individual priest could have the whole range of qualities that make for the full humanity seen in Christ. A scholarly priest, for example, might well have a broad and deep Christlike wisdom, but would she have the time for diligent Christlike pastoral care, and vice versa? Surely only in the whole body of Ch+rist – the Church with all the manifold gifts of its people – can the whole of Christ be represented. Paul never affirmed of any individual, but only of the whole Church in its varied ministries, 'you are the body of Christ'.

How can you as minister be mindful of whether you are representing Christ truly? Certainly not by some strong consciousness of being Christ for others. To focus on that could lead to the arrogance, narcissism and self-deception of an ego-minded ministry. The criterion is almost the opposite: a strong awareness of and focus on Christ in the *others* to whom you are ministering. The difference between a church council or other meeting in which the minister is representing Christ – even in tough decisions that may cause controversy and ill-feeling – and one in which he is not, is that in the former case the minister will be attending to the Christ in the others at the meeting, including those who take an opposite view and seem to be on the 'wrong' side of a debate. In the latter case, the minister will be all absorbed in his own ideas and ensuring they prevail, and Christ will be out of the picture.

That point brings us back to the interdependence of ministries, discussed in the Introduction (pp. xii–xiii). Priest and people represent Christ to one another, and find in one another the verification that they are indeed representing him truly (or not). The people see their priesthood focused in a tiny miniature, as it were, and clarified by being interrelated in one person, whom we call *the* priest. The priest sees his ministry unfolded and teased out on a broader canvas, dispersed to the ends of the earth (or at least the parish or institution he serves) by the royal priesthood of all.

In the passage noted in the Introduction, John Robinson distinguished between representative and vicarious ministry. Elsewhere he writes: 'The ordained ministry is representative, not vicarious. It does not stand over against the laity, mediating between them and God, and doing what they cannot. It is commissioned – by Head and Body alike – to do in the name of the whole what in principle all can do' ('Christianity's "No" to Priesthood', in Lash and Rhymer (eds) 1970, pp. 13–14). In the Introduction, the point was made that Robinson saw lay and ordained ministry vary in direct proportion: the stronger the one is, the stronger the other. But this, according to Robinson, is only the case when a representative ministry operates: the ministry of the baptized is strengthened through being reflected and focused in the priest, while that of the priest is multiplied by being reflected in the baptized. But in a 'vicarious ministry' the ordained take the ministries and the priestly services that belong to the baptized as a whole and monopolize them, offering worship and pastoral care, not as representing that of the laity but in their place, so they do not have to bother. Vicarious ministry gives the laity an easy life and the clergy a hard but honoured one. Clergy have the challenge of doing all the ministry of the baptized: the baptized need only honour the ordained and let them do the ministering. Here, the ordained and the rest of the baptized exercise ministry in inverse proportion: the more ministry the ordained do, the less the lay people have to bother.

The mindful priest, therefore, will need to take care that he acts in such a way that he is representing and illuminating the priesthood of all the people, rather than vicariously offering priestly ministry in their stead. What this might mean we now explore.

Representing the world through Christ

> Read **1 Peter 2.4–10**: a Royal Priesthood.
>
> What key things does this passage say about priesthood?

These final sections turn to the flip-side of the truth that Christ represents the holy God in the form of our flawed humanity. He also represents our flawed humanity in the form of his own holiness to God. Central to the letter to the Hebrews is the notion that Christ who has become altogether like us is able to present us holy to God (for example 2.17). He is not our vicar, but our *representative* priest. In him we see our sins transformed into his painful wounds and then, by the alchemy of the resurrection, into glorious scars: not just cancelled out and forgotten, but *glorified* in God.

It is the calling of all the baptized to represent humanity to God in the offering of the sacrifice of praise and intercession. The baptized are called not only to be ministers – which in the present context means representing Christ to the world in the energy of the Holy Spirit – but priests, representing the world to God in Christ, consecrated by the Spirit. In his sole use of explicitly priestly language, Paul neatly balances these two roles, speaking of: 'the grace given me by God to be a minister (*leitourgos*) of Christ Jesus to the Gentiles in the priestly service (*hierogounta*) of the gospel of God, so that the offering of the Gentiles may be acceptable, sanctified by the Holy Spirit' (Romans 15.15–16). Paul is a minister (literally one who 'liturgs' or offers a public service) representing Christ to the gentiles, and a priest (literally 'working the holy') enabling the gentiles to make an acceptable offering to God. As already noted, the passage in 1 Peter connects the priesthood of the baptized both with offering spiritual sacrifices, and with proclaiming the mighty acts of God: the representation here is two-way.

This is a profound mystery, no more manifest than in Christian worship, which consists in what the fathers, expanding upon the New Testament, called a reasonable and spiritual sacrifice: a sacrifice in the primordial sense of 'making holy'. It is of course not us but Christ who has made the holy offering, and the Holy Spirit who makes his sacrifice complete by consecrating our present offering. In worship, the ordinary world, with all its faults and frailty, and its violence and sin, is taken into God and transformed into what is peaceable and perfect.

In worship, it follows that both ordered beauty and flawed ordinariness need to hold together. The world and its flaws are being offered as represented in the medium of Christ's holiness. An analogy of how this happens may be found in the paintings of artists like Rembrandt and Van Gogh, who depicted ordinary people (and even in Van Gogh's case their old decaying boots) without any attempt to beautify them, or to hide their warts, but held in a kind of stillness that makes them holy and beautiful. Good worship is like those paintings: down to earth and welcoming to sinners like ourselves, but presenting us in an order and stillness – as well as music and movement – that glorifies with the glory of Christ, who represents us to God as found in him.

The beauty we have in Christ is no fiction, as if Christ were pretending to God that we are holy while 'really' we are sinners. Sinners we truly are, but we have no need to beautify ourselves and put on our Sunday best (or its inner moral equivalent) when we go to church. For Christ, by representing us holy and blameless before God, reflects something true about us human beings that is deeper and more original than our sin.

The good use of space in church buildings can help to give a sense of this reality: for the worship space is not so much made holy as revealed in its holiness as heaven and earth that are full of God's glory. Likewise time is not, as is sometimes said, 'sanctified' through the liturgical year; rather the natural cycles of time are revealed as holy through being refracted through the lens of Christ and his historical work of redemption (Thompson 2009).

Leading worship: occasional offices

It is as the minister leads worship that this aspect of the ministry of representing the world in Christ comes to the fore. It is important that this profound transformation is grasped as the essence of worship: that we offer not entertainment or beautiful ritual but the spiritual making-holy in Christ. The priest conveys her own mindfulness of this process, both through the forms and ceremonies, and through the way in which she herself carries them out.

This is especially obvious at those times when the priest or minister is called to lead occasional offices like weddings and funerals, or arranges worship at times of public crisis or celebration like the outbreak or cessation of war, or the death or marriage of public figures. At these times widespread inchoate feelings of sorrow, anxiety or joy can be given shape and form and 'held' in a public act of worship, rather as an artist gives his feelings form in a work of art. Christian worship will need to connect these feelings to the wider story of Christ, giving them a voice and a place and a beginning and end in that greater story, so that they become part of the sacrifice, presented through Christ to God.

The minister acknowledges the prevailing feeling in her own demeanour – sombre at a funeral, light at a wedding – but does not allow the feeling to overwhelm the worship. On such occasions many of those present are likely to be only partially familiar with the Christian story and the hope of the resurrection, and, in any case, however strong belief in the resurrection may be, it does not take away the appropriateness of sorrow at times of pain and loss. Strong protestations of explicit faith at such times may alienate many in the congregation, but by quietly embodying the belief she carries in her heart, and a sensitive leading of the liturgy, the minister is more likely to enable those present to suspend their disbelief and enter into its imaginative unfolding for this particular occasion.

If there are particularly painful circumstances like, say, suicide or estrangement at a funeral, it will need to be gently acknowledged, though within the broader picture in which the person is represented to God as he is in Christ. By the same token it is not hypocritical that at funerals we tend to hear only of saints, and rarely of criminals or other sinners; for the role of a funeral eulogy is to present the person perfect in Christ. That is not to say that it is not often very moving when there is a gently humorous allusion to some well-known frailty in the deceased, reminding people of his humanity. This can even happen inadvertently: a good deal of mirth erupted at a funeral when reference was made to how much a budgie enthusiast had 'loved his birds': the 'birds' he had a reputation for loving were evidently not only of the feathered kind!

Letting worship be worship

Most people – apart from those who specifically study theology – learn their theology not as they learn information in the newspaper, by reading and reflecting on it, but more as they learn a new song or dance, through repeatedly rehearsing it until it is 'in their bones', part of who they are as God's priestly people. For this reason, although there is a time for preaching, worship as a whole needs not to be overly didactic, but rather, allowed to do its own profound thing in which all can participate.

And it is equally important that the priest is not consciously or subconsciously saying, in effect, 'I am the icon of Christ: look at me!' To represent, as already noted, is to point to a reality beyond you of which you are just the flawed icon. When in worship the focus is entirely on the representation at the expense of the Represented One, idolatry results. In this context, one can understand the rage of the Puritan iconoclasts who smashed the images and many things beautiful in themselves. But without smashing the images, or hating the clutter of holy imagery from the past that can at times seem to weigh so heavily upon us, the style and bearing of the priest, and the ethos and even the layout of the worship can be designed and executed in order, not to call attention to themselves, but to point beyond.

Long ago Augustine laid down the principle – accepted in Catholic theology – that the sacraments work *ex opere operato* (by the working of the work) rather than *ex opere operantis* (by the working of the worker – the minister). The idea behind this is that the sacraments are not the priest's work, but God's. The priest's task is faithfully to reproduce the signs ordained by Christ – taking bread and wine, for example, and saying the Eucharistic Prayer, and breaking and sharing them out – and God in his faithfulness will make the grace of Christ available to those who faithfully receive it.

It is especially important in small and perhaps dwindling urban or rural congregations to recall that Christ and hence his body the universal Church is represented and present 'wherever two or three are gathered in my name' (Matthew 18.20) and wherever the Eucharist is celebrated. Despite calls, highly relevant in other settings, to focus on mission rather than maintenance, the importance of the maintenance of worship, and the representative, royal priestly role of those who share in it, should not be underestimated.

There is something here that can be applied to worship generally. The priest, rather than being strained or anxious about whether the worship is 'effective' or 'successful' – whatever that might mean – can simply be attentive to leading the worship in faithfulness and fidelity. It is God who achieves good worship in us, and again, the minister and the worshippers are just clay pots to contain and help pour out the treasure. The role of the priest in worship is basically to enable this to happen.

The mindful apostle

The Introduction suggested three ways in which ministry can fail to be mindful, and we suggest that we can fail to be mindful apostles in these three ways, which relate to the passage studied at the outset of the section 'Salt, Light . . .'.

- The absent-minded apostle is like **a light that does not know it is under a bushel.** This minister's apostleship is mainly in his own head. He is wonderfully literate in theology, and preaches elaborate sermons that entrance a few and lose the majority.

The worship of the absent-minded church is typically 'cerebral', academically highbrow and rather dry, but liturgically middle of the road to low, with little attention to the bodily movement and general atmosphere and feeling that give life to the dry bones of liturgy.

- The ego-minded apostle is **a light that refuses to be confined to a lampstand** and therefore gives off more burning heat than light. The ego-minded apostle refuses to be confined by traditions that seem to her outmoded. Romantically, she sees traditional symbols and seasons only as burdensome structures that inhibit the free expression of faith in the world of today. This is the great temptation, perhaps, of 'fresh expressions', which has been criticized (Davison and Milbank 2010) for treating the gospel as a disembodied essence that can be expressed in different ways to attract different kinds of people. Worship can then degenerate into a self-conscious indulgence in 'the worship we like best'. The homogeneity that is often encouraged in 'fresh expression' churches (because it has been shown that churches of like-minded people grow fastest) can mitigate against the human variety that is needed for the rainbow presence of the different ministries that, in their variety, represent Christ.

- The mindless apostle is like **salt that has lost its savour:** one whose behaviour lacks the 'taste' of the gospel. Here the opposite has happened: tradition is handed on blindly without regard to what it now presents to anyone, in denial of the way that once was awesome and challenging is now merely quaint and obscure, having lost the taste it once had. We sometimes feel this has happened to the Anglo-Catholic tradition we once loved. Meaning is not so inseparable from tradition that the latter cannot lose it in this way, and it is of course this slow seepage of significance from the old symbols that 'fresh expressions', for all its faults, is trying to tackle.

Mindful apostleship, then, is not only a broad theoretical knowledge of scripture and tradition (though that is a *sine qua non*), but also a kind of *practical* know-how. The priest needs to know the Christian tradition in her bones, in the way she knows how to cook or drive or ride a bike. That does not mean having the whole of scripture and tradition on the tip of her tongue, any more than knowing how to cook means having all the good recipes learned off by heart, or riding a bike means being able to describe to others precisely how it is done. It involves rather the tacit skill of being able to pass something of the richness of the tradition on to others, with or without words, so that they catch hold of its life-giving light and savour.

Being friends with tradition

And that involves something close to personal faithfulness. In a relationship of love or friendship, normally there are no rules to say what counts as faithful and unfaithful behaviour. But the friendship itself will involve a tacit knowledge of this. That is not to say that there may be times when the friends' or partners' expectations differ, leading to an argument in which things have to be spelt out. It is the same with faithful representation: ultimately it is about being a friend of Christ and the tradition that has represented him in the past and continues to do so.

Friendship is not blind, inflexible loyalty, for a friend is someone you feel able to challenge if you think he has got things wrong. Nor is it a situation in which 'anything goes', for a friend is someone whose opinion you respect and trust. Sometimes there may be times of breakdown when you do the equivalent of arguing things out with your friend, and maybe feeling reprimanded. Faithful and mindful representing is thus the kind of friendship in which tradition can grow in us as experience and reflection enrich it.

That way, in the end, we will not be left with the 'theologically correct' talent we buried to keep it safe in the ground, but with our own unique plant, living and flourishing, grown from authentic seed.

Conclusion

This chapter has explored the apostle's ministry, which involves 'handing on' the gospel through a living tradition and representing Christ. Three examples illustrated how, as 'clay pots', we hand on treasure greater than ourselves, while the image of the buried talent reminded us how tradition needs to grow. The images of salt, light and the flawed icon of Christ explored the concept of representing Christ. Minister and people represent Christ in each other, and as a priestly people represent the world to God through the lens of Christ, especially in worship. We have seen that the holiness on which the apostle needs to rely is not her own but that of Christ. But that does not let the minister off the hook. As a flawed icon she still needs to point with her whole being to Christ. And that demands the devotion of the Holy One and a commitment to prayer, which are the subject of the next chapter.

Questions to ponder

1 Reflect on some time when you have felt called upon to do or say things that are at odds with what you have believed or felt in yourself. Have you felt the same hesitation as Adam Smallbone did? Did you actually avoid doing the thing others expected, or did you comply without a second thought, or something in between? What was going on that made you respond as you did?

2 In what ways do you find it helpful and unhelpful for Christians to think of themselves as 'resident aliens'?

3 How do you respond to the suggested possible interpretation of what Jesus may have meant in the parable about the talent buried in the earth?

4 Which aspects of 'representing' come more readily to you, and which do you find more difficult? What might help you feel more comfortable with the latter?

2

The Holy One: Mindful Praying

Like the representative, the 'holy one' is a quiet person, but by no means as 'buttoned up'. One senses beneath the unassuming exterior, so lacking in sartorial elegance, a radiant richness of spiritual imagination, an inner expansiveness that denotes one whose priority is the joyful discipline of prayer.

The congregation and their worship reflect the same spirit of serving the world primarily by offering it to God in prayer. An austere liturgy, focused on a few icons and candles, employs symbols that radiate with all the more clarity for being used sparsely. And to this focus gather many not committed to explicit faith but hungering for a deep spirituality.

Such people will naturally take on a ministry of prayer and intercession, which like a backbone is unseen, but supports everything else that goes on in a church.

Focus: preparing for worship

One of us still regularly leads worship in our local churches. The other, who no longer does, still has a curious kind of recurring dream about preparing to do so. The bishop or some important dignitary is about to arrive. The congregation, larger than usual, is gathering, full of expectancy. However, the order of service is in some indecipherable script, I cannot remember who is doing what, and my sermon is unprepared, or else, on reading my notes, they do not make any sense at all. When the service begins, it turns out to be an absurd ritual in which weird banners and trophies are processed with great flamboyance and magnificent hymn-singing, to random points. And yet, despite my anxieties, and the meaningless paraphernalia, I am quite enjoying it all. And I awake with a certain nostalgia for the times when I did lead the people's worship of God in spite of the fact that in my dreams it seems so absurd.

I hope and trust that I was never actually as unprepared for worship as I am in my dreams, and that the worship I led had a little less banal pomp and a little more meaning and sense of God's holiness. But the dreams certainly betray the strange mixture of feelings that ministers often experience at that transitional moment when preparing to lead the people in the worship of God.

You might like to pause and focus on the feelings you have had at comparable moments. Or, next time you prepare to lead or share in worship, make an honest and mindful inward note of the feelings you have, both positive and negative. Don't edit the feelings or try to explain them, but at a later stage come back to the feelings you have noted and try to ascribe them to their causes.

When leading worship, the greater part of the preparation will have sent you into a fairly solitary world where you commune only with God and with your own thoughts: shutting the study door and switching off the phone so as to wrestle with God in scripture and produce a sermon; sitting in front of the computer, reflecting on the readings and the needs of the people and the occasion so as to prepare a worthy act of worship; saying morning prayer or meditating or doing whatever your rule of life dictates to help keep your mind on the things of God. Blended into this there will have been the intimate and domestic routines of dressing, tooth-brushing, having breakfast and so forth. But all of a sudden you have to forsake this personal, private world as you undertake what may be the most public thing you ever do: conduct the leitourgia, the public worship of the people. Whether you are an extrovert who more naturally relishes the moment or an introvert who struggles with it, the transition is stark and unavoidable.

In terms of the threefold tension explored in Figure 1, the 'I–you' relationship, the tender intimacy with God, is suddenly disrupted by the presence of a 'they'. It is quite easy for things to go wrong at this point. Even Moses and the prophets seem to have resisted the movement from intimate encounter with God to its implications in terms of public role. When Moses' beautiful contemplation of God in the burning bush (of which more later) suddenly turns into an expectation that he will lead God's people into freedom, his first reaction is not unfairly caricatured in a drama sketch as: 'Please – send someone else!' (Martin and Kelso 1986, pp. 22–6). (Moses' hesitation is suggested in the burning bush account at Exodus 3.11; but emphasized more strongly in the later account of his call, by the priestly editors, at 6.12, where Moses complains that his lack of eloquence makes him ill-fitted to the task God is assigning him.)

In terms of the three non-mindful alternatives suggested (pp. xxi–xxii), one is to approach the worship *absent-mindedly*, full of the lofty ideas you have just been contemplating in the study or the lady chapel, but failing to communicate them to the gathered congregation. (This was perhaps the besetting sin of one of us; when I had not prepared well for worship, people noted that on occasion I would preach in a quiet voice gazing at some point in the ceiling, engaged in some intellectual reverie which the congregation could not penetrate!) Or you may approach it *ego-mindedly*, too full of a sense of your own significance in the liturgy, or too anxious about it, and so – in the way discussed earlier (p. 18) – standing between the people and God, as a vicar rather than a repre-sentative. Or you may find yourself, in your anxiety or determination, *mindlessly* rushing around trying to make things happen for people in the worship, offering one trick after another, but losing that sense of flow and coherence and godly focus that is of the essence of holiness in worship.

In a nutshell, if you wish for worship that conveys the 'contagious mindfulness' of which we have spoken (p. viii), there is no alternative but to do what Paul (Galatians 3.27) calls . . .

'Putting on Christ'

We have described the vast shift of focus involved in the transition from preparing for worship to actually leading it. Not all traditions express this through the putting on of vestments for worship – but all, I suspect, have some subtle way of marking the movement, through vestry prayers and the like. (We are told – perhaps apocryphally – that even Billy Graham would sometimes ask those praying with him before preaching to the vast gathered throng, 'How do I look?') But it was a Baptist layman who first called our attention to the beauty of the prayers used by the priest in Catholic and Anglo-Catholic churches as he puts on his robes. Here are some of them.

With the alb (white robe)

Purify me, O Lord, and cleanse my heart; that, being made white in the Blood of the Lamb, I may come to eternal joy.

With the maniple (a band worn on the left arm, probably originally a kind of handkerchief, now seldom used)

Grant, O Lord, that I may so bear the maniple of weeping and sorrow, that I may receive the reward for my labours with rejoicing.

With the chasuble (the seasonally coloured 'poncho' worn over the shoulders)

O Lord, Who said: My yoke is easy and My burden light: grant that I may bear it well and follow after You with thanksgiving.

Through the robes, different aspects of Christ are being taken on: his purity and joy, his suffering and sorrow, his risen life, his burden of work, which is light. The imagery perhaps reverses that of the treasure in the clay pots discussed in Chapter 1. That was about people ordinary on the outside containing Christ within: this is about the ordinary person putting on Christ as an external garment. That could suggest hypocrisy, of course. But the hypocrite is in denial about his unworthiness; he is only concerned to make a good impression. The mindful minister knows he is ordinary and unworthy, but that when he leads worship he enters an arena of expectation in which he represents the people's holiness in Christ (as discussed above, p. 16). There is nothing hypocritical about the vesting prayers: all of them acknowledge – rather than deny – unworthiness, but the dominant note is joy in the real transformation that comes about by the putting on of Christ. Even if yours is a tradition that does not emphasize robes, or uses different robes, you might consider adapting these prayers to convey the putting on of Christ that is (unlike robes themselves) essential to leading Christian worship – and indeed to participating in it.

The use of robes was of course central in the Old Testament priesthood. In a beautiful poem, George Herbert uses the outward dress of the Aaronic priesthood as described in Exodus 28 – the turban on the head, the jewelled ephod on the chest, the bells hanging from the robe (not of course what Christian priests would outwardly wear!) – as images describing the inner holiness of the priest.

> Holinesse on the head,
> Light and perfections on the breast,
> Harmonious bells below, raising the dead
> To leade them unto life and rest.
> Thus are true Aarons drest.

Profanenesse in my head,
Defects and darknesse in my breast,
A noise of passions ringing me for dead
Unto a place where is no rest.
Poore priest thus am I drest.

Onely another head
I have, another heart and breast,
Another musick, making live not dead,
Without whom I could have no rest:
In him I am well drest.

Christ is my onely head,
My alone onely heart and breast,
My onely musick, striking me ev'n dead;
That to the old man I may rest,
And be in him new drest.

So holy in my head,
Perfect and light in my deare breast,
My doctrine tun'd by Christ, (who is not dead,
But lives in me while I do rest)
            Come people Aaron's drest.

(from 'The Temple', 1633)

Such a holiness is not a work of will to please God but a beautiful response to his love. It does not strive to safeguard the holy but (as we shall describe) wanders the borders of the holy and awakens and draws others to explore there too. It is a product, not of overcoming one's own 'profaneness' but of a radical self-emptying, letting Christ become 'my only musick, striking me ev'n dead . . .'.

Holy ones and prayer

By this roundabout route we have come to focus on the kind of holiness, and a related prayerfulness, that remains probably people's strongest expectation regarding the priest or minister. Indeed the holiness of the minister (ordained or lay) comes to her from all three dimensions: from the call of God; from the people and their expectations; and from the minister herself as a person created in God's image. Of course, there may well be tensions between the kinds of holiness that are meant in each dimension. The people may, for example, be looking for a certain kind of dependable respectability that is at odds with the sometimes zany and spontaneous spirituality of God's saints and prophets, and perhaps also at odds with the minister's particular gifts and personality.

As an exercise, write out the words 'be holy' as a command to you. Then in three columns write (i) the qualities you feel God means by this, (ii) the holy qualities you feel you possess or might acquire, at least in part, and (iii) the qualities you sense the people around you expect of those who minister to them, in relation to this 'command'. Look for the correspondences and divergences, and reflect on them.

The image of the 'holy one' (the holy man or woman, or saint – which means 'holy one') is an ancient and probably universal image or archetype. In India the holy men or *sadhus* are particularly prominent in their orange robes or their nakedness. The ideal of the man or woman who has given up everything to travel the earth, or live as a hermit in remote mountains or forests, without provision and wholly dependent on charity, is found in many cultures. It has been institutionalized in various ways, from the orange-robed monastic *sangha*, still held in awe in many Buddhist lands, through the Temple priesthood of Judaism, carefully dealing through complex rites with the dangerous and potentially lethal holy fire of God, to the *staretz* or spiritual guide and the holy fool who were once such important figures in Russia.

The 'holy one' in most of these cases is one who has renounced the pursuit of worldly gain and honour in order to focus on a life of prayer and/or meditation, focused on God or Ultimate Reality. In a Christian context, it is reasonable to equate the Holy One with the person of prayer, and this chapter will explore the place of the different kinds of prayer in the life of the minister or priest.

At the core of the Jewish torah, in the 'holiness code' in Leviticus, we hear the command, 'Be holy as I am holy' (Leviticus 11.34). The command is clearly intended for all God's people, not just the priests. All Christians and indeed all human beings have a vocation to holiness, and Chapter 1 noted (p. 15) what damage is done when the call to ministers to be holy is understood vicariously, as a call to be the designated holy ones in the parish so that the rest do not have to pray. Nevertheless, whenever we have asked lay people to identify what they see as the priorities for their priest, almost unanimously prayer and holiness have come out top. Given the centrality of this expectation of prayer, it is remarkable how often ministers confess, lament or protest that their prayer life is limited and stunted by the demands and expectations put on them. We hope the rest of this chapter will impart a fresh sense of the excitement and wonder of the vocation to pray and to be holy with God's holiness.

The holy fire and its four aspects

In a well-known story from the desert tradition, Abba Lot asked Abba Joseph what more he could do over and above observing his monastic rule. We can imagine a minister asking a similar question: 'I say the daily office, faithfully visit the sick and troubled, plan and execute worship with care, prepare for and attend many meetings, carry out weddings and funerals that are generally acknowledged to be well done, I proclaim the gospel from the pulpit and indirectly in the market place. Is there anything more I can do to be a good priest?'

In reply to Abba Lot, Abba Joseph lifted up his hands to heaven with fingers that blazed like lighted candles, and asked, 'Why not become wholly fire?'

Why fire? Fire gives warmth and light, but can also burn. It has the qualities that Rudolf Otto famously (1958) described as numinous, which he defined in terms of the *mysterium tremendum et fascinans* – the mystery that is both frightening, even daunting, and fascinating, alluring and attractive. Fire frightens us, for obvious reasons, but attracts us too, which is why people from ancient times have gathered in circles around camp fires, each maintaining the careful distance that gives warmth without burning.

Fire, then, stands as an image of the holy. The Bible describes God as a consuming fire (Hebrew 12.29) because his glory and beauty attract us, but he also daunts us, disturbs us, even frightens us. In one tradition of Hebrew thought, you cannot see God and live; and certainly, you cannot encounter God in the depths of your being without being transformed, and catching fire with something of the divine holiness yourself. But change is something we all fear and resist.

Abba Joseph is suggesting that the task of the monastic life is more than that of becoming good and doing all the correct things. It is to catch light with the divine fire. Can we say the same of those who minister? Are they called, not just to be good and respectable, but to be saints or Holy Ones?

In Orthodox theology, the image of fire is used to describe the sacramental work of the priest and the consecrated gifts themselves.

Meanwhile, in his poem 'The Chapel', R. S. Thomas captures an evangelical aspect of holiness, using the same image of fire. The poem describes how once in a darkened chapel

> . . . a preacher caught fire,
> and burned steadily before them
> with a strange light . . .
> with the result that the people
> sang their amens
> fiercely, narrow but saved
> in a way that men are not now.
> (1995, p. 276)

['The Chapel', © R. S. Thomas, *Collected Poems 1945–1990*, Phoenix, an imprint of the Orion Publishing Group. Reprinted by permission.]

How do you respond to these images of 'holy fire'?

Where do you find the equivalent of 'holy fire' at least beginning to be kindled in your church?

In what activities does something of the consuming glory of God blaze out?

Where and how have you found it evident in the lives of others?

In what follows, with the help of some Hebrew patriarchs and prophets, we will look at four aspects of the holy fire.

1. Fire draws our attention. With the help of Moses, we consider holiness in relation to the ability to stop in our tracks, turn aside and contemplate what God is and does amidst the everyday.
2. Fire gives light, but can also hurt. With the help of Jacob, we consider the enlightenment, but also the risk, involved in the vocation to make our home on the borders of the holy.
3. Fire kindles through hands uplifted as in prayer, and gives warmth to a cold world. With the help of Abraham, we consider the vocation to intercede.
4. Fire can be dangerous; it can kill us; it burns away to nothing and goes out. With the help of Elijah, we consider the vocation to simplicity, the voice of silence and 'sunlit emptiness'.

Turning aside to see the fire

Read **Exodus 3.1–15**. Imagine yourself as Moses, paying particular attention to:

- what you are doing;
- what you see – try to imagine this in full detail;
- what you resolve to do;
- what God first commands you to do, and what you actually do. Attend to your feelings at this point;
- the task God sets you;
- your response to this task;
- what God reveals about himself to encourage you in your hesitation.

Now try and think of some experience of your own in which some of these same elements were present. Think this through in the light of Moses' experience.

There is a huge amount to learn from this famous passage, which represents the earlier of the two accounts of Moses' call. It is an encounter with God in his holiness. It illustrates how any place may become the holy of holies in which God is present. God reveals to Moses his essence, his name, 'I am who I am' – a name which has been interpreted in many ways but which denotes God's freedom, his refusal to let his being be named by any name other than being itself. God, we might say, is not this or that; God just is. But with that name goes a call to freedom, and a call to lead people into freedom. God's freedom is not an aloof, detached freedom but a freedom that issues in compassion and struggle for those who are not free, to bring them to a place where they can, like God, just be who and what they are.

But all this ontologically and historically momentous communication can only happen through Moses' very particular turning aside to see. He is at his ordinary daily work of shepherding. He might well have just noted the unusually bright bush nearby, and then got his head down and continued in his work. His concentration and dedication might well have been commendable. But no, he *turns aside* from the task and *looks* with wonder and curiosity. And he is able to see the divine energy in the creation, the supernatural in the natural. Whether what he saw was an actual fire which did not burn the bush up, or whether he was simply able to see the divine fire in the wonder of this beautiful piece of God's creation, we do not know. And it does not matter. Either way he saw a wonder, a miracle: either the miracle of creation behaving strangely, or the miracle of creation itself, the miracle that the bush *was* – evidence of a God who *is*. In either case the key is Moses' mindfulness: his ability not to let his projects and labours determine him, his ability to attend to what is there under his nose.

Such mindful attentiveness does not come easily. In fact to attend in this way, while doing work that requires focus and concentration, is perhaps the most difficult of all things. Simone Weil writes (1959, p. 72):

> There is something in our soul which has a far more violent repugnance for true attention than the flesh has for bodily fatigue. This is something that is much more closely connected with evil than is the flesh. That is why every time we really concentrate our attention, we destroy the evil in ourselves.

The shift of attention involved is the opposite of that described at the outset of the chapter, when we turn from our inner reverie with God to our public duties. Here we lay aside our duty for a while to attend to what is going on around us, in order to see God at work. Both movements happen in the passage: for Moses, having stepped aside from his shepherding duties to look at the bush, will soon have to step back from his encounter with God in the bush to embrace a very different and more challenging public task. But the art of moving from one mode of attention to another and back again is the core skill that makes ministry mindful. We see it at work in:

- turning aside to sing or say the Daily Office, or meditation, or whatever discipline you use to make yourself, at least once or twice a day, turn aside and attend to the things of God;
- turning aside, perhaps from your journey to say your prayers in church, to notice that the daffodils have opened, and the churchyard is beginning to shine with the cool, pristine fires of spring;
- the quiet word offered at a meeting where the stronger voices are prevailing, which, as you turn aside from the agenda and listen to it, may help to provide the clue to resolve the issues being discussed. Turning aside holds one of the keys to good leadership and management;
- the outwardly dull and unassuming person in the congregation who will never put herself forward, but who, if you turn aside and attend, may be found to have just the gifts needed for a certain task. Turning aside holds one of the keys to good collaboration;

- the word or phrase in the passage of scripture which you have not particularly noticed before, and which is not mentioned in your commentary, but which is suddenly calling for your attention because it begins, like the bush, to seem strange and worth investigation. You look up the Greek or other translations. You ponder. And gradually this rejected 'stone' becomes the keystone that relates this passage to what has been going on in your congregation, or in the news, or in your life. Turning aside holds one of the keys to good preaching and evangelism;
- the odd thing the person said, casually, when you were talking to her. You thought no more of it at the time, but something about the words makes you wonder now. Was she trying to communicate something more important than the more apparently central features of the conversation? You feel a need to open up opportunities for the person to say more if she wishes to. Turning aside is one of the keys to good listening and counsel.

How do we increase our use of this all-important skill of turning aside to see? Like all skills, through practice. Keeping to a regular daily discipline of turning aside to pray, both as part of a regular rhythm and through being willing to turn aside for momentary prayer when events beckon, helps the skill to become habitual – especially if it continues despite any inner resistance. Mindfulness can be practised too, in and among the events of a busy day: noticing, as you walk along, what is going on around you, what you are seeing, feeling, hearing, smelling, thinking, what nature is doing, and how people are looking. Eventually it can become second nature, even when you are very focused on achieving things and meeting deadlines, to attend at the same time to what you are experiencing and learning in small ways, and to what God may be saying through them.

Living on the borders of the holy

Read through, meditatively, **Genesis 28.10–22**: the story of Jacob's ladder.

As you did with Moses, imagine yourself as Jacob, tired, at night, with only a stone for your pillow. You may find it helpful to do this exercise late at night in an open place, with only a candle by which to read. Awaken to imagine this amazing sight of the ladder filled with angels, through which you encounter God. You may find Blake's picture helpful – an internet image search on 'Blake Jacob's Ladder' will easily find it for you.

Once again, as with Moses, a remote place becomes the holy of holies, the altar and temple of the living God. You might try repeating to yourself the phrase 'Truly the Lord is in this place, and I never knew it', and with this phrase turning to the world around you.

Then read through Jacob's other dream, **Genesis 32.23–33**. Like the earlier dream, this takes place at night, but Jacob is now on the run from his brother Esau, intent on revenge. The passage feels more primitive and brutal. Imagining yourself as Jacob, you wrestle all through the night with an unknown being. You prevail and demand to know the being's name. Though the being does not give it, you realize that you have been wrestling with God. As you walk away, you limp from the wound you have received. The wound testifies to your encounter with the holy long after the experience has vanished.

Finally reflect. Are there experiences of your own that have been like the enchanting, almost fairytale light-in-darkness of Jacob's ladder, or the much more sombre and painful wrestling of his other dream? If so, you might like to call them to mind and relate them to these dreams of Jacob.

The passages show how encounters with God's holiness can vary immensely. The first passage is in some ways a precursor of Moses' encounter: in both cases God is encountered in a vision of light; both take place in a wild and remote place, and both lead to a revelation of God in his name YHWH and his promise of abundance of life. On the other hand, whereas Moses makes an effort to turn aside and see, Jacob's vision comes without effort, by sheer grace, and the only work involved is the setting up of the altar to mark the experience. In the other dream we see the very opposite: the vision involves struggle. God (by implication) does not give his name, but he does give a new name and identity to Jacob, who is to be called 'Israel', 'the one who strove with God'. The divine nature is given implicitly, in that the name reveals that the opponent is God, to whom Jacob's wound bears witness. A classic by Rowan Williams took up this theme of the second dream in its title, *The Wound of Knowledge* (1979). That book relates the wound to the experience of many spiritual writers, including Luther's theology of the cross and St John of the Cross's dark night of the soul.

When we pray, and especially when we meditate on the scriptures, sometimes there is an effortless revelation; at others an inchoate fumbling and wrestling, full of doubt and maybe despair, out of which nothing seems to emerge. And yet the encounter has changed us, and the cost bears witness to the divine nature of our 'opponent'. The important thing is to welcome both kinds of experience (hard as it may be in the latter case) as instances of what William Countryman describes as the core vocation of the priest (by which he understands all Christians, and even all human beings). This is to 'live on the border of the HOLY'. Countryman capitalizes 'HOLY' as one of the names of God:

> It can be helpful to imagine our human encounter with the HOLY as life in a border country. It is a country in which, at privileged moments of access, we find ourselves looking over from the everyday world into another, into a world that undergirds the everyday world, limits it, defines it, gives it coherence and meaning, drives it. Yet this hidden world is not *another* world, but the familiar world discovered afresh. It is the everyday world seen at new depth, with new comprehension. It is like discovering that the small part of the iceberg we are familiar with is buoyed up by a much larger mass of ice beneath the surface. In the border country one discovers connections, roots, limits, *meaning*. To live there for a while is like having veils pulled away. In the long run we find that the border country is in fact the place where we have always lived, but seen in a new and clearer light. (1999, p. 8)

The holy seems like another world that borders on this, but is in fact this world when we turn aside from our worldly projects, to see it as it is. We might say that we are all called to live on the border between the 'worldly' world and the world of true insight. And this calling to make our home on the border is the vocation – universally human, but responded to by some more than others – to be a priest of the HOLY.

In a similar vein, John Pritchard describes the priest as a 'spiritual explorer', as fascinated by God as explorers were by certain mountains they just had to conquer or lands they risked their lives to find:

> For the priest prayer is a matter of life or death. It's a tale of love and loss; it's an experience of joy and bewilderment; it's dancing and struggling with the divine lover. Sometimes it's sitting in the dark thinking that this is all folly. Sometimes it's all that life can hold. It's all part of the God-directedness of our lives. And it's irreplaceable. . . . The practice of ministry will often leave us feeling like a compass in a room full of strong magnets. Everywhere there are attractive

possibilities into which we could put our energy, but one magnet above all must direct our life . . . People have a right to expect this from a priest. Certainly, we need to beware of and resist the projections which can be placed on a priest – perfection in life, faith, prayer and the behaviour of our pets is hard to live up to – but they are right to expect the priest to be fascinated with the holy. (2007, p. 23)

Pritchard goes on to relate the story of Abba Lot and Abba Moses (see above) which reminds us that living on the border of the holy can burn and demand costly transformation. But this cost will be the consequence of being on familiar terms with a Holy One who, like Christ, had nowhere to lay his head, but was always on the move . Just when we were getting comfortable, he invites us to journey with him somewhere else.

So the priest makes his home wandering on the borderlands as the albatross is at home flying across the oceans. He is familiar with the move between worlds – public and private, ordinary and holy – described in our focusing exercise. Yet albatross pairs always find their way back to last year's nesting site, even if in the meantime they have circumnavigated the globe. In the same way the priest comes back to a faithful rendezvous with her people and to the places where she is needed.

At home with the uncanny

The vocation to be at home on the borders runs throughout ministry, but is especially apparent, perhaps, in the need to be at home where people today are often very ill at ease, with the dying and the departed. The priest needs to navigate with confidence the passage from this life to the next, in the last rites, in comfort for the dying and bereaved, and in dealing with apparent haunting by departed spirits. Few ministers can have avoided the request to 'exorcise' a house believed to be haunted. Exorcism, of course, is a popular but inappropriate term here, since demons possess people, not houses. If it is really a demon possession that seems to be involved, the matter is beyond the ordinary minister's competence. Most churches have experts – diocesan exorcists and the like – to whom the matter should be referred if the frightening goings-on relate to one particular person who is not obviously psychotic. And if they affect a person who does seem to be disturbed, the matter should be referred to doctors and others able to give appropriate diagnosis and care.

But it may well be a case where somewhat disturbing and out of the ordinary (but not directly harmful) manifestations are going on that have the ring of truth, but are not ascribable to the activity of a living individual. Such phenomena may arise from a local death in troubling circumstances. In such cases suitable prayers for the departed, with rites like sprinkling with holy water of haunted places, have always – in our experience – seemed to work, to an extent that has taken us by surprise. Whether you understand these things in a realist way – that an actual departed spirit has found rest in the next world thanks to your prayers – or in a psychological way – an aura of disturbance or a bad memory which the living inhabitants have latched on to has been dispersed by the priest's peace and confidence and prayer – may not matter. What matters is that the priest herself is neither 'spooked by the spooks', nor dramatizes them, nor by her antics encourages the people's own horrified fascination, but lives at home on the borders of the ordinary and the holy, the familiar and the strange, the living and the dead, and acts soberly with a matter-of-fact confidence that Christ is stronger than any harmful influence, able to overcome and to heal matters that lie, frankly, beyond our own understanding.

Interceding

> Read **Genesis 18.16–33** where Abraham intercedes on behalf of Sodom and Gomorrah.
> In what ways is this like and unlike your own experience and practice of intercession?
>
> - To what extent do you reason with God or try to persuade God in your prayers?
> - Do you see God in the same way or differently – and in what respects?
> - It may help to write some notes about your own practice of intercession.

Abraham, here, reminds us of a Middle Eastern trader haggling over the price of his goods. God is angry with the people of Sodom and Gomorrah and determined to destroy them. But Abraham is a friend, chosen of God, in a position to mediate. He appeals to God's 'better nature', reasoning with God about the injustice of destroying fifty . . . twenty . . . and finally only ten just men. We see, perhaps, an antecedent of the eighteenth-century judge Blackstone's principle that 'it is better that ten guilty persons escape than that one innocent suffer'.

Doubtless we would be uncomfortable with the idea that God has a 'better nature', since for Christians God's whole nature is unified and consists of mercy through and through. A lot of ink has been spilt arguing whether in interceding we are trying to persuade God to change God's mind, or submitting ourselves to the immutable will of God. It is beyond the scope of this book to enter those arguments. Nevertheless, there is quite clearly an unresolved tension between the all-good nature of God and the pain and suffering we see in this world. Intercession springs from a desire to heal that discrepancy and channel the energies of God into the healing of the world, and the energies of the world into the glorification of God. Though God and the world cannot be regarded as hostile forces between which the intercessor has artfully to mediate after the manner of Abraham, the one who lives on the borders of the holy will wish to open the space where the two interact, thus sharing in the bringing of healing to the world and glory to God.

And there is the key. Interceding springs from interbeing. Christ is called, in the letter to the Hebrews (2.17, 3.1, 4.14–15, 5.1, 5, 10, 7.26, 8.1, 9.11), the great High Priest because he crossed the borders between the holy and the 'profane'. As God, incarnate as a human being, he felt the full weight of the world's harm; as the man, risen and ascended into God, he showed the way to the transfiguration of the world, in all its ill and pain, into glory. God's priestly people are called to enter that go-between space he opened up, and ordained priests and ministers are reasonably expected to pioneer that path and show the way. Elsewhere one of us defined intercession as simply:

> . . . thinking of and being with God in his glory, and thinking of and being with others in their pain. It means steeping ourselves in the holy mystery of God, which is where . . . we now belong, where we are now 'hidden with Christ'; and steeping ourselves in the suffering of humanity, which is equally our own. The more we know the joy involved in the former, the more we will be able to be naked and open to the latter. Intercession means moving between these two points, taking the divine energy with us into the healing of the human world, and taking the sufferings of the human world into the passion of the divine, so that a third, new point will be reached where the will of God is done. (Thompson 2009, p. 147)

We therefore cannot intercede aright unless we first contemplate, and enter the borderland, feeling the full weight of the glory of God and the pain of the world simultaneously. If we feel the glory of God but deny the plight of the world, our intercession will degenerate into blind submission to God and a desire to overrule the world's legitimate claims on God. If we are conscious of the pains but insufficiently attuned to the holy, our intercession will degenerate into a desire to manipulate God or present God with a shopping list of needs. We will fail to 'see our prayer within the context of [the] great and eternal divine passion for our well-being', and instead we will 'bind it to our own limited vision and limited hope' (Williams 1994, p. 140).

From feeling both the glory and the pain we are able to utter both in true intercession. Abraham's own intercession, businesslike as it was, sprang from an acute sense both of God's holy anger against the inhospitality of the two towns, and an acute sense of the suffering and injustice that would be done to the innocent in a blanket destruction. (If we feel the holy anger to be unjustified, it is perhaps partly because hospitality is not the sacred duty for us that it is in Middle Eastern culture.)

So Pritchard describes the priest in his calling to intercede as a 'pain bearer, keeping vigil with a troubled world' (2007, Chapter 7), feeling the weight of the sufferings of those he prays for. In that sense, the work of the priest as intercessor feeds back into, and draws from, his work as carer and servant. But the intercessor does not merely bear pain for the sake of it, hoping that it will in some way alleviate the sufferer. He bears those pains as the pains of God, yearning for the healing and liberation of the victim, yet knowing that there may well be factors in the situation that will tragically resist that fullness. In this sense, the work of the intercessor relates to that of the representative and the evangelistic witness to the love of God, vulnerable but real.

Intercession does not infallibly 'work', any more than any other ministry does. In the event, Abraham was unable to avert the destruction of Sodom and Gomorrah. Though we can be with God and be with the world as best we can, we cannot know either fully enough to represent each to the other perfectly, or predetermine the future outcome. But intercession remains integral to the calling and being of a priest.

Sunlit absence

Read **1 Kings 19.1–13:** Elijah on Mount Horeb.

Imagine yourself into the story. You have just performed a spectacular public miracle on Mount Carmel, by which your fame seems assured. But you have fled into this lonely place, a wilderness full of aridity and despair. Eventually you come to a great mountain, and sit in a cave.

You see great sights and sounds pass you by: earthquakes, mighty winds, and blazing fire. But they are empty: you see nothing of God in them. They are just a 'tale . . . full of sound and fury, signifying nothing' (Shakespeare, Macbeth, 5.5.26–28).

And then there is silence, an audible silence, a tangible breeze . . . and you sense the presence . . .

The passage tells of the lowest point in the ministry of that great prophet of fire, Elijah. He has just had his greatest public success, calling down God's fire to consume his burnt offering and so proving God's superiority to the gods of the prophets of Baal, who failed to do so. But far from seizing this moment of triumph, Elijah is overcome with fear of retribution, and flees alone into the desert, where he wants to die. His success has burnt him out. But God continues gently and quietly to provide for him, even in his despair, until he comes to the holy mountain where long ago the Law was given to Moses. There his despair deepens into something more profound: a realization that God is not in the spectacular outward events of earthquake, wind and fire. By implication this might even mean that God was not in the fire by which through the prayers of Elijah on Mount Carmel he had apparently proved his superiority.

Later, St John of the Cross would take up this theme. On the mountain of God the person of prayer encounters many new experiences. But she has to learn to say 'nada, nada', nothing, nothing of this experience is God. The saying is reminiscent of the Hindu 'neti, neti' . . . neither this . . . nor this . . . is God; or the Mahayana Buddhist insistence that nothing has existence in itself, all forms are empty.

Only then comes the experience of God . . . in the paradox of the sound of a breeze, which makes no noise: Simon and Garfunkel's 'sound of silence', perhaps; or translated into visual terms, a 'sunlit absence' (Laird 2011). It is the radical alternative to the idolatry which on Mount Carmel Elijah had opposed, but not radically enough: for there he proved God to be just a bigger and better wonder-worker than the gods of the idolaters. Only now, through painful experience, does Elijah realize the full radicalism of his struggle: all idols, including those mighty events in which we imagine God to be, must be overcome. We must find God without form at all, in the glorious spaciousness of emptiness, in the mysterious sound of silence.

This was the fruit of hard struggle. Elijah's public triumph had burnt him out, in the same way that many ministers, at the height of a very active and 'successful' ministry, find themselves burnt out. Yet as with

Elijah, this burning out may bring the minister closer to the living fire of holiness, the heart of her calling.

Many traditions have affirmed this. In Orthodox, Roman Catholic and Anglo-Catholic theologies, the priesthood involves suffering because it is 'sacrificial'. The priest is to lead a life 'plainly consecrated to God, a life of loneliness, of prayer, of work' (Fr Briscoe at the first Anglo-Catholic Priests' Convention, Oxford 1921, cited in Billings 2010, p. 101). This vocation to holiness, including incessant toil and a kind of isolation from the flock (which the priest tended but did not befriend) has inspired, but also sometimes burdened, many priests in these traditions. Hard work, loneliness, celibacy, constant availability, lack of time he could call his own, and the bearing of the pain of others, were all part of the ideal, even if many priests inevitably failed to live up to it. J. H. L. Morrell's *The Heart of a Priest* (1958) emphasized self-surrender in all walks of the priest's life. The chapters on 'Self-surrender in Endurance', 'Longsuffering', 'Work', 'Study' and 'Self-Denial' make up the greater part of the book. Only in the final chapter do we hear of 'The Priest's Reward and Joy'. But this joy is itself founded on self-surrender. 'Detachment from the earthly means attachment to the heavenly', it is argued, so that 'no calling is so full of abounding joy' (p. 178).

Of course, this sacrificial understanding requires an awesome self-discipline. But it is a discipline of action, in Elijah's terms the discipline of Mount Carmel, a discipline of hard work and effort leading to public acclaim, but also in many cases to burn-out. What we are talking about, the discipline of Mount Horeb, is different. It is not a discipline of action so much as one of contemplation. It is not a matter of doing a lot but of keeping still, so as to reflect the light of God as still waters reflect the sun or moon.

In an oft-quoted passage, Monica Furlong has described the kind of priest she looks for.

> Clergy are in for a growing loneliness, of being misunderstood. I suggest that this will only be endurable if they expect this, understand the reasons for it, and do not cast too many envious glances over their shoulders at the circumstances of their predecessors.
>
> I am clear about what I want from the clergy. I want them to be people who can, by their own happiness and contentment challenge my ideas about status, success and money and so teach me how to live more independently of such drugs.
>
> I want them to be people who can dare, as I do not dare, and as few of my contemporaries dare to refuse to work flat out and to refuse to work more strenuously than me.

I want them to be people who dare because they are secure enough in the value of what they are doing to have time to read, to sit and think, and who face the emptiness and possible depression which often attacks people when they do not keep the surface of their mind occupied.

I want them to be people who have faced this kind of loneliness and discovered how fruitful it is, and I want them to be people who have faced the problem of prayer.

I want them to be people who can sit still without feeling guilty and from whom I can learn some kind of tranquillity in a society which has almost lost the art. [Paper at Wakefield Diocesan Conference, 1966]

Whereas the hard-working, 'sacrificial' priest may be pleasing to people because he manifests a vicarious salvation – people can appreciate and celebrate their priest's good works instead of having to be holy themselves – Monica Furlong's contemplative priest may be a threat. Eugene Peterson describes many of the features of Furlong's ideal in his account of the 'contemplative pastor' (1993). Such a pastor is, he argues, unbusy, apocalyptic and subversive. The unbusiness is described well in the passage just quoted, and we can see why it is subversive, as it challenges the business by which people clutter themselves and run away from their own emptiness. 'Apocalyptic' for Peterson names the ultimate values that will persist until the end of time and when everything we cling to collapses. It is what the pastor is always looking for through the darkness of his contemplations, in the vigilance of the 'watchman' – one of the key terms with which the Anglican ordinal describes the ordained. Peterson writes:

Being a pastor who satisfies a congregation is one of the easiest jobs on the face of the earth — if we are satisfied with satisfying congregations. The hours are good, the pay is adequate, the prestige considerable. Why don't we find it easy? Why aren't we content with it?

Because we set out to do something quite different. We set out to risk our lives in a venture of faith. We committed ourselves to a life of holiness. At some point we realized the immensity of God and of the great invisibles that socket into our arms and legs, into bread and wine, into our brains and our tools, into mountains and rivers, giving them meaning, destiny, value, joy, beauty, salvation. We responded to a call to convey these realities in Word and Sacrament. We offered ourselves to give leadership that connects and co-ordinates what the people in this community of faith are doing in their work and play, with what God is doing in mercy and grace . . . We have an obligation beyond pleasing somebody; we are pursuing or shaping the very nature of reality, convinced that when we carry out our commitments, we benefit people at a far deeper level than if we simply did what they asked of us. (pp. 131–2)

So it is that the vocation to holiness pushes the way in which we serve people (the subject of the next chapter) in a direction that is subversive (of which more in Chapter 8).

There is a memory from our own ministry that poignantly conveys something about this deeper level of reality – the sound of silence and the sunlit absence. We had, at that time, a small but remarkably mixed choir of all ages, and it contained some very new younger voices. The choir leader had rehearsed the Taizé chant, 'Stay with me, remain here with me, watch and pray'. This was to introduce the great Vigil of Gethsemane that follows the Maundy Thursday Eucharist. The chant was to be sung ever more quietly to lead into the silence, but nobody had thought of how to decide when to stop. So when the time had come, and we had stripped the altars, leaving the main church in darkness, and were gathered in the side chapel, full of lights and flowers and the sacrament representing Christ, the choir sang the chant over and over again, quieter each time. We thought they had finally stopped, when two of the younger girls piped up again in their fragile, faltering voices. At last there were some moments of silence . . . but then, one of the voices sang yet again. It was not in itself ethereal singing, but by the time there really was outward silence, the silence itself was singing: 'watch and pray . . . watch and pray . . . watch and pray'.

The Holy One is one who is like that singing.

Conclusion

The previous chapter described the fundamental relation ministers are called to bear, or the fundamental meaning their lives are to have: that of representing God in Christ to the people, and the people in Christ to God. Bearing this significance requires memory, steadfastness and steady momentum. This chapter has described what the minister needs to be in order to do that: holy, able to turn aside to see the holy in the ordinary and hence to live on the border between the two, to intercede on those borders and to be open to the fiery emptiness of God. For this she needs courage, lightness and inner orientation.

In the rest of the book we turn to the various things the minister is called to do: to care, to teach, to manage, to communicate, to share the gospel and to set people free. These are the activities through which she represents Christ, and leads people on the borders of the holy.

Questions to ponder

1   Reflect on times when you have found *turning aside* richly rewarding and times when you have found it a real struggle.

2   How far does the metaphor of living 'on the borders of the Holy' connect with your experience, and how do you respond to it?

3   It is suggested in this chapter that intercession is taking the sufferings of the human world into the passion of God and allowing God's glory to shine in the dark places of the world. How far does this resonate with your own experience and with the way intercessions are led at your church?

3

The Pastor: Mindful Serving

The minister who epitomizes the ministry of serving sees herself as firmly placed within tradition, but as a servant rather than a leader. For she sees what needs to be conserved as being ultimately not an abstract faith or tradition, but the faithful themselves. The faithful people are, for her, the tradition she seeks to guard and pass on to posterity. Her quietness and humility are the classic qualities we call 'pastoral': they encourage people to trust her to guide them, like the good shepherd, to good and healing pasture.

The liturgy of 'serving' churches, though often traditional in style and full of richness and depth, is not ostentatious or triumphalistic; more ancient or medieval in feel, perhaps, than baroque. It feels rooted in the healing ministry of Christ, offering a place in which to be, to heal, and for each member to grow in his own way.

Natural 'servants' will obviously make good lay pastoral assistants; they will be the people to call upon for hospital and bereavement visiting.

Focus: reckless rehabilitation?

For several weeks you noticed an anxious-looking middle-aged newcomer sitting at the back of your congregation. A couple of times he slipped away before you reached the porch. Then you managed to speak with him. Though he refused the invitation to stay for coffee, he readily responded to your offer of a visit. You found his council flat, where he lives alone, in considerable disarray. So far in the conversation he has told you that he has just come out of prison after a three-year sentence, but he has not disclosed what for. In prison he 'came to Jesus' and began a new life, putting his past behind him. His past, he says, is no longer relevant since he is a new creation in Christ. Now he wants to get involved in church life but finds it difficult relating to the respectable people who come. He also needs help finding a job, which won't be easy given his record.

Where will you take the conversation from here? What might you suggest for him or offer to do? What will be your main considerations, and what theological, scriptural and other models will be your guide? Choose two or three words that would express how you see your ministerial duties in relation to this man.

Servants and deacons

Tell any Anglican priest in any part of the world that he is no prophet and he will cheerfully agree that this is indeed so. Tell him he has no gifts of leadership and while he may not like it he will not greatly resent it. But tell him that he has no pastoral sense and he will be really hurt, and feel deeply wounded and insulted in the house of his friends. (Roger Lloyd, cited in Billings 2010, p. 118)

In recent times it has often been taken for granted that the priesthood is one of the 'caring professions'. Ministry was taken to be synonymous with pastoral care, and constituted the focus for a burgeoning 'pastoral theology'. It was, as this passage suggests, at the heart of an Anglican priest's self-definition. But the terms 'minister' and 'pastor' suggest that for many denominations the models of servant and shepherd have always been at the centre of how the calling of their leaders has been understood.

There are indications that this hegemony of the pastoral is changing. More recently the focus seems to have shifted to other areas like mission, management and leadership, in which the minister is expected to be more proactive and even directive. The Anglican criteria for selection for ministerial training (Archbishops' Council 2011, see www.churchofengland.org/clergy-office-holders/ministry/selection/ddos.aspx) have incorporated new sections on 'leadership and collaboration' and 'mission and evangelism', but appear never to have had a section denoting care, loving concern, or a desire to serve others, central as these are in the ordinal. There appears today to be a real dilemma for the Church of England at least as to whether its task is (as traditionally understood) to be a 'chaplain' serving a nation broadly understood as Christian, or, nowadays, to evangelize and convert the nation to the Christian faith (Billings 2010, pp. 75–6).

However, although there may be more of an emphasis on one or other approach, mindful ministry surely requires both. For, as this chapter suggests, a ministry of service to others, carried out in a theologically reflective way, proclaims and reflects the servanthood of Christ which is at the heart of the Good News of the gospel.

The vocation of servant has deep roots in the Old Testament, though mostly the service encountered there relates to the service of God rather than people. The central part of Isaiah, generally known as 'second Isaiah', contains four well-known 'songs' about a mysterious suffering servant of God. Mostly the servant serves God by proclaiming God's name and bringing justice, but in the last song (Isaiah 52.13 — 53.end) he also serves the people by offering himself to be punished for their sins. This was probably the intention of the saying, 'The Son of Man came not to be served but to serve, and to give his life as a ransom for many' (Mark 10.45; Matthew 20.28). In John's Gospel Jesus acts out a parable of this servant role, discussed below.

In the New Testament, among the charisms or gifts of the spirit, 1 Corinthians 12 lists 'healing' (v. 9) and later on 'healers' (v. 28) and also 'helpers' (*antilepsis*, support, succour, protection or charitable giving). Romans 12.6–8 includes serving (*diakonia*), the giver or – more precisely – the one who shares out (*metadidous*), and the one who shows mercy or loving-kindness (*eleos*). All of these are arguably aspects of the ministry discussed in this chapter. By the end of the first century these varied ministries had been subsumed, by and large, into the ministry of the deacon.

Deacons are mentioned several times in the New Testament. The later instances, in the Pastoral Epistles, describe deacons alongside the bishops, whose role is not described but assumed as if it were already well established. The concern of these passages is to clarify not the diaconal role itself but the moral characteristics expected of the deacons. In Catholic tradition the diaconate is traced back to the appointment of seven men in Acts 6.1–6. It was argued at the time that the apostles should not have to busy themselves with the distribution of food to the needy, but focus on their task of 'prayer and the ministry of the word'. The apostles authorized the seven by the laying on of hands for a role that was clearly pastoral, charitable and administrative.

However, the passage in Acts immediately goes on to tell the story of the two men first mentioned among the seven. Stephen preached a long sermon, before becoming the first Christian martyr (Acts 6.8 — 8.3). Philip, meanwhile, went to preach the Good News in Samaria (8.4–8) and converted the first gentile, the Ethiopian eunuch, before continuing on his way preaching as far as Caesarea (26–40). If these men were deacons, the Acts of the Apostles seems to be clearly underlining an evangelistic role. In fact the term 'deacon' has a variety of meanings: servant, waiter, butler, steward, manager, messenger, or one who attends to or ministers to need. This chapter focuses on the servant and ministering roles, but the ministry of the evangelist (Chapter 7) can also be considered to be diaconal.

Butler or slave?

Read **John 13.1–13**.

As you do so, imagine yourself as Peter. Focus on the feelings that come to you as Jesus kneels before you, looks you in the eye, and starts to pour the water over your feet. Attend to the feeling of the water. Allow yourself to say something to Jesus that expresses your outward and inward feelings – it may be very different from Peter's recorded response – and hear what Jesus replies to you.

Now re-read the passage and imagine taking on the role of the one who washes the feet of others. (Imagine yourself as you remove some outer clothes in order to do this – how does this feel?) Picture the faces of the people whose feet you might wash: they may be people you know and care for, some may be strangers, or people you find difficult. Perhaps there are people there whose feet you do not really want to wash – if so, reflect on that. Look each person in the face, and attend to what their faces and perhaps their voices are saying to you, and you to them. Finally stand for a moment, and then sit down with the people around the table. What is the atmosphere, and what effect has the washing of those people's feet had on your relationship with them?

Jesus' action here, for many, epitomizes a radical ministry of service:

> You cannot claim to worship Jesus in the tabernacle if you do not pity Jesus in the slum . . . You have your Mass, you have your altars, you have begun to get your tabernacles. Now go out into the highways and hedges, and look for Jesus in the ragged and the naked, in the oppressed and the sweated, in those who have lost hope, and in those who are struggling to make good. Look for Jesus in them; and, when you have found Him, gird yourself with His towel of fellowship and wash His feet in the person of His brethren. (H. Maynard Smith (1926), *Frank Bishop of Zanzibar: Life of Frank Weston*, London: SPCK, cited in Billings 2010, p. 109)

It is, perhaps, significant that when Jesus refers to himself as 'one who serves', the word used is *diakonos*. But when in the above passage Jesus says 'a servant is not greater than his master', another, stronger word is used: *doulos*, a slave. The washing of feet was certainly the duty of a slave rather than a waiter, butler or minister.

There is actually quite a difference between these contexts. A slave obeys a master without question, and is liable to be punished for any sign of insubordination. A butler or waiter, on the other hand, holds quite a dignified and responsible position in a household. He manages the household and is trusted with the day-to-day decisions about its running. If the master asks him to do something he deems unwise – ordering the wrong sort of wine for the meal, for example – he is entitled to question the master and suggest a wiser course. Overall he takes the burden of management and organization from the master.

Now when we speak of service, in our society it is the diaconal model we have in mind. Public servants, ministers including prime ministers, employees in the 'service' industries, the people who 'service' our cars, along with doctors and nurses and the like, all act more like butlers than slaves. They serve with wisdom rather than blind obedience or overwhelming compassion, keeping a professional distance between themselves and our felt need. Their demeanour is not that of cringing submission to our will, but a dignified offering of what to them seems the best way of bringing well-being to us (or our car).

It is easy to find examples where the minister definitely needs to be this sort of *diakonos* rather than a *doulos*. A colleague on a council estate parish told of a time when the doorbell of the vicarage rang in the middle of the night. Sleepily at first, but with an adrenaline rush that helped him wake up, he pulled on his dressing-gown and ran down the stairs, prepared to cope with some kind of emergency. Perhaps someone was on their deathbed, and the last rites had been requested. Perhaps a neighbour had been talking to someone on the brink of suicide, and was looking for help. When he opened the door, however, there was a large and rather menacing-looking youth with a glazed expression. He asked the vicar if he had any tin foil to spare. The vicar was savvy enough to know this was not some last-minute catering need – the foil would not be used to wrap a chicken in the oven, but for snorting cocaine. So he refused the request. Whereupon the young man snapped resentfully, 'Hmph! Call yourself a Christian!' and turned away.

If the minister were a *doulos*, his duty would have been to do the young lad's will. But as a *diakonos* he is entitled to respond by treating the addict with respect and responding with a dignity of his own, suggesting politely that colluding with his habit might not be the best service to offer right now.

However, it is not quite so simple. Though it is different from slavery, there is clearly something more to Jesus' washing of the feet than mere table waiting, Though what he does is the act of a slave, it is not offered either as a table waiter would offer the best option on the menu, or as a slave would do it, in response to command. In the context of the Passion the whole action is clearly a Johannine sign of the *kenōsis* or self-emptying involved throughout Jesus' ministry. Jesus is the one who chose to lay aside his garments of divine glory and come among us to touch those parts of us that are most soiled by the earth, those parts that we are often ashamed of, offering the baptismal waters of dying and rising with him, before he himself rises and reassumes his robes of glory.

Letting the emptiness flower

The ministry of service, then, is not just a kind of soul-service; its agenda is set neither by the demands of the 'clients' nor by professional training in a large body of learned professional expertise, but by the kenosis of Christ. That is not to say that we should see ministers as gentlemen and ladies who lay aside their own great status to get alongside the 'lowly'. It is rather that they are able to let go of something of their own egos, their own preconceptions, while yet not being totally dominated, as a slave would be, by the demands of the other. It is to allow a letting go in which the great service that Christ has done and still does for us can intervene. It is to allow the emergence of a void – the *kenos* or empty space of *kenōsis* – that is not filled by the needs and desires of either party; a pain or sorrow that is not resisted but felt for what it is, which Christ and the Holy Spirit alone can fill with healing and renewing power.

We are back with mindfulness again. And again, there can be a temptation for the minister to serve the other in unmindful ways:

1 He can fill the void with his idea of God's plan for everyone, leading to an absent-minded ministry in which – to take our example – the person is simply lectured on his need to turn away from drugs to God.
2 He can fill the void with his own need to do something impressive or at least credible in the other's eyes, leading to an ego-minded ministry that is really about meeting his own needs. He might have invited the young man in and offered him coffee and

sat and chatted, feeling very chuffed about his generosity and failing to notice how bored and desperate and fidgety the man was getting. (The same kind of sensitivity is needed, we have often found, with men of the road, who appreciate a meal and a chat, but not always 'counselling' or tender loving care.)

3 Or he can let the need of the other fill the void, in an absent-minded ministry that is a slave-like response to the other's presenting needs. The vicar might have got sucked into the young man's feeling of urgency, and felt impelled to go and fetch some foil so that his visitor would be thankful rather than angry.

The mindful option is to resist any of the impulses to fill the void, and simply attend to it with non-judgemental compassion, letting God hold it in his love. When this happens, just sometimes the other person will follow suit. Sometimes through this process, God opens up a solution which emerges on the lips of either the minister or the person in need – curiously it seems not to matter which, because it comes from somewhere neither of them could have invented. More often there is no solution, but the sorrow is transformed beyond personal sorrow and woven some-how into the torn and healing fabric of the world.

This resistance to filling the void does not come naturally, and we can think of many examples of failure, like the one just cited. But one of us remembers visiting the family of a child who had died, whose funeral I was to take. I remember being met by a room full of relatives and an atmosphere of stony, resentful silence. By the time I left there was warmth and gratefulness. What had I done? Literally nothing. I had just let them pour out how painful and unfair it was to lose their baby. But what they warmly thanked me for was, as they put it, not preaching to them. I had not tried to fill the void with words of defence of God or comfort for them, but let the void be the void, until it weighed on me too, though not in any self-conscious way. I left them with that void, but it had somehow become a softer void, which, though without any identifiable hope, was perhaps a little more open to the future. Prob-ably you can think of similar examples from your own ministry.

In the following we will look at this work with the void through two traditional images that tease out the meaning of the ministry of service: the shepherd and the healer. We shall see what this ministry has in com-mon with counselling and therapy, and how it differs, exploring how in Christian service the emptiness of sorrow opens out more fully in the breadth of community, the course of time, and the theological perspec-tive of Christ's self-emptying.

The Good Shepherd and the counsellor

> Read **John 5.5–14** from the point of view of the man at the pool.
>
> You have been crippled for 34 years. You can see where healing lies, but your very illness prevents you reaching the healing source.
>
> Note Jesus' question to you. Are there physical or mental conditions or habits that you have given up wanting to change, because change seems impossible and wanting it only gives you pain? Or does the question seem unfair, because over all these years, you have continued your struggle to reach the source of healing?
>
> And note his command to you. Feel the power of that command transmuting into energy in parts of you that have grown weak over the years. How do you walk now: strongly and confidently, or feebly and fearfully?
>
> Now shift your attention to your own desire to bring change, perhaps among people who have grown accustomed to weakness . . . ; and your own need for change.

At first Jesus seems to work like a counsellor, getting the man to identify what he really wants. But once he knows from the man's own words that he really does want healing, he seems to become completely different, issuing a command in the way no counsellor ever would. He is more like a doctor, perhaps, writing a prescription and saying, in a tone that brooks no contradiction, 'Take this four times a day!'

According to the ideas just advanced, we see this transition in the following terms. By asking the question, Jesus forces the man to face head-on the full sorrow of his condition. 'Sir, I have no one to put me into the pool when the water is stirred up; and while I am making my way, someone else steps down ahead of me' (v. 7). The void of sorrow has been opened up. But it is this very void that opens the path for the divine command of healing. If we understand things this way, we can chart a path between two misleading models of the pastor.

On one model – that employed in professional counselling – the client is the only one with authority to disentangle the needs he really feels and the aims he really wants to have. The counsellor is there, specifically, to help the client do his own work. Such an approach is typically modern in the way it respects the autonomy of the human ego.

On an opposite, more traditional or pre-modern and certainly less fashionable model, the minister is the one given the spiritual wisdom to discern true from false in terms of needs and aims. The client comes to the minister as to a shepherd or pastor rather than a counsellor. A shepherd does not ask the sheep where they would like to go. He is the one who knows where the fresh waters and green pastures are, and how to negotiate the valley of the shadow of death (Psalm 23); he leads the sheep and they follow, as their very survival is at stake. Or changing the metaphor, like the sheepdog he needs to attend both to the sheep and to the master who knows the sheep's best interests. He cannot simply do the bidding of the sheep.

So which model should the minister follow in her offering of care: the shepherd/sheepdog or the counsellor? Or something else? Alan Billings (2010) makes a strong case for the former. He criticizes the 'listening' or counselling model of the pastor, which he sees as advocated in a work popular when he himself trained for ministry, Alistair Campbell's *Rediscovering Pastoral Care* (1981). He criticizes the vogue for the minister as 'social activist and personal therapist' (a somewhat odd combination – activists seldom make good therapists and vice versa!) which he sees as rising from a loss of confidence in the directive role of the traditional pastor.

> The pastor's task was to prepare souls for heaven, to help – in Herbert's words – shrivelled hearts to recover greenness. At some point in the Church's recent history, this emphasis changed: the cure of souls ceased to be central, and concern for people's emotional and material well-being assumed priority. (p. 134)

Herbert's 'greenness' – opposed to the 'shrivelled' – is an evocative image of what the pastor seeks, but it needs interpretation. To us it suggests the green pastures and still waters of Psalm 23, and the 'life in all its fullness' of John 10.20, and hence something akin to what Aristotle – using the same kind of organic analogy – called 'flourishing'. And that was his term for well-being. So it is not at all clear how the goals of the counsellor and the pastor can be opposed. What may be different is how well-being and fullness of life are to be achieved, and by whom they are to be discerned.

In fact, Campbell included in the book his own critique of a simplistic model for the pastor as counsellor. He sees this as evidenced in a generation of American pastoral theology, epitomized in the writings of Seward Hiltner, for whom 'a tender and solicitous concern' was central. Campbell argues (pp. 31–3) that Hiltner transfers uncritically to pastoral care the methodology of non-directive counselling and client-centred therapy. Whereas in counselling we attend to our pains and traumas in order that they may find release, and we may begin to be able to order our own lives according to our ideals free from buried pain, in authentic pastoral care our pain may initially get worse. For the good shepherd may lead us to confront issues like sin and the need for remorse and repentance (*metanoia* – transformation of mind and intent), and that may mean challenging and changing the ideals by which we have led our lives. It is a mistake (though one often made) to expect the assistance the doctor or surgeon or even the counsellor offers us inevitably to lessen pain in the short term; why should we expect this of the pastor?

On the other hand, Campbell (p. 44) concurs with Hiltner (1959, p. 44) in his abhorrence of the 'pastoral bulldozer' approach which Hiltner parodies in the way a (mythical, we hope!) Pastor Barton consoles a widow.

> So now his life with you is ended, and you cannot add to nor take away from it. Thus I want to tell you that all your thoughts about him must be self-analysed the moment they begin to cause you what is commonly called 'grief' . . . Then if you find elements of self-pity, terminate them at once and force yourself to breathe a prayer of gratitude that your life with him was so beautiful and that he lived so complete a life in so short a time.

Pastor Barton is here trying, by his rhetoric, to force the poor widow through a process that can only happen, in that beautifully rich phrase, 'in her own good time'. He encourages her to repress feelings that are a natural and important part of grieving, and to feel instead feelings he considers to be more 'Christian'. One wonders whether, at root, Pastor Barton is afraid of pain, and that his words spring from a compulsive need to fill the void of grief in himself and others.

By contrast, Jesus opens up that void and draws attention to it. That is how his otherwise rather brutal question to the crippled man is best understood. In John 3.14 Jesus likens himself to the bronze serpent lifted up in the wilderness, which enabled the Israelites to be healed of the bites of the real snakes. That sounds like a model of counselling, which enables us to see uplifted into consciousness the things that have wounded us, so that we cease to be harmed by them. In Jesus we see the things we most fear and repress – brutality, suffering and death, and our own part in them – lifted up, presented to full view on the cross, so that we begin to be set free from their compulsive hold on us, being 'born anew' (John 3.3) to new possibilities of choice and life.

When, at an Anglican ordination, the bishop requests future priests to 'set the example of the Good Shepherd always before them as the pattern of their calling', this is not just saying that the minister should guide and lead people like a shepherd (though it is saying that). The decisive reference is to John 10.11 where Jesus describes himself as the shepherd who lays down his life for the sheep. He is probably referring to the way a Hebrew shepherd would lie down at the opening to a sheepfold so that wolves and thieves could not get in without first killing him: it refers too of course to the cross. Moreover, shepherds in Jesus' days were not a prestigious profession: they dealt with messy, unclean animals which they had to kill; their life was tough and they were not well paid; they were on the edge of decent, law-abiding society. Campbell points out that they were more like cowboys than kings. So the good shepherd is the image of a tough, marginal and suffering leader and carer, rather than a well-respected professional.

The good shepherd, therefore, is one who has the courage to lead those they care for through the void – the valley of the shadow – to the green pastures and the table of companionship. This image, Campbell suggests, challenges the pastor to speak to others:

> ... with both tenderness and strength. It matters too much to us whether the other is pleased and too little whether we speak the truth as best we see it. We cannot be shepherds so long as comfort is our main concern and so long as the roads through the wilderness are too lonely and too dangerous for us. Thus, far from giving us a simple paradigm for our caring concern, the image of the shepherd seems merely to reveal our inadequacies. If it is the sacrificial love of Jesus that the pastoral relationship demands of us, we know before we begin that the goal is unattainable ... (1981, pp. 34–5)

In this context, the minister who simply serves the other's agenda is acting mindlessly. But the Pastor Barton who lectures the other on the ways of God is absent-minded, and maybe also ego-minded, wanting to avoid pain and be thought of as a fount of wisdom. In either case the pain of the void is sidestepped. The shepherd's strength, by contrast, comes from a deep attentiveness to the pain the other presents, and a hunger for her flourishing, which overrides the shepherd's desire to be well thought of and pleasing. We begin to see why the good shepherd needs to be tough and fearless in his caring, and why he will suffer with the other in the only place where the divine command to flourish can be heard.

The soul-healer in the world of professional therapies

Important as they are at a deep level, the images of the servant and the shepherd only surface explicitly a few times in the Gospels. Much more frequently Jesus' serving and pastoral work is expressed in his ministry of healing. In a broad sense, the minister is called likewise to be a healer.

This calling finds expression at that most moving moment in the Catholic or Anglican licensing service, when the bishop says to the priest, 'Receive the cure of souls, which is both mine and yours'. In fact the *cura* of the original Latin is better translated by words like 'care', 'concern', 'charge', and even 'management'. The bishop as he says these words is sharing with the priest his concern for the parish, his burden of responsibility for it. So 'care' is altogether appropriate. But inaccurate as it is, 'cure' may be a welcome translation, because it suggests a dimension of healing, of dealing with the wounds of the soul, and of making people whole.

The image of the healer is very ancient, of course, going back to the tribal witch-doctors and medicine men. Healing was one of the duties of the shaman, who was often someone who had been initiated into the understanding of healing by his own experience of wounds and sickness. The local pastor, in former times, as well as being responsible for poor relief and certain aspects of law and order, was often expected to act as the doctor too – especially for the poor who could not afford fees. George Herbert advised clergy to 'mix a little physic' and keep it with them for the purpose (Billings 2010, p. 65).

These days we would certainly not respect a minister who indulged in a little amateur medical care along with his pastoral visits. The work of healing in our society is undertaken by a varied host of professionals – doctors, surgeons, nurses, therapists of various kinds – who can leave the minister feeling like a professional without a well-defined profession: a 'priest of the gaps' holding the remnants left behind by the professionalization of the main pathways of care. If the priest represents herself as just another carer and curer in the community, she is likely to be experienced – by herself and others – as a very inadequate and unprofessional one alongside well-trained others. The threefold temptation for the minister can become strong: to plough on absent-mindedly, unaware of this perceived lack of a definable profession; to stage 'healings' in an ego-minded way that makes up in drama what it lacks in scientific basis and real long-term well-being; or mindlessly to rush about attending to all sorts of needy people, making up in quantity what might appear to be lacking in quality.

Each of these alternatives betrays a lack of mindfulness of, and quiet confidence in, what is neither inferior nor superior to the care offered by the other professionals, but certainly different and special. The remainder of this chapter will explore three aspects of this distinctiveness, arguing that:

- the minister's healing has a social dimension, which may involve conflict and subversion;
- the minister is not a crisis manager or quick fixer, but a fellow traveller aware of the tragedy and comedy of life;
- the minister heals theologically by helping people 'mind the gap'.

The community of conflict and healing

Read **Mark 5.1–20**: the healing of the Gerasene demoniac. Imagine yourself as a villager watching this story unfold.

What are your gut reactions to the demoniac in his chains; to Jesus; to what happens to the pigs (your own pigs, perhaps, just ready for the market?); to seeing the man clothed and in his right mind? What do you find yourself saying – to your fellow villagers; to the man, perhaps; or to Jesus himself?

One thing that is often remarked as special about the pastor is simply his presence in the community he serves. On many inner-city or outer estate parishes, he will be the only professional who lives in the same area as the person in need. The pastor may also know the person outside the context of the need, so that he or she is not simply a 'case' he must solve, but the person he meets at the fish and chip shop or at the school or community centre, or perhaps the person he prepared for confirmation, or someone who regularly attends worship.

The pastor is also likely to know and be known by friends or family of the person in need and may well herself have a vested interest in the outcome of decisions he or she makes. This means the pastor simply cannot be a counsellor to the person in the professional sense. If a need for professional counselling arises in a parishioner, then whether or not the pastor has the training of a counsellor or is actually counselling people outside the parish context, the parishioner needs to be referred to someone else for counselling. The local pastor cannot offer that pressure-free space of unconditional regard which the counsellor offers. The pastor will inevitably and rightly, consciously or subconsciously, *want* things of the person. Such things as remorse, reconciliation, 'getting on' with other parishioners, conversion, love of God and neighbour – these are matters a counsellor has to leave open as options for the client to choose or not, but which it may be appropriate for the pastor to desire and strive for intensely.

The pastor, as well as seeing problems from the client's point of view, will see them also from the other perspective, the perspective of those who may be oppressing that person, or being oppressed by them, or both. He has to attend not just to one life as it sees itself, but to many lives, and that means that one person's healing is not the only issue at stake. As well as griefs that need alleviating there may be griefs that need to mature into remorse and the seeking of forgiveness, or into understanding and the offering of it. In the process for a time, the pain may be greater.

In counselling and therapy, the focus of loving concern is the client; it is his or her story that has to be freed from the stories others have made them tell of themselves. However, as Rowan Williams argues, 'the story that can be told of me does not *belong* exclusively to me' (2000, p. 104) but also to the others with whom my life is entwined. Unravelling a person's own story from shaming descriptions others have imposed on him or her is, to be sure, part of the minister's healing work; but another part is to weave together that person's story with the story of others in an authentic and mutually enriching way within the life of the Church. For we do not belong only to ourselves: recall how Paul describes us, quite mysteriously, as 'members one of another' (Romans 12.5; see p. xiii).

This unravelling and something of this re-weaving is at work in the account of the Gerasene maniac, a story considered in great depth by James Alison (2001, pp. 125–43). In his declaration of the name of the spirit that possesses him – 'Legion, for we are many' – the man may be referring to the many names and stories people have used to imprison him and exclude him in shame. Perhaps what is in the Gospels often described as 'possession by an evil spirit' can be understood as the imposition on us of alien names and demeaning stories – something in the experience of many of us, for sure. The name 'legion' suggests an analogy with the Roman forces who had taken political possession of the land, imposing their own alien story on the people. All of this Jesus is able to liberate the man from, allowing him to become clothed and free from shame, reposing in his right mind. But the villagers will not have it. The man's new-found peace disturbs them, so that they urge Jesus to leave. They do not like to see this man, whom they have placed in a pigeonhole labelled 'mad', walking about quite normally among them.

Something similar happens when someone labelled 'convict' or 'murderer', having undergone real change of heart and mind, is released from prison to live among people in the community, and perhaps, as in our focusing example for this chapter, even to go to church . . .

Perhaps the greatest pain and sense of helpless inadequacy we ourselves have experienced in ministry has arisen from occasions when one person's flourishing seems (rightly or wrongly) harmful to others. A person recovering from deep psychological problems, for example, longs for the healing affirmation that comes with being given a small responsible role; but that person may cause distress to others in that role or those affected by it. Should the person be persuaded to stand down, with all the harm that may do to their progress toward wholeness, or should the colleagues be persuaded to work with that person despite their hesitations? The same kinds of possible conflict of interest were, of course, what made this chapter's focusing exercise of the ex-prisoner so difficult.

We live in a world that is beautiful and often funny, but also has a tragic aspect. There are huge conflicts of interest, and often one person's flourishing seems to be at the expense of others. In such a situation it may not in practice be possible to serve both parties equally, and bring about fullness of life for both. For the pastor can only persuade, and not command. In such cases, nonetheless, the *wounded* healer offers solidarity in pain and sin, analogous to that which Christ offers, as the pastor who suffers and is tempted alongside us (Hebrews 4.14—5.10). While the counsellor makes his client feel special and unique, the pastor makes her people feel ordinary and human – and so God-bearing: as the two sections that follow suggest.

The tragicomic companion

> Read **John 4.4–26**: Jesus and the Samaritan woman at the well.
>
> Note down the stages by which each person in this dialogue becomes disclosed to the other at progressively deeper levels.
>
> Reflect on a conversation you have had, apparently casual – on a bus or train or in a pub or at a party, or on a pastoral visit, perhaps – at the end of which you felt you were deeply known and knew the other deeply. What is it that makes some conversations superficial 'small talk' and others deep encounters? What might you do – or refrain from doing – to make pastoral encounters deeper?

The professional carers are more often than not crisis managers. Doctors see patients when they are ill, not very much when they are well. The counsellor and the therapist deal with specific issues, and when their clients feel that their problems are resolved, they depart. These healers deal with specific malaise. The local pastor by contrast will know many of the people she serves through large chunks of their lives, sometimes from the cradle onwards, sometimes to the grave, and she will know them through thick and thin. (Of course some pastors, like chaplains in hospitals, hospices, prisons, are more like the professional carers in this respect.) The healing which local pastors strive for is entire wholeness of the whole person through the course of their life as a whole. Though at times the person they care for may be more 'sick' than others, they can never be regarded as outside the pastor's care or concern. The charge (*cura*) of souls does not culminate in a point of 'discharge'.

This means that the pastor will sometimes be involved in the whole process of healing at times of loss, including (in the most common pattern) initial shock and denial, through rage, bargaining, grief and sorrow and acknowledgement of irreparable loss, to healing and new beginnings. Most professionals will encounter people mainly at one or another stage, and have their specific tasks to do to foster healing, but the pastor may accompany the person through them all – and beyond. That will supply a different perspective. Doctors and nurses encountering people with intense depression in bereavement or loss often see the depression as a problem that needs to be solved by counselling or drugs or both. The pastor will see it as part of a process and may know from experience whether the person is 'grieving well' but needing sympathetic accompaniment, or whether something morbid is happening that needs special expertise. And probably, though the energies of pastors are very often taken up with the stage of grief and loss, their real strength may lie in their presence and assistance at the later stage, when patients are discharged from hospital or offenders from prison, or those who have been bereaved begin to move on, and face the task of 'rebuilding their lives' with the help of a community that can support and encourage them. One of the most moving aspects of ministry is the accompanying of people in this way. We think in particular of a couple whom one of us first met in grief, through taking the funeral of the wife's mother, who went on to become first members and then 'pillars' of the church, and remain, now in later life, good friends.

However, just like the person in need, the pastor herself will never be entirely 'well'. She ministers to the wounded as a wounded healer, sharing the sins and failings of those she ministers to. Of course, the doctor may be suffering from a severe illness himself, and the good therapist is likely to be in therapy for his own complexes. The difference is that the doctor or therapist would be unprofessional if he started talking to the client about his own problems. He has to present himself as an unknown space circumscribed by his own expertise, if the client is to trust him and feel he is being properly attended to. But, though some would advocate the same professionalism of the clergy, it does not seem, as a general rule, appropriate to the pastor. The Good Shepherd, after all, preserved no such aloofness. Several times he is described as expressing, or otherwise evidencing, how vexed and deeply troubled he is by people's lack of response, or by his own coming death. In this sense the good pastor is, as Pritchard puts it (2007, Chapter 8), the 'wounded companion, sharing the journey' of his people.

But though a great deal of pastoral theology concerns helping people in their pain and sorrows, the pastor does not accompany people only through the valley of the shadow. Being with people means sharing their joy, too. Jesus spent a great deal of time with outcasts and wrongdoers, and there is no reason to think he spent all the time counselling or admonishing them. He had a reputation for eating and drinking with them: enjoying life together. It is worth reading through all of Psalm 23 with Jesus' ministry in mind, and then your own.

Even in the bad times there may be healing in laughter. Stephen Pattison devotes a whole chapter to 'Laughter and Pastoral Care or, The Importance of Not Being Earnest' (2000, Chapter 8). Pattison looks at various theories of humour and concludes that laughter at its best (when it is not cynical or derisory) serves to offer 'the sense of distance and perspective' (p. 184). When we laugh at ourselves – we note – we 'see ourselves as others see us'; without a heavy self-condemnation we shift out of the often narrow perspective offered by our own distress.

> Humour and laughter can be enormously enriching. They can reveal and reinforce a sense of humanity, rediscover a sense of mutuality, redefine and relieve even the most difficult situations, help reconcile people to themselves and others and help them to recognize the reality of themselves and others and help them to recognize the reality of situations and selves from a different angle. (p. 186)

Campbell, similarly, appreciates the humour of the 'wise fool', an image he adds to that of the brave shepherd and the wounded healer. We will look at the wise fool more in Chapter 8, but here suggest that, to be a good servant, pastor and healer, the minister needs to be a kind of tragicomic companion. He is one who journeys with people to the point where he is able to see and share the good potential in the sad times and the tragic edge to some of the apparently good times (especially on occasions when our blessings come at others' expense).

When Jesus sits by the still waters of the well, talking with the Samaritan woman, we see him teasing out with humour the dark and tragic side of her life. Gradually she comes to acknowledge the huge gap in her life that she has tried to fill with a succession of men. Perhaps some have died, some have divorced her – we are not told. But in either case there is sorrow, as well as the shame incurred in such a community by her present adultery. But the story has its funny side too – so many husbands, and the present one is not a husband! Meanwhile, by talking about the hole in the ground where water lies, Jesus gradually opens her up to the possibility that he himself is the gulf through which living, healing water flows without ceasing. He is only there with her for a few moments, but in those moments he has managed to be the companion of her whole life in all its tragedy and comedy. Scripture does not often contain overt humour, but we imagine these two people laughing a little together, and perhaps crying at certain points too. Her whole past life, now fixed and unalterable, and the future, now alive with new possibilities, are all there in this short encounter which shows what it means to be a tragicomic companion.

Minding the gap

Read **Mark 14.3–9**: the anointing at Bethany. (The parallel account is in Matthew 26.6–13; with variants in Luke 7.36–50 and John 12.1–8.)

Imagine the scene from the point of view of Mary, focusing on your feelings especially at the point at which you break the jar of ointment over Jesus' head. Stay with those feelings for a few minutes. Then consider whether there are other occasions (whether in ministry or not) when you have felt similar things.

People are not sheep. There is a hint of the parable of the lost sheep (Luke 15.3–7) when the Anglican bishop commands those to be ordained priest 'to search for [God's] children in the wilderness of this world's temptations, and to guide them through its confusions, that they may be saved through Christ for ever'. The good pastor cannot simply carry the wandering 'sheep' on his spiritual shoulders back to the fold. The sheep in question may have a different idea from the shepherd as to what constitutes good pasture, and may not feel that his natural 'home' is in the fold of the church. And the good pastor must recognize this. However much he may, as noted, *'want* things for the person', like remorse, reconciliation, conversion and healing, they can only come through the person's own seeking and desire, and in the person's own way, not necessarily the way the pastor is familiar with.

The Anglican theologian W. H. Vanstone argues that the love of God waits, riskily, for a response that may or may not come. Chapter 7 will have more to say about his understanding; but it is perhaps here that the pain of the pastor connects in some small way with the Passion of the Good Shepherd. The pastor mirrors God's risky love, which holds back from forcing any response, however subtly, because a *free* response to God's love – the person's *own* response in her *own good* time – is what is so passionately desired. Passionately the pastor 'minds the gap', not trying to close it either by conforming the other to his agenda or submitting himself to the other's.

The contemplative's love of God empties her of all preconceived ideas of God, because she wants union not with her preconceived idea but passionately with a God who transcends all understanding and takes her by surprise. Perhaps we should speak of the pastor's love of her people as contemplative in the same way. It is a love that passionately wants neither the advancement of her own idea of what constitutes healing and salvation, nor the other's achievement of preconceived goals, but the other's coming to the fullness of Christ in her own unique way, which may take both the pastor and the other by surprise.

That brings us to the third element that is positive in the care of the pastor: the ultimate perspective in which it is offered, and which it demonstrates. Jesus' healings were not isolated demonstrations of power, nor were they *only* acts of compassionate service. Challenged as to the power by which he heals, Jesus declares, 'if it is by the finger of God that I cast out the demons, then the kingdom of God has come to you' (Luke 11.20). Jesus' miracles represented the presence and nature of the reign of God, in which all find wholeness. They represent the Kingdom, and focus its eschatological thrust.

So the ministry of the healer presents to the world the healing and salvation, the process of coming to healing, integration, wholeness of life, that comes to the world through Christ. The ministry of the servant represents Christ the servant, and the service we will offer one another, in mutuality, in the Kingdom of God. The ministry of the shepherd represents the Good Shepherd through whose guidance we ourselves become, in the beautiful phrase of the philosopher Martin

Heidegger, 'shepherds of being' guiding all beings towards their proper flourishing.

Stephen Pattison defines pastoral care as 'that activity, undertaken especially by representative Christian persons, directed towards the elimination and relief of sin and sorrow and the presentation of all people perfect in Christ to God' (2000, p. 13). We may want to qualify the word 'elimination' here with a tragicomic sense of the persistence of sin and sorrow which more utopian, secular carers may not share. But what according to Pattison sets the minister's care apart is its *representative* nature, and its *eschatological* thrust towards presenting people 'perfect in Christ'. Jane Leach writes of this thrust in terms of the 'minding the gap' between the now and the not yet:

> There are certain tube stations in London where, as the doors open, you will hear the incantation, 'Mind the gap; stand clear of the doors please. Mind the gap.' . . . I am suggesting . . . that it is the role of the presbyter to mind the gap – the gap between the now and the not yet – self-consciously, publicly and articulately to struggle to discipline ourselves to live in that space in between what we know and what we do not yet know, where God is weaving the future, and to draw others into the kind of attending to the moment that makes room for God to work. (In Luscombe and Shreeve 2002, pp. 25–6)

In the case of the Christian minister this attention involves seeing and serving the *Christ* in the other. That is why the deacon is a messenger as well as 'servant'. The minister is a herald to the other person, representing to them the presence of Christ within them; and an eschatological sign announcing the perfect flourishing to which Christ is calling them. That is why, though they have often been opposed as alternative priorities, service and evangelism – the bringing of good news, the subject of Chapter 7 – belong together.

One particularly moving image of this is the anointing of Jesus by the woman, just considered. This rich, costly and ambiguous act of service – an anointing on the head like that of kings, but also an 'anointing for burial', and anointing was also an ancient part of healing, used by early Christians – seems to mean a recognition of the Christ as king in his coming sufferings. Unlike the disciples, Mary did not refuse to acknowledge the painful things Jesus was saying about his destiny. She 'minded the gap', holding the pain of Jesus' future self-emptying until it led her to her own present act of self-emptying compassion. When we offer costly service to others, we acknowledge their present sufferings as sufferings, minding the gap; but we also witness to their ultimate royalty-in-Christ which is discovered both through and beyond their suffering.

Conclusion

This chapter has explored the serving ministry of the pastor. Diaconal service, it argued, is not slavish obedience to people's needs, but the discriminating ministry of the butler. Rather than trying to fill places of emptiness and pain, the pastor helps the person find God in those places. Similarities and differences between the pastor and other professional helpers were explored: the pastor helps the individual within the context of a community where others' needs have to be balanced; she is a long-term 'tragicomic companion'; she heals within the ultimate context of the divine healing. But as a soul-companion her ministry borders on the ministry of the soul-guide and teacher, considered in the next chapter.

Questions to ponder

1   How do you respond to the differences as described in this chapter between the role of a professional counsellor and that of a shepherd or pastor? How far does this accord with your own experience?

2   How comfortable are you with 'holding the void with non-judgemental compassion'? Think of examples when you have done this, and other times when you have not done so, and how this has affected the people concerned.

3   What part does humour play in your understanding and experience of ministry, and how helpful do you find the notion of the minister as a 'tragicomic companion'?

4

The Teacher:
Mindful Nurture

The teacher possesses the representative's deep knowledge and respect for tradition, but while the Representative saw his task as being to pass the tradition on intact, the teacher sees it as treasure to be mined as needed, or to change the analogy, a map to help people trace their own journey. The teacher finds the core of ministry in the nourishing of Christians of all ages, and sees worship primarily as spiritual nourishment and inspiration. The resources of tradition are mined deeply but in an innovative way that is almost post-modern, bringing out of the storehouse things old and new combined in striking and imaginative ways.

Members of teaching-focused churches are explorers, eager to learn and grow through each act of worship, and disappointed if they come away without some kind of transformation. They like learning more about Christianity, and are keen on home-based groups provided discussion is genuinely free and open. They bring to bear a critical edge that more tradition-based Christians may find as threatening as teaching-focused folk find traditionalist-based approaches stifling and naïve. The liturgy of teaching-focused churches seeks to combine approachability with depth, in a tension not always easy to resolve. Without approachability and a degree of explanation of the liturgy, new attenders will not be able to learn anything; without depth there will be nothing of real substance to learn for either them or the longer-standing worshippers; and explanations, if simplistic, will irritate this type with their understanding of many depths of meaning.

Focus: Christianity in three sessions

> You are staying for a month with friends in India, partly as holiday but partly to help your friends in 'home-schooling' their three children, aged seven, nine and twelve. Though agnostic themselves, your friends are

concerned that their children, who know a little of the Indian religions practised locally, have absolutely no knowledge of the Christian faith. Knowing of your involvement in Christian ministry, your friends invite you to spend three hour-long sessions to teach their children about the essentials of Christian faith. They are insistent that you don't try to proselytize or convert the children, but they want them to know enough of the basics so they can decide for themselves whether they want to learn more.

- What are the essentials you would cover in each of the three sessions?
- What methods would you use (straight teaching, questions and discussion, activities etc.)?
- What would be the key 'learning outcomes' you hope the children will accomplish by the end of the three sessions?

Teaching, nurture and guidance are all, to a degree, involved in this exercise. And these are the ministries this chapter will explore, moving steadily in emphasis from the first to the last. They are aspects, we shall argue, of one ministry, which is fundamentally that of helping Christians to relate their experience of life to the traditions of faith so as to make sound decisions about how they live. In teaching, the emphasis is on imparting knowledge and understanding of the scriptures and traditions; in nurture, the emphasis is on enabling the experience of faith to nourish people; in guidance, the emphasis in on helping people make good decisions. But these three aspects belong together.

This ministry is part of what we call pastoral ministry, along with those ministries discussed in the previous chapter. In both cases there is an element of guiding people through life as the shepherd guides the flock. But it is helpful to distinguish those cases that emerge from a person's felt need for care and support, and those in which the driving force is their need to grow in faith. In the latter case, a Christian agenda (however tentative and exploratory) can be presupposed, and there is some element of transmission of what one person understands to another whose understanding is less. The goal is insight, understanding, wisdom (though not in a purely cerebral sense). In the former case Christian faith may not be there, and no transmission of faith may be sought; the goal is care, support, enabling of fuller life.

Of course, the Church has always understood that experience of care is often what leads people to seek nurture in faith. But the ministries of carer and teacher are different, and call for different skills and qualities. The person gifted in the one is not necessarily gifted in the other, and it is often appropriate for different people to offer the different ministries. And it is important not to offer the one when the other is what is being sought: to start teaching the faith to someone who only wants some support, or conversely, to offer no more than kindness and care to someone who wants to learn or be spiritually guided.

In the opposite direction, as it were, teaching shades off into evangelism. Some practices, like preaching, may involve both ministries. Nevertheless the ministries are distinct. Perhaps the simplest way to clarify this distinction (of which more in Chapter 7) is to say that the teacher and guide can assume and build upon a desire to learn more about, to grow in and be changed by Christian faith, whereas the evangelist seeks to arouse and inspire just that desire. The art of the preacher is to arouse that desire and then build upon it, and in building upon it to arouse it all the more.

Shamans, sages and rabbis

Teaching and guidance are probably both as old as humanity, but the traditions of each have been distinct. Present-day hunter-gatherer cultures often have 'soul-guides' responsible for guiding souls into the world, through life, and even beyond the grave safely into the next world. In many peoples to this day the task is assigned to the 'shaman'. As a guide familiarizes himself with his territory before guiding people through it, so the shaman familiarizes himself with the spiritual world – including the dream world – so as to be able to guide people through that world and relate their dreams and aspirations to their daily life. In the prophetic tradition the skills of the soul-guide are also evident – the encounter with the divine in visions, journeys to different realms (Moses' mountain, Elijah and Ezekiel's chariots), the interpretation of dreams, the development and application of practical wisdom. Prophets, like shamans, were charismatics existing 'outside the system' rather than inheriting their posts like the priests and kings, or being appointed by the latter.

At the same time, any culture will need its teachers, those who pass on to the next generation its traditions and accumulated wisdom. In earlier societies it was often the elders of the tribe who did this, but by the time of the Old Testament we see the rise of the sage or wise man, exemplified by King Solomon, who offered teaching and guidance of the kind we find in the wisdom tradition, expressed in pithy proverbs. In contrast to the prophets, wisdom was associated with the aristocratic ranks of society. In India and China we witness a series of great teachers including Gautama Buddha, Lao Tzu and Confucius, imparting insight into the nature of the universe and how to live in it for the best. The early Greek philosophers were, as the term describes, 'lovers of wisdom', living austere, eccentric, itinerant lives dedicated to bringing others to wisdom.

The first millennium BC saw the development of teaching institutions: the Greek academies and the Jewish synagogues, presided over by the teacher or *rabbi*. Jesus himself is recorded as often being called 'rabbi', and teaching, alongside healing, was certainly a major feature of his work. Yet he seems to have told his followers not to use the term (Matthew 23.8) and there is no evidence that he was trained as a rabbi, though he often preached in the synagogues. He is reputed to have taught in a different way from the teachers of the law, more idiosyncratic and authoritative, allowing himself a bold freedom of reinterpretation. In him we see prophet and sage combined to give a distinctive mode of teaching, which we will examine in the next section.

Among other teachers in the New Testament, Paul is obviously preeminent as he tries to guide and nurture the newly formed Christian communities in a way that resorted to scriptural tradition interpreted through a convoluted and often paradox-loving process of reflection: his own distinctive brand of the rabbinic culture in which he was taught. As we have seen, it was Paul who cited teaching among the spiritual gifts (1 Corinthians 12.28 and Romans 12.7). 'Words of knowledge' and 'discernment' are listed among the gifts in 1 Corinthians 12.8–10, and these gifts seem to relate especially to teaching and spiritual guidance respectively.

The rest of the chapter begins by considering preaching, the main opportunity in most churches for teaching the whole congregation, mixed as it is in age, background and spiritual maturity; here the agenda is mainly focused by the readings that precede the sermon, as well as national and local events that may need interpreting in a Christian context. The chapter then moves to consider Christian nurture, where the groups are generally smaller and more homogenous in terms of stages on the journey, and there is more opportunity for dialogue and interaction. It considers the kind of teaching appropriate at the Pastoral Offices, before moving on to the one-to-one engagement involved in the ministries of confession and spiritual guidance.

Despite the difference of contexts, we shall see a common theme emerge. In all these situations what the mindful teacher, nurturer or guide is fundamentally seeking to do is enable people to reflect theologically. She faces the familiar three temptations to be mindless, absentminded or ego-minded. And these temptations come in the form of a disproportionate attention to one of the three main ingredients of theological reflection: experience, tradition and response (decision or transformation).

Theologically reflecting together: the preacher as teacher

Read **Matthew 5.17–48**: part of the Sermon on the Mount

What do you notice about Jesus' approach to:

- scriptural tradition (in his case the law and the prophets);
- imagery and examples;
- the audience he is addressing.

How far do you think Jesus' approach should be mirrored in the approach of preachers today – perhaps including yourself – in relation to each of these three factors? Or are there important differences; and if so, why?

The collection of Jesus' sayings and teachings familiar to us in Matthew's and Luke's Gospels as the Sermon on the Mount manages to be, at one and the same time, conservative and radical, and to be urging those who heard them simultaneously to acceptance and to action. It is interesting to note that Fr Elias Chacour, a Palestinian Christian priest with a long record of extraordinary achievement in the struggle for transformation, education, hope and peace with justice, in his local community, has an interpretation of the earlier part of the Sermon quite different from that normally understood by the 'Blessed are . . .' sayings of Jesus. As an Aramaic speaker himself, he traces the word used by Jesus, normally translated as 'Blessed', back to an Aramaic word, '*ashray*', meaning 'get up, go ahead, do something' (2001, pp. 143–4). Perhaps even in this part of the Sermon on the Mount, therefore, Jesus was enjoining radical action together with acceptance, rather than passivity?

Although we cannot possibly get inside the mind of Jesus in his preaching, nor even the minds of his followers who have presented his teaching in the form we now have it, we can, perhaps, seek to replicate elements of his approach so as to enable a 'mindful' response. For 'mindfulness' in preaching applies as much to the hearers as to the preacher – except that the preacher not only needs to be mindful herself, but also has responsibility for enabling mindfulness in her hearers. She needs not only to have reflected theologically, but to enable a process of theological reflection in her hearers, helping them interpret their experience in the light of the scriptures so that they make their own resolves about future action.

Sermons can fail to achieve this demanding goal in the familiar three ways:

1 They can be 'mindless', consisting of a lot of anecdotes and examples from personal experience, or wonderful illustrations, but fail to engage at depth with the scriptures just read, and the tradition of interpretation, and so lead nowhere. We were told of one sermon from long ago which was still remembered by many people, not for anything the preacher said, but because he had started it by riding up the nave on a bicycle – the point of which had long since slipped into oblivion!

2 They can be 'absent-minded'. The preacher shows her mastery of theology by expounding at length on the scriptures and the different traditions of theology related to the passages in question, and what some scholars say belongs to Q, and what the *sitz-im-leben* of the passage was, and what form criticism has to say. But all of this is addressed, as it were, to empty space, with little of what is so often called 'relevance' to people's lives and the questions they are asking today. According to one probably apocryphal anecdote, there was once a preacher who addressed a beleaguered congregation of three in a council estate parish with brilliant rhetoric. 'And I know what you're all thinking about the point I just made,' he declared, lifting a wise and knowing finger: 'Sabellianism!'

3 Finally, sermons can be 'ego-minded'. The preacher wants to assert himself and make an impact. He may well have reflected deeply on the passage in question himself, but he lacks the patience to take the people through the process, and offers a set of pre-digested directives, lecturing people about what they should do in the light of the scripture passages.

All three errors betray a lack of mindfulness, especially concerning the congregation. The preacher has belittled the people's part in the sermon, not trusting them to enter with him into the process, either failing (as in 1) to enter the reflective process himself, or assuming (as in 2) they are thinking and feeling exactly what he is, or (as in 3) assuming he can bully and exhort them into going where he has gone before them. All three fail to bring people to that *kairos* moment where scripture and experience interilluminate (Thompson 2008, Chapter 5) and people experience an inner 'Eureka' or 'Ah! Now I see it anew!' providing the crucible in which new desires and resolves are forged.

At first sight, Jesus' Sermon on the Mount looks like a case of 3. Jesus seems very directive, telling people with authority what they should and should not do. But at a second glance things are much more complex and rich. This section of the sermon consists of a series of sayings always containing (i) and (ii) of the following elements, and usually (iii) and (iv) also.

i   A command from the torah introduced with words like, 'You have heard it said . . .'
ii A command of Jesus, 'but I say to you . . .' which intensifies the application of the torah command.
iii An example drawn from daily life illustrating how this intensified command might apply.
iv A final command summarizing the application of the parable.

For example, in the last saying, vv. 43–48, we read something like:

i   *You have heard it said*: You must love your neighbour and hate your enemy.
ii *But I say to you*: Love your enemies.
iii Your father in heaven causes the sun to shine and the rain to fall on the just and unjust alike. It's easy to love those who love you – even tax collectors and pagans do it. Loving enemies is the hard thing.
iv Be perfect as your Father is perfect.

The sayings contain the three core ingredients of theological reflection: a saying from scripture (i), reference to ordinary life experience (iii), and resolve for future action (iv), related back to scripture at (ii). Though Jesus is authoritative and commanding, the actual application of his commands is left to the hearer. Jesus gives an example from ordinary life to help him ponder how to apply the command. But how it will actually apply – who his enemy is, what it might mean to love him, and what it might mean to be perfect in the way the Father is, and how that might be achieved – are huge questions. The hearer is left, as after any good sermon – and indeed after any good act of teaching – with a lot of homework to do.

The best sermons, therefore, are not those in which the minister offers the pre-digested fruits of his own reflection, but draws the congregation into the reflective process itself. There is a sense, after a good sermon, of having worked hard with the preacher to produce results that may not be the same as everyone else's, or the preacher's, but which are a valid way of integrating the scriptures read in the service with your own experience to produce intentions and resolves that are relevant to your own life. Though everyone will have heard the same scriptures read, they will bring to it, with the aid of the preacher's reflections, different experiences. The art of good preaching (in its teaching aspect at least) is to allow this to happen – to allow everyone to hear a different sermon, the one that relates to them – yet retain a discipline that ensures that each person will have been engaged in reflecting theologically on their experience and discerning God's presence in their lives.

This is of course *the* big difference between Jesus' teaching and the rabbinic tradition, which tried to pre-digest the process of application by working out how to follow the law in the minutiae of daily life. Later on, the Church would revert to a legalism that is closer to the rabbinic approach than Jesus' – but that is another story. The job of the Christian preacher, we believe, is not to tell the people what to do, but to enable them to work it out for themselves through reflection on scripture and tradition.

Linking lives to the saving life: Christian nurture

Whereas preaching normally takes place in the large and heterogeneous group of the gathered congregation, Christian nurture usually occurs in smaller and more homogeneous groups in terms of stages on the journey, such as:

- a group of people preparing for confirmation;
- a house group meeting for Bible Study, a Lent group or other Christian nurture group;
- youth groups which include elements of Christian nurture;
- a group preparing for some liturgical event such as the baptism of their children, or marriage.

These contexts clearly provide more opportunity for dialogue and interaction.

Read **Acts 8.26–40** (omit the later addition at v. 37 if it is in your text).

What prompts the eunuch to want to be baptized? Why do you think he is so curious about the passage he is reading?

- What does Philip do in terms of baptism preparation and follow-up?
- How does this compare with how people are initiated as Christians in your church?

In 'nurture groups' of whatever sort, the essential task is to enable the kind and level of theological reflection that is appropriate to the members of the group, linking their particular life experience to the universally saving life of Christ in a way that leads to the next stage of their transformation. To be sure, the example of 'baptism preparation' undergone by the eunuch looks at first sight like a case of instruction rather than theological reflection. We are not told what was going on in the eunuch that made him so interested in the piece of scripture that he was reading, nor what prompted him to be so keen to be baptized. But surely there must have been some resonance between those words of scripture and experience of his own, and the Gospels must have been expounded by Philip in a way that built on that resonance and led to a readiness for a life-changing moment. Note too the decisive part played by Philip's spiritual discernment that led him to go to the eunuch at precisely the *kairos*, the right moment for him to be awakened.

And finally note the flexible informality of it all; there is no series of classes for baptismal preparation, and nothing suggested by way of follow-up. It all happens in the course of one longish conversation.

In preparation of this kind, the initiative needs to come from the seeker: the minister's task is to encourage the initiative, feed it with reflection together on appropriate scripture and tradition, and help the seeker to discern the *kairos*, the right moment for the next step forward.

The risks in groups for Christian nurture and courses designed for them are, as usual, threefold:

1 They may be 'mindless' – too experience-based with not enough scriptural and theological input, leading to a woolly pooling of ignorance or a kind of vague co-counselling. This is, perhaps, the typically modern error.

2 They may be 'absent-minded' – all instruction in scripture and theology churned out without any regard to the experience of the participants or what they are receptive to. This is the error of old-fashioned catechesis.

3 They may be 'ego-minded' – too quick to try and change lives according to the leader's mould, rather than allowing people in their own good time to make the connections between text and life in their own way. We have heard it said of a theological college principal of some years ago that he told his students that the purpose of their studies was to be broken and refashioned in his image! That may be an extreme case, but we have noted in ourselves and other ministers a temptation to want to make clones of yourself in those you nurture; this needs resisting.

Ages and stages

The age and stage of faith of those you nurture obviously makes a difference to the style of teaching that is appropriate, and this is a matter not only of ability to master new and subtler kinds of information, but also the way the imagination works, and the amount of life experience there is available to draw in to the reflection. This means that whereas standard educational theory often assumes that people develop with a linear, steadily increasing ability that levels off in adulthood and declines in old age, in terms of faith the curves may be much more wavy and not necessarily stabilizing at adulthood or declining at the end. James Fowler (1987) is particularly helpful here.

Young children, it has been noted (Hay and Nye 2006; Richards 2009), have unsullied minds open to experience and a sense of wonder, and can be remarkably adept, if suitably guided, at contemplative forms of prayer. At junior age comes a love of story and ritual; we have found that drama in church can provide an excellent way for children to engage with the biblical narratives through acting them out, while participation in the liturgy as servers and acolytes provides a different way of engaging through action.

With adolescence comes a self-consciousness that mitigates against such participation and a scepticism that can become cynical; the Church can be seen as another parental figure against which the teenager has to fight for his own independent identity. Frequently attendance at church declines or ceases at this point because the church is associated with the childhood world of myth. If confirmation is undertaken at this point, rather than an attempt to retain young people in that fading world it needs to provide a chance to bring doubts, criticism and rebellion to bear on the creation of a more truly adult faith. It is also an opportunity to create solidarity for those who will find themselves a minority within the Church (because of their age) and among their peers (because of their faith). In youth groups this creation of solidarity and friendship in faith may be the most important factor, outweighing the need for more explicit teaching. Perhaps the most important thing is sometimes for the members to see, in those who lead them, Christians who are not trapped in a naïve world of religious fairy tales, but capable of combining reason, doubt and rebellion with firm commitment.

With adulthood come the pressures and opportunities of work and family, and the need to order priorities according to faith. It is often a time for coming to faith, but pressures are such that this may not be reflected in frequent church attendance. The adult nurture group, exploring scriptural texts and faith issues through discussion, may be extremely important at this point. By contrast, in later life there may arise an awareness of the limitation of words and discussions in matters of faith, and for some (not all) the contemplative prayer group may provide a better way of simply dwelling in the presence of God aided by a simple text or a guided meditation based on a Bible story. In one sense this means a return to the childhood world of wonder at sheer existence, and delight in story; but with the intervening richness of experience meaning there is no longer a need to talk about faith, much more of a need to ruminate and allow faith and life experience quietly to meld in ever deeper formations.

For all these differences, it is important that we do not completely segregate the different styles of nurture and the ages that are best attuned to them, as at a school. One of the most moving services we have ever organized was called 'the seven ages of faith' in which seven people of different ages spoke simply and briefly, without any preconceived stereotype, about what their faith and church meant to them. We began with a baby, recently baptized, whose parents obviously had to speak on its behalf. Then there was a schoolgirl of about nine who had recently joined the choir (she later became confirmed and very involved in the drama club). Then there was a teenage youth, if we remember rightly, a young parent, someone in mid-life, an older person who had recently started attending church after a bereavement, and finally a gracious lady in her nineties who had attended church all her life. What was so moving, we feel, was the sense the service gave of the changing nature of faith through life, and yet also the deep thread of continuity.

For there is a sense in which we can all only approach spirituality with what the Zen masters call 'beginners' mind'. So there is great merit in the styles of Christian nurture in which those at different ages and stages travel together. In miniature, this mix of ages (and also cultures) was what we found surprisingly valuable when we were called upon by our niece to do the opening exercise of this chapter for real!

But it is possible to enlarge on such an approach and make it integral to the life of the whole congregation. It is not – we have found – desirable for youngsters and adults to learn together all the time; the adults with their greater confidence and sophistication tend to dominate. But it is good to come together at specific points, making use of the Christian year as something those of established faith can begin again and travel with those coming to faith for the first time.

This is the approach which has been developed in the Roman Catholic RCIA (Rite of Christian Initiation of Adults) and the ecumenical Emmaus Courses, and which was recommended in the Anglican report, *Stages on the Way* (Church House Publishing 1995). In its original form this was, as its name suggests, a way of bringing adults to Christian faith through baptism, but we have found that it adapts well to adults and young people coming to explicit faith anew and seeking confirmation.

The process allows for an initially tentative enquiry of faith leading to a service in church where those who decide to go ahead are accepted as 'catechumens' or learners. This leads after several months to a service of 'election' – in the RCIA most often at the beginning of Lent – in which the candidates resolve to go ahead into a final period in which the emphasis shifts from learning about the faith to enlightenment and transformation. Key texts like the Creed, the Lord's Prayer, the Beatitudes and the Command to Love are taught and entrusted to the candidates. This leads to the decisive act which may be baptism, confirmation or both, as well as first Communion. In the RCIA this takes place at the Easter Vigil. Finally there is a follow-up period in which the candidates reflect on their experience and relate it more fully to their future life. The process aims not at indoctrination or instruction but at a deep, carefully phased and theologically reflective integration of the candidate's life and experience with the stories and images of scripture and tradition.

The RCIA and models like it represent a profound shift in the culture of a church, and probably need years to become truly established. Nevertheless the process came to be valued immensely: it gave the whole church a sense of being a learning church, always beginning again and growing anew in faith alongside the newcomers; it gave dignity to those exploring and discovering faith for the first time, as the centre of the process supported by the Church as a whole. We valued also the restored sense of the liturgical year fostered by this approach, and especially Lent and Easter, as a time of journey together; and the new role of sponsor, which involved at best a quite profound friendship in Christ, whose essence was not teaching so much as companionship in learning and support in prayer.

This section has considered the need to adopt 'beginners' mind' in order to grow in faith. We now consider a very different ministry in which innocence is likewise restored, setting us free to grow anew.

Forgiveness and challenge: the confessor

> Read **2 Samuel 11.2–5, 14–21, 12.1–14**: David's sin and repentance.
>
> Consider the process by which David comes to repent.
>
> What do you make of the 'absolution' given by Nathan, and the qualification?

Today the ministry of absolution is regarded as an important part of the work of the priest in the Catholic traditions. There it forms a decisive part of the representative role of the priest; in absolving from sin, he is the ambassador of the forgiveness of Christ. At times, however, this ministry has trespassed from the representative into the vicarious, the priest absolving as if he himself were dispensing Christ's forgiveness. The doctrine that in cases of mortal sin, salvation is impossible without confession to a priest, has given confession a fearful, compulsory aspect that has only relaxed recently. It is this, of course, that has led to anger and suspicion in many Protestant circles. But sadly, that has often led to the abandonment of a core part of the repertoire of the minister as guide and nurturer of the soul in Christ.

The Church of England does not regard confession and absolution as essential to the Christian life, and is less clear in any case about the distinction between venial or transitory sins that heal of themselves, and the mortal sins that, unchecked, destroy the soul. The former Anglican Archbishop Michael Ramsey comments, 'As for the term "mortal" sin, who knows whether the pride or complacency of the devout may not be as deadly as the scandalous acts of the profligate' (2008, p. 47). In terms of objective forgiveness itself, sincere confession directly to God is regarded as being as effective as confession to (or more properly, through) a priest. But in terms of the subjective assurance of forgiveness, in some cases only sacramental confession may bring peace of mind. Hence the well-known Anglican saying about confession: 'All may, some should, none must'. This means that in Anglicanism the sacrament belongs in the context of the healing and guiding of the soul. (In the Anglican Book of Common Prayer the ministry of absolution forms an option within the Visitation of the Sick – along with soul-guiding, and preparation for death, as appropriate.)

Meanwhile, in the earliest, patristic traditions, to some extent preserved by the Orthodox Church, the emphasis is on restoration to the community of faith, from which serious sins (adultery, apostasy or murder) exclude the sinner.

So there are at least three traditions concerning confession:

1 The Catholic understanding that it is *objectively necessary* in cases of serious sin, to restore a right relationship with God; or in the Orthodox case, a right relation to the community the sinner has offended.
2 The Anglican understanding that it is *subjectively desirable* in some cases, to quieten the conscience.
3 The stronger Protestant position that it should not be practised at all, as it interposes an undesirable layer of mediation between the believer and God.

We note, however, that there are at least three dimensions of sin. It involves *hamartia*, a 'missing of the target' or falling short of the glory and beauty intended for us by *God* when he created us; this is what the Catholic tradition focuses on. It involves *guilt* and *remorse*, suffering in *ourselves* as a consequence of sin, which the Anglican approach seeks to deal with. And it involves *opheleima*, the debt we owe to *others* because of injustices and harms we have done to them, which is what the old and Orthodox traditions emphasize.

This third element should not be sidestepped. In Jewish tradition, recompensing others for the harm we have done to them is an inseparable part of true repentance. And it is clear in Jesus' teaching, in the Lord's Prayer and in parables like the unforgiving servant (Matthew 18.23–35), that forgiveness by God is contingent upon our forgiveness of and by one another. It is this element that is so prominent in the story of David and Nathan. The story enables David to come to understand just what he has done in terms of harm to Uriah and Bathsheba. His anger against the man in the parable declaring him worthy of death is turned back by Nathan on David himself, in the powerful declaration: 'You are the man.' Only after remorse at the harm he has done can absolution come: 'The Lord has put away your sin; you shall not die.'

Obviously, which approach a minister takes toward the ministry of absolution will depend on the tradition and context within which he works. But we suggest that this ministry has the same potential pitfalls as the others.

1 The Catholic stress on objective restoration of right relationship with God has great power, but it is 'absent-minded' if the priest proceeds formally according to the rule books defining the supposed seriousness of different kinds of sin, rather than bringing the person, as Nathan did, to a true remorse, a true sense of the harm he has done to others. In *God's Callgirl* (2006) Carla van Raay relates how she longed to hear words of remorse from her dying father, who abused her as a child, so that she can forgive. But on his deathbed he merely informed her that he had confessed to the priest all the bad things he did, so it is all right now. Here, part of the process where the father might come to genuine absolution has been short-circuited by an unmindful priest. For if in the confessional the priest represents Christ in his unconditional forgiveness, he surely also represents Christ in the other, in those the sinner has harmed. This is surely part of the point of having three parties involved: not just the sinner and God, but also another, the priest, who is able to bring the sinner to a

just sense – neither excessive and obsessional, nor deficient and evasive – of the harm he has done. This in turn suggests what God's forgiveness might mean in terms of future actions of restitution and restoration and seeking forgiveness from those he has harmed, that the sinner now needs to undertake.

2   For the same sort of reason, the Anglican approach would be 'ego-minded' if it were to suggest that confession and absolution are just therapeutic methods to restore the ego of the sinner to peace of mind. The sinner may well come to the confession deeply burdened and absorbed by a troubled conscience. But bear in mind Rowan Williams' comment (cited on p. 58) that our stories are not our own property; what is brought to the confessional is not just a soul that is hurting, but a soul that hurts for the harm it has done. Part of the confessor's role may well be to bring the penitent out of her self-absorption to see herself in a more objective light. This third-party perspective is exactly what Nathan instils in David. In that perspective the burden for some penitents may be lightened, because the person begins to see that she has intended and done no harm, to others or to herself. Or something else may happen: the crippling sorrow of guilt, which is in a sense fundamentally narcissistic, relating to a damaged sense of self-respect and self-worth, may give way to the more potentially enabling sorrow of remorse, which concerns harm done to the other. Absolution may then be conditional upon putting those wrongs right.

But of course, that may be impossible. Ian McEwan's novel *Atonement* (2002) explores the remorse of a girl whose lies incriminated a man about involvement in rape, leading to a prison sentence that prevented the love he had for her sister ever coming to fulfilment. Both he and the girl's sister are now dead, and the girl, now an old woman, has had to live her life with the knowledge, not only of harm done, but of goodness she prevented from ever happening. Nothing can be done to right the wrong she has done. In such cases, absolution would probably be unable to quieten the conscience, yet the priest might suggest pathways of restoration. This might be a public confession that would posthumously clear the man's name; or perhaps dedicated work to prevent similar future miscarriages of justice. In the novel, the way of atonement is through art and its power to 're-write' wrongs.

3   Finally, if you are in a tradition where confession to a minister is not a possibility, then it would be 'mindless' to imagine

that all the deep and difficult issues which confession strives to deal with are not there, or are always possible to resolve in the private lives of people's prayer to God. This will be especially apparent where people in the congregation are harming others in it, or outside it, bringing scandal upon the Church. The priest would be 'mindless' indeed if he colluded with those alleged to be doing harm by leaving the question to their personal relationship with a God who forgives them (if indeed they need forgiving); or at the other extreme, resorting to processes of exclusion and excommunication before reconciliation had been seriously attempted. In the absence of a defined ministry of reconciliation and absolution, the minister needs other ways of engaging in dialogue with the person in the context of the ultimate issues of sin, forgiveness, judgement and salvation.

In the above we have stressed that sin is not a purely individual matter but involves harm to others. But it may affect others beyond the individual in other ways too.

The first is that it is often caused by others. Victimizers are often people who have been victims, and in a lot of sin there is an element of imprisonment and compulsion. Actions arising out of compulsion, rather than being freely chosen, need not forgiveness but healing. Most of us, of course, need a bit of both. 'When we have repudiated every voluntary sin,' wrote St Mark the desert ascetic, 'then we shall begin the real warfare with the impacts of suffering ('the passions') which fill us' (Kadloubovsky and Palmer 1954, p. 83). Once he has found forgiveness for the bad choices he has made, the penitent is liberated to confront the bad that has chosen him, the memories of hurt that incline him to those foolish choices.

The confessor, though not just a kind of healer, needs to be healer as well as absolver; otherwise he will leave the soul's wounds forgiven but intact. The discernment of the need for healing vis-à-vis forgiveness is one of the most delicate arts the confessor needs. She needs to imagine herself as having two hands: a right hand held up to protect others and declaring a firm 'No' to harm done to them, and a left hand reaching out to the penitent, laying on him the sign of healing, and drawing him up from the abyss. In the story of Christ and the adulterous woman (John 8.2–11) we see both hands at work: the healing hand protecting the woman from shame and indicating the collective nature of sin, as involving the woman's persecutors as much as her; and the firm hand forbidding future indulgence: 'Go, and sin no more.'

Finally, individual sin is often a collusion in collective sin. We sense that many people these days have a weaker sense of personal sin than in the past, but a stronger sense of collective sin and their participation in it. They are less likely, on the whole, to feel troubled in their conscience by having too strong desires or having told white lies, but more burdened, perhaps, by the way their relatively rich lifestyle is premised on the exploitation of the third world poor. The confession of collusion in this kind of collective sin needs a strong, imaginative response.

The matters discussed so far have tended to be sombre, and might suggest that confession is a gloomy sacrament. But, of course, reconciliation with God and our neighbour are ultimately supremely positive aspects of the gospel. For this reason, although the close examination of harms we have subjected ourselves to and caused for others is a serious discipline, it is also a turning from the shadows to the light; a restoration of baptismal innocence and joy. Something of this is conveyed in the quotation in the box that follows.

Welcoming, birthing, guiding: the soul-friend

Read the following account of Cuthbert's practice of spiritual direction:

> No-one left unconsoled, no-one had to carry back the burdens they brought with them. With a word from God he would rekindle spirits that were chilled by sorrow. He brought back the joys of heaven to those weighed down with worry . . . To people beset with temptation he would skilfully disclose the ploys of the devil, explaining that a person who lacks love for God and others is easily caught in the devil's traps, while a person strong in faith can, with God's help, brush them aside like so many spiders' webs. (The Venerable Bede, cited in Simpson 1999, p. 109)

Imagine yourself in conversation with St Cuthbert in his hermitage on the remote island of Lindisfarne. You have travelled far overland and then on a boat across the sea. Think of the burdens you might come with.

List three qualities you would like to see in St Cuthbert. (You may want to affirm those in this description, or you may wish to critique some of them.)

Add two qualities you would hope *not* to find in your soul-guide.

All ministers will be called upon to act as confessors and absolvers, whether or not in the formal sacramental sense defined by the Churches. Likewise, all ministers will be called upon as soul-guides, even though only some will be spiritual directors in the formal sense of having undertaken special training, and then making time for regular appointments with particular directees over an extended period. Much has been written about spiritual direction in this formal sense; in this section we apply what one writer, Mary Guenther, has said about spiritual direction to the more general ministry we call soul-guidance.

The previous chapter described the ministry of caring and healing, while the preceding section examined aspects of the confessor, and suggested that the confessor needed to be a healer too. Soul-guidance is the ministry of one who is both confessor and healer, in the context of a long-term ongoing ministry to particular people seeking to grow in Christ. In this context the hurts and harms that people have experienced and done, which stand in the way of that growth, will clearly need to be addressed. Confession in soul-guidance may or may not be expressed in a sacramental ministry of absolution, but there will be a need to 'disclose the ploys of the devil', because all people are sinners and all are sufferers.

However, this needs to be done in relation to the more positive task of enabling people to grow in Christ, and leading them to pasture (good books, good traditions of prayer and meditation, good life, good experience) that will nourish that growth.

Margaret Guenther (1992) describes spiritual direction in terms of three key tasks: teaching, hospitality and midwifery. We have looked at teaching already. The task of hospitality brings into focus the importance of the place and atmosphere where the minister receives those who come to her. Soul-hospitality demands that we provide a space where the soul can rest and expand, and where (to use a Tibetan Buddhist image) the snake of consciousness can unfurl from its tense coils. There needs to be sense of space and austerity with a few simple focuses: an icon or painting, a vase of flowers, and a sense of being in the desert. If this cannot be readily achieved in the study, with all its business and electronic gadgetry, the church may be suitable, or some other quiet space may need to be found.

But perhaps the most vivid of Guenther's chapters is that which deals with the soul-guide as midwife. Both Jesus (John 16.21–22) and Paul (Romans 8.22–23) use birth as a primary image of the coming-to-be of people (and indeed, in Paul, the whole creation) in Christ. Guenther teases out the way the soul-guide helps the person to 'give birth' to new life and resolve, first by 'story-telling . . . exploring . . . depths unhurriedly . . . exploring ways of praying in a gentle and unhurried way' (p. 96). There can follow 'a time of transition, which can be frightening . . . The birthgiver is gripped by a tremendous force and feels she has somehow lost control' (p. 99). The task of the soul-guide at this point is to 'see pattern and form in seeming formlessness' (p. 102). Finally, as with birth-giving, active work must be encouraged, to accomplish and bring to completion the new birth taking place in the soul.

So what can go wrong with soul-guiding is closely linked with what can go wrong with birth-giving.

1 It can be a 'mindless' and ultimately indulgent chatter about spiritual experience, in which the soul-guide abandons her duty to guide. She fails to provide apposite imagery with which to reflect on the experience, and colludes entirely with the directee's perspective, so that nothing new comes to birth.

2 It can involve an 'absent-minded' theological lecturing, in the absence of any true listening to the directee or any attempt to share her perspective, so that there is no organic relation between the 'teaching' and her experience, no spark of interillumination in which the directee gasps, 'Ah, now I see what has been struggling to birth in me . . .' This is like a midwife whose knowledge is theoretical and distant, unable to work empathetically with the woman to enable birth.

3 The soul-guide may be 'ego-minded', too bound up with her own need to be a good and productive director of souls. Riding roughshod over the feelings of vulnerability and potential shame that people have about new things that emerge from the depths, she will race the directee on to a premature birth in which everything is decided too quickly, and resolutions are hastily made but unlikely to last.

Concluding note: 'When two or three are gathered in my name . . .'

In this chapter, we have moved from preaching week by week to the large group or congregation, through the nurture of smaller groups for generally shorter periods, to soul-guidance which in its traditional form of spiritual direction was always an ongoing one-to-one ministry. In the ministry of Jesus we find analogies for the first two: his preaching to the crowds, and his teaching of the twelve and of groups gathered around the table (which would presumably have been about the same size). But though we do see Jesus in one-to-one encounters, these encounters tend to be one-off encounters with those he healed, or with people like the Samaritan woman at the well, and Mary Magdalen in the garden. There is no evidence that he ever met regularly with anyone for one-to-one spiritual guidance. On the other hand we do find him meeting in very small groups, typically of four. Repeatedly he does so with Peter, James and John, while Mary, Martha and Lazarus probably represent another instance, as does his meeting with Cleopas and the other disciple on the Emmaus Road. It was with the first of these groups that he shared his most intimate moments: his glory at the Transfiguration and his agony in Gethsemane.

Spiritual direction in the strict sense is a one-to-one relationship best pursued – for the same reasons as counselling is, see Chapter 3 – outside of the parish setting. In any event, time would not permit this kind of relationship for a minister with many individuals in the congregation, and those whom the minister had to turn down for time considerations might feel rejected. But a kind of mutual spiritual direction can be developed within a church community based on groups of three of four, bound by strict confidentiality so that sharing can be deep. In this context, though the minister or other leader might act as enabler or facilitator initially, an interchange of roles often works very well. A group such as this, based on Smith and Graybeal's *Spiritual Formation Workbook* (1999), provided, for one of us, an extremely challenging and enlightening as well as supportive and encouraging experience. This was a self-arranged group within a church community consisting of three people only, meeting every two or three weeks for an hour. Some may have an equivalent experience through 'prayer triplets' or more informal groupings. (See also Pickering 2008, pp. 194ff.) Such models of soul-guidance can be helped to flourish within congregational settings and can have a profound indirect effect on the life of a church community.

Conclusion

This chapter explored the ministry of the teacher, which includes aspects of the shaman or soul-guide, the wise man and the rabbi. The chapter considered the teaching aspect of preaching as the enabling of theological reflection, and looked at Christian nurture as enabling people to link their life experience to the narrative of salvation. It then looked at the role of the confessor, who represents Christ the forgiver of sin, but also Christ in the other who has been harmed; and that of the soul-guide, suggesting that though the minister cannot offer members of the congregation spiritual direction in the strict sense, there is potential in soul-friending small groups of three or four.

But the ministries considered here can easily expand into those considered in the remaining chapters. The guide of a whole faith community is the leader, considered next. The soul-friend, as well as being akin to the tragicomic companion of Chapter 3, is fundamental to the conviviality considered in Chapter 6. The preacher, as well as having the teaching role considered here, has as noted an evangelistic role, which is the subject of Chapter 7. And the confessor, who pronounces words of forgiveness and absolution, delivering people from the bonds of sin, is doing part of the overall work of liberation, covered in the final chapter.

Questions for discussion

1 How far do you agree or disagree with the suggestions on pages 71 and 74 about what can go wrong in preaching, or/and in nurture groups? What are the elements, in your experience, that make for a more positive experience in each context?

2 From your point of view and experience, what are the main pros and cons of sacramental confession vis-à-vis personal confession? How do these relate to those suggested in this chapter?

3 What has been, for you as the recipient, the most fruitful soul-guiding experience, and how might you enable an equivalent experience for those in your care?

5

The Leader:
Mindful Oversight

A typical 'leader' carries an inherent authority, is energetic and busy, and has little time for fools – of which you fear you may be considered one!

The leader is perhaps less interested in people for their own sake, but has a remarkable ability to find the right person for the right job, and to educate people and make them feel confident in taking on new tasks. She is good at enabling the PCC to share and own her vision, and though she does not always communicate the plan well, and feels impatient with dissent, she generally finds ways of keeping the peace.

The services in her church are brisk and efficient, always over in an hour, well organized but some would say rather unimaginative and middle of the road in content. The mainstream people enjoy being part of a well-run show, making their own well-appreciated contribution. But those on the fringes may feel that their hesitancy about commitment renders them second-class, because they are not yet ready for 'muscular Christianity' – the hard but well-rewarded graft that is the church's norm.

Focus: The youth club and the hall

The run-down building used by the local youth club, much vandalized by the youth themselves, has been condemned, and the youth club is looking for new premises. The committee that runs it has approached you as minister regarding use of your recently re-furbished church hall. Indications are that they might welcome a church-based professional youth worker to replace or supplement their currently demoralized leaders, especially if the package included the use of the church's excellent premises. However, at least two out of the four leaders are quite hostile to the Church.

Another difficulty is that the evening they meet – apparently the only evening possible – clashes with the evening when the dance club (as they have done from time immemorial) uses the hall. The latter is a secular group but pay better rent than the youth club could afford. You feel strongly that this is a God-sent opportunity for the church to develop its presently non-existent mission to young people, and there are several people in the congregation who share your enthusiasm. Two of them would even be prepared to volunteer as assistant leaders provided funding for a professional leader could be found. But a majority on the church council is exceedingly reluctant to risk the newly furnished premises, pointing out that if these were vandalized, or if the youngsters started congregating around the hall on other evenings, other groups might be put off. The dance club has indicated that it would go elsewhere rather than change evenings, in which case their revenue would be lost.

Being very proud of their new hall, which brings revenue to the church and enables it to be generous in its giving, people fear that this move might mean a return to the bad old days when the church subsidised an ill-maintained and ill-used hall. Meanwhile the two local papers have – as usual – opposing headlines on the matter. One runs 'Youth Club from Hell Seeks Next Victim: The Church' and the other 'Will Church Spurn Young People Yet Again?'

In a week's time the church council will meet to make a decision on whether to start moves to accept the club on its premises.

- Who will you talk to, what will you say, and what other preparations will you make beforehand?
- What do you plan to say at the meeting?
- Consider the degree of priority you would give to each of the following in this situation, indicating how you see your role at this time:
  - Leading.
  - Planning.
  - Representing.
  - Challenging.
  - Reconciling.
  - Encouraging.
  - Collaborating.
  - Listening.

Ministers as managers?

From fairly extensive reading about pastor and priest predecessors, I was impressed that everyday pastoral life was primarily concerned with developing a life of prayer among the people. Leading worship, preaching the gospel, and teaching Scripture on Sundays would develop in the next six days into representing the life of Christ in the human traffic of the everyday.

With my mind full of these thoughts, my pastor friend and I stopped at a service station for gasoline. My friend, a gregarious person, bantered with the attendant. Something in the exchange provoked a question.

'What do you do?'

'I run a church.'

No answer could have surprised me more. I knew, of course, that pastoral life included institutional responsibilities, but it never occurred to me that I would be defined by those responsibilities. But the moment I became ordained, I found I was so defined both by the pastors and executives over me and by the parishioners around me. (Peterson 1993, p. 58)

Peterson's dismay will be familiar to many who have felt called to a ministry concerned with prayer, spiritual guidance, preaching and leading worship, and find that much of their time is spent running a church! A page earlier, Peterson writes:

Until about a century ago, what pastors did between Sundays was apiece with what they did on Sundays. The context changed: instead of an assembled congregation, the pastor was with one other person or with small gatherings of persons, or alone in study and prayer. The manner changed: instead of proclamation, there was conversation. But the work was the same: discovering the meaning of Scripture, developing a life of prayer, guiding growth into maturity . . . The between-Sundays work of American pastors in this century, though, is running a church. (p. 57)

Peterson makes a plea for restoring the cure of souls – or soul-guiding – to the heart of ministry: a plea that we would echo. Meanwhile, given the amount of time most pastors have to spend these days 'running the show', it is very important to ensure that this 'running' is not just management, or the maintenance of the church apparatus for its own sake. It needs to be 'mindful management' – management that is theologically reflective and enables this in others. Is not the whole purpose of managing the church to ensure that the whole 'show' presents the gospel, represents Christ, is informed by prayer, serves those outside the Church as well as those within, and helps to guide all into fullness of life in Christ?

Among the charisms listed in Paul's epistles we find *kybernēseis* (1 Corinthians 12.28), which literally means pilots or helmsmen, translated 'governments' in the Authorised Version, 'leaders' in the Jerusalem and Revised Standard versions, and 'those with gifts of administration' in the New International. In Romans (12.8) is listed *proïstamenos*, meaning one who is set over others, an overseer, manager or director. Interestingly, in this passage the Jerusalem Bible translates the familiar word *diakonia* (Romans 12.8) as 'administration'. There is a cluster of related gifts and abilities here that is listed after the more authoritative and primary gifts like apostleship, prophecy and teaching.

These days a managing director's role tends to be regarded as the 'top' job, and in fascist systems the 'leader' (*führer* or *duce*) is the most powerful person. There is also, as noted, a current vogue for considering the minister primarily as leader. The lists of charisms suggest that we should not regard the leaders and managers as having the most important gifts in the Church. But on the other hand, we should not downplay these roles as somehow 'unspiritual', since they are listed among the charisms. The minister is indeed called to be a kind of leader, but that is not her defining role: for the leader is to be defined in terms of representing, praying, serving, teaching, nurturing, guiding. This chapter will try to show how the spiritual gifts of leadership in the Church flow from and back into the other gifts suggested by Paul and described in this book.

Leadership in four styles

In the focusing exercise there are a number of ways in which a minister could understand his leadership role, leading to different courses of action:

1 He may see himself as the person with the best **overview** of the situation, balancing the competing claims in his own mind and coming up with a solution. His approach will then be to use his authority to impose this solution on all in their best interests, taking the flack for his decision rather than seeing those with opposing views pitted against each other.

2 Or he may see himself, as an **administrative servant** of the community, allowing the church council, which he understands to be the body with responsibility for the church premises, to come to its own decision. He will then do his best to help in the implementation of the decision, whatever it is, and to deal with any problems and conflicts that arise.

3 He may see himself as a prophetic **visionary** for God's Kingdom, not ultimately accountable to the church council but to Christ and his gospel. Passionately he will argue and persuade and if necessary challenge and cajole the parties concerned until this vision is accepted and implemented.

4 Or finally, he might see himself as the **enabler** of all concerned, seeing all parties as having important contributions to make to the solution, which has to emerge through good communication and negotiation. He will talk to all the groups involved, listen carefully to their concerns, and enable them to listen to one another. He will help people identify shared interests, seeking to convert what seems to be an 'I win, you lose' conflict into a 'win–win' solution.

For any minister there is likely to be a core understanding of what it means for her to lead the parish, and a way of leading with which she feels most comfortable. Hopefully these will be the same, but not necessarily: we have encountered ministers who feel they are failing to be good leaders as they understand it, yet are quite able at leading the congregation in a different way which sadly is not their ideal. There is also the understanding of the congregation and how they expect and desire (again not necessarily the same) to be led. And finally, there is the question of what kind of leadership will actually work best in a situation in the sense of leading the congregation forward in the ways of the Kingdom. This is likely to involve a mixture of styles, with the balance varying according to the situation.

Simon Walker (2010) argues that the good leader is the 'undefended' one who does not react to criticism or failure by retreating into the style of leadership with which she feels most secure. Rather, she is fully aware of the different leadership approaches and has learnt to use the different styles – even those which do not come naturally to her – flexibly, as occasion requires. Walker (pp. 188–9) likens the process to riding a bicycle, in which you have constantly, in the light of the road you are travelling on, to shift the balance between pushing the pedals, freewheeling, and applying the brake; between turning the handlebars to the left and to the right; and (we might add to Walker's image) between shifting the gears down, for a slower but easier ride, and up, for a faster but harder and perhaps riskier one.

Walker discerns three variables at work in determining the four leadership styles outlined above. These concern, first, control and the use of power in the process, which may be 'strong' and top-down or bottom-up and 'weak' – we prefer the term 'gentle'. Second, there may be a tendency for the leadership approach to push towards 'conserving' and keeping things as they are; or it may be more 'expansive' and innovative, seeking new opportunities. Third, the leadership may be more 'presented', transparent and up-front, or it may be more reserved and keeping a low profile. As we describe the four leadership styles in the rest of this chapter, it should become clear how the planner by natural inclination is strong and conserving, the steward gentle and conserving, the visionary strong and expansive, and the enabler gentle and expansive. However, what the mindful minister needs to do is work outside his natural comfort zone when the situation demands, moving mindfully in all three dimensions.

Our forebears in Old and New Testament times would clearly not have used such concepts in their perception of leadership, but exploring the four leadership styles identified above in the context of biblical models both deepens and illuminates the mindful practice of leadership. Each style can, of course, be distorted by becoming absent-minded, ego-minded or mindless. If this begins to happen, the minister needs to be able to recognize it and provide a corrective, perhaps by moving toward a different leadership style, or seeking someone with gifts that complement her own.

Overviewing: the planner

Read **Proverbs 8.1–31**: the call of Lady Wisdom.

Spend a time imaginatively visualizing Lady Wisdom as here depicted.

List the qualities of Wisdom as here described.

List the qualities that, for you, make for a wise leader, worthy of respect.

What similarities and differences are there in the lists?

Where have you learned wisdom in the past, and where would you turn in the future to grow in wisdom?

This section considers the style of leadership that is strong and hierarchical, and oriented to conserving and passing on the inheritance of faith. Typically this kind of leader has an overall plan or map in his head of what the basic elements of parish or congregational life ought to be. He is willing to share this plan with his people, and to graft into the plan insights from the people that are compatible with it, but he is unlikely to welcome a head-on challenge to the plan itself. He sees his task as finding the right people to whom elements of the plan can be delegated. He is uncomfortable with people who 'rock the boat' – a ship needs many workers of different kinds, but if there is more than one helmsman, chaos will ensue. (*kybnernēseis* – pilots or helmsmen – as noted, constitute one of the spiritual gifts, and it describes this style of leadership well.)

By the late first century these leadership gifts had become focused on the bishops (*episcopoi*) charged with oversight (*episcopē*) of the churches in a city and its surrounding regions. The term 'overseer' has some very negative connotations – for example, the taskmasters who supervised the work of the Hebrew slaves in Egypt were overseers; and in the ancient world the term frequently referred to the 'inspector' who checked to see if people, and even things like drains, were functioning as they should. The Latin equivalent of *episcopos* gives us the related terms 'supervisor' and 'supervision'. Ironically 'oversight' can also mean the opposite – a failure in your overview that leads you to 'overlook' something crucial.

In recent Anglican thinking about ministry (for example Croft 1999) *episcopē* is very often cited as an increasing part of the priest's task, as he or she has to take on more and more parishes and the job becomes administratively much more complex. It is certainly true that the more lay ministries and gifts are recognized and enabled, the more there needs to be a person who holds the use of these gifts together and has an eye for the big picture. *Episcopē* is perhaps better translated as overview than the ambiguous term oversight; it suggests the essence of this ministry, which is having a deeper overall understanding of what the Church is for and where it needs to go, and being able to put the pieces together to enable this to happen.

Though there are plenty of other places in the Bible where we might have looked for understanding of this kind of leadership, we have drawn on the tradition of Wisdom. This strong Old Testament and Apocryphal tradition (running in parallel with that of prophecy) seems to have grown from among society's leaders, emerging from an aristocratic and court-based setting; indeed, traditionally the Wisdom writings are ascribed to King Solomon, who chose the gift of wisdom above all other gifts (1 Kings 3.1–15). It arises not from any visionary apprehension of God, but from a more rational pondering of creation and society, and above all from a deep love of the Wisdom of God, which is often personified (as above) as an adorable woman. Typically it expresses itself in pithy proverbs, contrasting the wise man who, guided by wisdom, is able to guide others, with the fool who spurns all guidance.

The Greek word for wisdom, *Sophia*, and the Hebrew *hokhma*, both convey an essentially practical know-how, even cunning and cleverness, rather than the armchair ruminations we have perhaps come to understand by 'philosophy'. The core art of the leader we are considering is not just having good ideas, but being able to put them into practice in the life of a congregation.

But the image of Lady Wisdom suggests something even more crucial. Lady Wisdom is a close friend – even some might say a consort – of God:

> I was beside him, like a master worker;
> and I was daily his delight,
> rejoicing before him always,
> rejoicing in his inhabited world
> and delighting in the human race.
> (Proverbs 8.27–31)

This delight in God and God's creative work needs to be the core energy of the Christian leader. In the book of Wisdom the qualities used to describe Lady Wisdom clearly show how she partakes in of the nature of God:

> In her there is a spirit that is intelligent, holy, unique, manifold, subtle, mobile, clear, unpolluted, distinct, invulnerable, loving the good, keen, irresistible, beneficent, humane, steadfast, sure, free from anxiety, all-powerful, overseeing all, and penetrating through all spirits that are intelligent and pure and most subtle. (Wisdom 7.22–23)

Though there are a few qualities here we would *not* wish to see in the leader – 'invulnerable' and 'all powerful' we would surely prefer to leave to God alone – the rest constitute an idealized portrait of a perfectly mindful minister.

It should now be clear why Table 1 (p. xv) identifies 'words of wisdom' as a charism of leadership. In *Wisdom and Ministry: The Call to Leadership* (2008) Michael Sadgrove looks to Solomon, Joseph, Daniel and David for models of the wisdom needed in the leader, and draws extensively on writings in the Wisdom tradition (Proverbs, Psalms 1 and 73, Job, Ecclesiastes and the Song of Songs) to glean an understanding of all that wisdom means.

Mindful overviewing and planning contributes to a congregation a clear sense of priorities, with everyone pulling together in a co-ordinated way that maximizes the efficiency of their efforts and helps them see relatively quick results to reward their hard work. It helps everyone feel they have a place in the overall plan.

Walker describes two kinds of overviewing planner. The 'presenting' or front-stage type is the more typical 'commander' exemplified according to Walker by Roosevelt and his top-down plans. The 'reserved' or back-stage type is shown in the 'foundational' strategy of men like Lincoln, who draw not on explicit plans but on foundational ideas that all take for granted: in Lincoln's case this was the American constitution and the equal rights it gave to all. In our terms this kind of leader merges into the representative, discussed in Chapter 1, who contends not for his own plans but the deep and longstanding traditions he represents.

Mindful overviewing and planning can go wrong in the usual three ways.

1 The 'absent-minded' planner is the **armchair philosopher**, whose wonderful plans remain in his head or on paper, because he is unaware of the disparity between them and reality. One of us confesses to guilt in this respect: ideas for him prove so absorbing in contrast with the painstaking work required to make them become a reality! In particular, he helped develop some wonderful plans for developing the church as a centre for the community. The brochures we sent to potential funders were works of art, and the whole conception was – though we say it ourselves – brilliant. But we spent so much time on developing them that we lost the initiative. The school opposite the church was closed and suddenly provided ample facilities for the local community, rendering our contribution redundant in the eyes of funders. It also has to be said that we probably only won over about half of the congregation to support the plans. To correct his deficiency, the armchair philosopher needs to become or enlist a **visionary** leader who can inspire people on a gut rather than intellectual level, and get things moving.

2 The ego-minded planner is the **dictator** who is too personally attached to his plans, and cannot tolerate criticism. Highly defended, he has no concept of a loyal opposition, but sees all disagreement as dissent aimed at undermining his position. If he is not to alienate

crucial areas of support, the dictator needs to move to or enlist the more rational, detached approach of the **steward** who can enable people to weigh up plans more objectively, without any suggestion that those who disagree with the vicar are enemies of the Church!

3 The mindless planner is the **meddler** who cannot truly delegate parts of the plan to others, or trust people to carry them out, but is always interfering with their work and making sure they 'do it right'. It has been argued that one important factor in the shift of fortunes on the Eastern front was that Stalin, who had been a meddler, learnt to trust his generals with the war effort, while Hitler, who had trusted his generals, lost that trust when battles began to be lost, and increasingly interfered with ill-thought-out orders from the top. The meddler needs to become or enlist the **enabler,** who trusts and empowers people to do their part of the task.

Administration: the steward of mysteries

Read **Genesis 41**: Joseph becomes Pharaoh's steward.

Reflect: What led Pharaoh to promote Joseph?

What fitted Joseph for the task?

What tasks did Joseph's post involve?

Evaluate Joseph's performance.

Paul urges his people to 'think of us in this way, as servants of Christ and stewards of God's mysteries' (1 Corinthians 4.1). The Greek is *oikonomous mystēriōn theou*. The first word, from which we get our word 'economy', derives from the word for a house or household and means the important kind of servant who was put in charge of managing the household affairs, ensuring that necessary supplies are bought, administering the budget and balancing the books. As often in Christian thought, the barrier we usually place between the common and the holy is here broken down. 'Stewards of mysteries' conjoins the humdrum tasks of household management with the mysteries of God.

In this section we are dealing with tasks like managing, planning, prioritizing, organizing, administering, administrating, funding, and looking after buildings. All of these involve a style of leadership that has to do with serving God's people rather than guiding them, and with maintenance rather than expanding in new directions. It is very ordinary and humble, and it may seem to be beneath the dignity of the man of God. But the gospel demands that we do away with two-tier thinking and conjoin the holy mysteries with the most ordinary acts of service.

Churches use the word 'stewardship' a lot these days, mainly in two connections. One is encouraging people to help the church financially, to make ends meet, to manage their own finances in a way that takes partial responsibility for the church's financial viability. Yet we have witnessed stewardship campaigns that have shied away from the humdrum issue of people's pockets and preferred to talk about more 'lofty' things like people's spiritual gifts. The other is the 'stewardship of the earth', the notion that God has appointed human beings as managers of the 'household' of the earth, so that we need to take care that the 'household budget' is well kept and resources do not run dry. Stewardship, then, is about the spirituality of ecology and economics. In the ministry of stewards in congregations, a sense of the spirituality of the mundane tasks that keep the church going – architecturally, financially, practically and personally – needs to be fostered and appreciated.

In business, managers tend to work on a dualist (and often sexist) basis, with the (more often male) managing director having the bright ideas and overview, and the (most often female) secretary dealing with the down-to-earth management of his affairs. Larger parishes and congregations may be able to appoint parish administrators or secretaries, but in many cases the minister has to be both overall planner and day-to-day administrator.

Some ministers may find such administrative work an uncongenial distraction from what they understand as their true calling, but it is significant to note that Jesus himself, according to Walker (pp. 255ff), epitomizes the 'steward', in the more reserved 'self-emptying' variant, which, of course, also relates to Jesus' role as 'servant' discussed in Chapter 3. The more extrovert and front-stage 'consensual' variant of the steward Walker sees exemplified by Nelson Mandela whose other gifts relate him to the 'communicator' discussed in Chapter 6.

As a biblical model we have just considered Joseph, who came to be Pharaoh's chief steward. Yet Joseph had been a slave and a prisoner, and he was also a dreamer and interpreter of dreams. It is interesting to see how all these factors worked together to make him a good steward of Pharaoh's land.

1 He was an isolated stranger, an outsider, not an Egyptian but a Jew. This enabled Pharaoh to trust him, presumably because

he was distant from the rival factions among his own people, having no hidden power agenda of his own. In the same way the minister, typically, comes from outside the community. She does not belong to any of the factions that often subtly operate in a church community, as in any other. As Joseph rejected the seductions of Pharaoh's wife, so the minister needs to ensure that the friendliness and good qualities of some members do not lure him 'into bed' with any particular sub-group in the congregation. The mistrust and imprisonment that Joseph had to undergo because of his rejection of Pharaoh's wife is not un-like the pain and rejection a minister sometimes has to accept in order to remain impartial, and therefore trustworthy as a guide for all.

2 He interpreted dreams. It was his ability to interpret Pharaoh's dreams convincingly that led Pharaoh to trust him as a close guide. In the same way the minister listens carefully to the 'dreams' of her people, both in the sense of their deepest hopes and aspirations, and in terms of the experience they find dark, puzzling or confusing, as Pharaoh found his dreams to be. She then helps the person interpret those dreams in the light of the Christian tradition, so that they can become a force for change rather than consternation. To do this the minister, like Joseph, must be a deep dreamer herself. Her own vision needs to be intense, her own dark and confusing places familiar and not frightening. And she must be open to wherever the vision is coming from. Vision is by no means limited to church councils or parish plans, let alone to the minister herself! It may be that the individual or group (even the youth group of our example?) which the community finds most confusing or difficult or embar-rassing holds the truth the community needs to face up to, just as it was the awkward and often despised prophets (see later) who did so in Hebrew culture. Two 'fringe' members of the congrega-tion in the council estate parish where we worked had a 'dream' of a community fayre to be held on the green close to the church, with the intention that it should be a meeting-point between church members and the wider community. Some of the longer-standing church members were fearful . . .

3 But Joseph was not a head-in-the-clouds dreamer. His interpreta-tion of Pharaoh's dream led on to some very practical guidance as to measures that could be taken to see the people through the famine that was coming. The guide likewise is a practical dreamer, eminently able to translate vision and obstacle into practical steps.

If he is more of a dreamer by nature he will need to access them through the more practical members of the community – just as a minister who is more practical and organizing by nature will need to access the dreaming and guiding skills of others.

If Joseph epitomizes the mindful steward, these three aspects may suggest the remedies for what can go wrong for the minister as administrator.

- If absent-minded, he becomes the **bureaucrat**, obsessed with drawing up parish plans and policies, but indifferent about implementing them or monitoring whether they are carried out. One of us remembers trying to deal with recurrent disputes about how much rent different organizations using the hall should pay, drawing up a formidable list of criteria for what counted as a church organization and hence lower rent, and a highly complex scale of rents according to different users' needs and deserts. However, once the document was created and circulated, and admired by its creator for its elegant justice, not much else happened and things went on much as before, because nobody had thought through how it would actually be implemented! To overcome his absent-mindedness the bureaucrat needs to learn the arts of the **enabler**, so that people actually do things in response to blueprints. He needs to learn the third lesson from Joseph, concerning his down-to-earth practical skills.

- If ego-minded, the steward becomes something a bit more sinister: the **commissar**, a bureaucrat with a mission, ego-invested in his plans and feeling personally affronted if his policies are not strictly adhered to. He needs to learn the broader picture of the **overseer**, with his stronger sense of priorities and goals that policies serve, understanding that policies are made for people and not people for policies. The perspective of Joseph's first qualification, his detachment as a stranger without any power of his own, may help here.

- If mindless, the steward degenerates into the paperholic – who may in fact be largely paperless these days: the priest who sits forever in front of his computer screen making plans and rotas, and running off endless lists to pin here and there, without any ability to prioritize where to give his time and attention, and what is sufficiently unimportant to let go. He needs to become more of a **visionary** to see the wood from the trees, and to generate motivation to achieve what serves the vision. Here the steward needs to learn from Joseph the dreamer.

Inspiring: the visionary

Read **Revelation 10**: the angel with the sweet and bitter scroll

Summon this vision to mind in all its detail.

- Imagine the scroll the angel gives to you. What do you think the message is that *you* are given to proclaim?
- In what ways is your message sweet and in what ways bitter?
- Can you recall times when the role of imparting a vision has been delightful, and times when it has been bitter, or painful?
- You may like to compare this passage with the passage with Ezekiel 2.1—3.15, on which it is partly based.

Both the planner and the steward base their leadership on plans they hold in their heads. The plans may have emerged from consultation with the congregation, but the minister needs to hold in his mind an overview of how they fit together. The steward may have a more complex set of plans, the detail of which lies on paper lists or computer, but still he needs to hold in his mind the fact that these lists are there and where they can be found. And though there may be a strong element of forward movement and change involved in the plans, the important thing is that they have been worked out so as to hold together and *maintain* that forward momentum.

With the visionary and the enabler, we move to a different kind of energy, one that burns in the heart rather than enlightens the mind; which draws on symbols and images rather than literal-minded analysis; and which focuses on emotion and motivation rather than rational decision. And rather than maintaining a forward thrust by a rational order that all can see and assent to, here it is the other way round: the forward thrust or draw, generated by the vision, is what pulls people together in corporate action.

So in this section we move to the all-important realm of vision and the visionary leader. Here we are on dangerous ground, because false visions abound. Hitler could be seen as a visionary who brought the people together around a powerful ideal ablaze with imagery and rhetoric; but it was a false vision based on deep resentment and irrational hatred, and it led (after initial success in healing a broken economy) to war and genocide. It is vital that the vision of the visionary leader is grounded in love not hatred, and in a God who transcends reason without being irrational; a God who gives the prophets visions, but also says through his prophet, 'Come, let us reason together.' It is a false leader who refuses to reason with people on the grounds that he alone has the inspiration of God.

In the book of Revelation we encounter vision upon vision, entrusted according to tradition to an elderly John the Evangelist sitting in a cave on the prison island of Patmos. The visions are powerful, and they lead the recipient to write words of immortal beauty and hope, but also, it has to be said, sometimes of anger and resentment. These days, wary of the pitfalls of arrogance and false vision, most books on ministry fight shy of vision and prophecy, preferring to focus on care or oversight. As R. S. Thomas noted (Chapter 2), our preachers no longer catch fire and burn.

And yet one of us remembers that it was when at one church council meeting he got angry and passionate, that people commented afterwards that at last they understood. A vision that had stayed, rather absent-mindedly, in my head, suddenly descended to my heart and guts, and people could begin to feel the fire and be motivated by it in a way they had not been able to before.

Anger is risky. It can easily descend into violence, leading us to say bitter, hurtful things we later regret but cannot unsay; and habitual anger (like habitual tears) instils embarrassment if not resentment. But occasional mindful anger (like occasional mindful tears and sorrow) may have its place at meetings. The scroll of vision, delightful as it is to the mind and in spite of its spiritual 'taste', has its bitter edge. Without that edge, we might just want to contemplate it, rather than engage in the conflict involved in bringing the vision to birth.

Walker describes two kinds of visionary. There is the reserved visionary who carries the vision within, sharing it powerfully and effectively on occasion – exemplified by Martin Luther King (and perhaps, we suggest, also the original Martin Luther). And there is the presented visionary or 'pacesetter' – exemplified by Winston Churchill – who translates the vision explicitly into targets for the people to strive for. The ministry of the reserved visionary is close to that of the teacher, while the pacesetter is more like the evangelist.

The mindful visionary is able, like the teacher, to help the people relate their practice as a congregation to the inspiring images and teachings of the scriptures. Her passion for the gospel then proves contagious and begins to motivate people's decisions even about 'mundane' matters like the hall and the church building. But the leader can fall short of this mindful ideal.

- The absent-minded visionary is the **idle dreamer,** who sees the reality of the Church through the spectacles of her own rosy-tinted vision. Historically theologians have quite often been idle dreamers, speaking of the unity, holiness, universality and apostolicity of the Church, and taking no notice at all of the Church's frequent fragmentation, corruption, nationalism and betrayal of gospel values. In the same way idle dreamers can see their own churches as incarnations of their own ideal; they need to develop as **stewards**, or call upon the ministry of stewards, to provide more accurate feedback on their church's shortcomings, and cash out the vision in terms of practical changes.

- The ego-minded visionary is the **primadonna**, over-attached to her personal part in the vision, and unable to recognize others' insights, dismissing them not because they are wrong but because they are not hers. We remember someone saying of a particular bishop that you could only persuade him to take a course of action if you made him think it was his idea. But there is something of that in many of us, caricatured in the TV series *Yes, Minister*, where the civil servant – something of a 'commissar' – persuades the MP that he is just being a 'yes man' to all his polices, when in fact the policies have all been fed to him by the civil servant, being the policies that have always been in place! What the primadonna really needs is not a steward so much as an enabler; she needs to strengthen her own regard for others' gifts and enable others to contribute their vision, even if it is different.

- The mindless visionary is what we might call the **disturber**, who has random fragments of powerful inspiration but cannot co-ordinate them into a coherent plan that people might own and trust. People do not understand where the disturber is coming from, so they just feel disturbed by his seemingly random fits of rhetoric. What the disturber needs is a bit of the rational coherence and planning ability of the **overseer**, enabling random acts of disturbance to coalesce into a coherent plan for transformation according to the vision of the Kingdom.

Discerning: the enabler

Read **John 1.40–51**. This passage, from the middle of the first week of Jesus' ministry according to John, describes Jesus giving Peter his name, and calling Nathanael (a disciple unique to this Gospel, whose name means 'God given') whom he had previously noticed under a fig tree.

Imagine yourself as Jesus in this passage.

First focus on Simon, being introduced to you early in the morning in the house where you are staying. Picture Peter standing there in the early morning light – what does he look like? What about him enables you to entrust him with being the Rock on which the Church is founded?

Now imagine yourself walking along and noticing one man in particular sitting under a fig tree. What makes you single him out from the crowd?

Finally, imagine yourself meeting Nathanael. Picture this man whom you had noticed yesterday. What makes you think him worthy of his name? What vision do you share, and where does it come from?

The God of the Bible is a God who works through people, whom he calls and entrusts, even though they are not always worthy of trust. Consider the call of the following, and what they have in common.

- Moses – considered in Chapter 3.
- The prophets – especially Isaiah (Isaiah 6), Jeremiah (Jeremiah 1), and Ezekiel (Ezekiel 1 – 3), Jonah (Jonah 1 – 4).
- Mary (Luke 1.26–38).
- The disciples by Jesus (one example just considered). (See also Matthew 4.18–22; Mark 1.14–19; Luke 6.12–16; John 1.35–45.)

In most of these cases God does not command imperiously: his call is often awesome, accompanied by vision, but also courteous and reasonable, considering and dealing with the hesitation of the person called. The call runs with, not against, the grain of the person's experience so far: the disciples have the gift of fishing already, now Jesus calls them to put their fishing skills to a new task: 'Follow me, and I will make you fish for people' (Matthew 4.19; Mark 1.17).

And the entrusting persists through failure – and even disobedience (as in Jonah). The most striking case of this, however, is the way, after Peter's threefold denial, Jesus does not, as many a manager would, say to him, 'OK Peter, this looks like too big a task for you. Thank you for your services, and we know you tried hard, but I think you'll appreciate why we'd better get someone else for this job . . .' Instead (John 21.15–19) he asks a question no manager would: 'Do you love me?' and proceeds to say how in the future Peter will be strong enough not to disown him again, even in the face of death.

Discerning who is reliable and right for a task is a big part of leadership generally, and of ministry in particular. As well as envisioning and motivating others with her own vision, the minister needs to perceive the vision and the qualities that are there in others, and how they may be built on and developed further. She calls people to do more than they feel *and currently are* capable of, trusting to a process whereby they may grow to be worthy of things they are not yet. This goes beyond what a secular manager might do: because God is involved, the minister can envisage possible grace and growth where the manager would be more sceptical and cautious. Yet she must not be reckless here, since failure on the part of the entrusted person may damage both that person and his fellow-travellers.

A third difference from many managers is that the latter are delegating tasks 'from above', fitting people to the plan, whereas enablers will typically arrive at plans from a consensus among the people, fitting plans to the people and the gifts they bring. In either case, of course, there has to be some kind of negotiation between plans and people, but there is a difference in balance.

Walker's two enabling strategies are serving, typified by Jimmy Carter – offering a gently supportive and encouraging presence on a one-to-one basis, as in the ministry of the servant described in Chapter 3; and the consensual, typified by a rather different president, Ronald Reagan. This strategy allows consensus on goals to aim for to emerge in a more explicit and corporate way, expanding into the approach of the liberator as described in Chapter 8.

Enabling others to flourish in ministry may at times require a deliberate stepping aside from using all your own strengths and skills, so that others may fill the vacuum. Walker notes how Jesus declared, in the context of his own coming sacrifice, that 'it is expedient for you [disciples] that I go away' (John 16.17) – for only if Jesus goes can the Spirit (and all his gifts) arrive.

Self-sacrifice is the conscious choice not to use force or to exercise power but instead to allow something to be done to you. Inevitably, therefore, it involves a degree of suffering and risk. It may be the emotional suffering of letting a loved one walk away, and the risk they may not come back. It may be physical suffering under persecution or even torture. In this regard, self-sacrifice is the weakest, most powerless course of action: it involves doing nothing, abdicating your right to impose yourself and choosing to allow others to impose on you . . . When it's employed deliberately, it obliges followers to take responsibility for their choices: there is a genuine withdrawal of the leader's presence that leaves his followers to cope without him. (2010, pp. 278–9)

Jesus' own costly withdrawal, allowing himself to be 'handed over' at the time of his passion, is beautifully explored in Vanstone's *The Stature of Waiting* (1982). The mindful enabler will not be able to emulate Jesus in this regard, but will find inspiration in holding his example in mind. The enabler who loses mindfulness may do so in one of these ways:

- The absent-minded enabler is the **star-gazer**, the one who looks on everyone in her congregation as a star, perfect and free from all faults, and so gives them tasks that not only are they unable to do now, but are way beyond what they could ever achieve. The result is a church let down and a person demoralized. The star-gazer needs the corrective of the **overseer**, to make a more fruitful marriage between 'below' and 'above'; between people and plan.
- The ego-minded enabler readily becomes a **fence-sitter**, leading from the back not because of awareness of people's gifts and insights, but from a fear of being criticized, and a wish to tell people only what they want to hear. He needs a stronger element of the visionary, to impart a more overt and passionate approach.
- The mindless enabler becomes the **anarchist**, who absolutizes individuals' gifts and needs, and helps everyone 'do their own thing' regardless of the needs of the church or any overall plan. Something of this seems to have been at work in the chaotic laissez-faire worship of the Corinthians, which sounds (from Paul's criticisms) as if it amounted to a cacophony of individuals determined to inflict their gifts of prophecy, tongues or whatever on everyone else. The anarchist needs to learn from the careful balancing act of the steward, who sensitively co-ordinates what people have to offer to the demands of order and mutual respect.

Conclusion

This chapter considered the minister as leader charged with organization and oversight. With the help of Walker, four styles of leadership were considered: oversight or overall planning, which involves a top-down delegation; administration or 'stewardship', in which the minister works out the detail of the plans the people he serves have decided on; inspiration, in which a visionary motivates people to follow her vision for the gospel; and enabling, in which the gifts of the people are discerned, encouraged and co-ordinated into a vision that develops 'bottom-up'. The mindful leader will combine these styles but also draw on the gifts of leadership in others.

However, we need to return to the point made earlier: although leadership and administration do appear in the Pauline lists of ministries or spiritual gifts, they are not the primary gifts listed. Leadership is not the essence of ministry but needs always to be predicated on other spiritual gifts. For this reason, a minister who has (or has developed) few of the other gifts described in this book, and attempts *only* to be a leader, is unlikely to be able to share and proclaim enough of the substance of faith and love and holiness to gain the confidence of a congregation. At least some of the fundamental gifts of ministry will need to be developed and fostered, so that this leader can become more than 'a sounding gong or a tinkling cymbal'. And if a leader is to be *collaborative*, he will need in particular the gifts explored in the next chapter.

For reflection and discussion

1   Which of the four styles of leadership described in this chapter comes most naturally to you? How far do you feel you need to develop aspects of other leadership styles, and how might you do this?

2   What examples of visionary leadership can you think of, and what have these leaders contributed to the church communities they have served?

3   Which of the qualities of Lady Wisdom described in Wisdom 7.22–23 do you recognize in yourself and in other ministers you know or have known? How might such gifts be fostered?

6

The Go-Between: Mindful Collaboration, Conviviality and Communication

A busy extrovert, bubbling with obvious energy, the communicator has leapt up to you after the service and found out the intimate details of your life before you realized that you had given them away, and introduced you to like-minded people, and got you on the intercession rota to boot! The communicator seems all over the place, a merry chaos, and yet next time you visit the church your name is remembered with pretty well everything else.

The church services are full of media magic, though some might find the approach superficial; the sermons expertly delivered, a little simplistic in content, but conceived as a basis for discussion and the provocation of thought. The noticeboards are full of information about parish and local community meetings, well organized and up to date. This minister leads energetically but from the back, seeing her main task as enabling the many able and energized members to pull together in a consensus.

The church has an atmosphere of transparency and conviviality, though some might criticize it for not going deep enough, and not raising radical questions for fear of rocking the boat. The church is based around the people who are willing to commit energy, and at meetings the attempt is always made to find consensus.

Unlike the roles of lay administrators and pastoral assistants, 'go-betweens' are seldom acknowledged or appointed as such. Nevertheless the role of ensuring good communication between priest and people, and among the people, remains vital, since forming a vision is not the same as sharing it with others, and pastors will seldom do both things well. In Anglican churches the go-between role is often carried by the churchwardens; in free churches and the Catholic and Orthodox churches it may be the deacon or elders.

Focus: a new rota

It is announced at the morning service that a new rota for readings and intercessions is being prepared, and people should tell Mabel if there are any Sundays they cannot manage. You are relatively new to the congregation, and beginning to feel you'd like to get more involved. But you are not sure what the protocol is, whether new readers are wanted, or indeed who Mabel is. You wonder, from the announcement, whether the rota is a closed shop, open only to those who know Mabel.

Reflect on what is being *communicated* in this announcement, intentionally and non-intentionally, by what is said, by what is not said, and by the way it is said (or not said).

Going between

Read **Acts 2.1–13:** Pentecost.

Imagine yourself, as vividly as you can, as one of the disciples. Focus on:

- the gathering in one room – what feelings do you have at this stage?
- the wind – what does it sound like – *feel* like?
- the tongues of flame – imagine one of them settling on you – what is *your* flame like – does it 'speak' to you, literally or metaphorically – what change in you does this effect?
- the tongues of different languages.
- the crowds gathered around you. Note their comments.
- How do you feel after the experience? In what way has it changed you?

Let the particular imagery fade. Probably nothing *exactly* like this has ever happened to you, but as you are left with the general feelings, if you can remember a time when similar feelings were evoked, or a similar change in you took place, you may like to reflect on that event and the effect it had on you.

Finally, how might the passage and your reflections on it connect with conviviality, communication and collaboration?

As noted in the Introduction, collaborative ministry has become very central. When we trained for ministry, it was becoming important: it was the model we tried to follow in our ministry in parishes and elsewhere, though it was not always the model of the people we served, which occasionally caused problems. By the time we taught in a theological college, some 25 years after being trained ourselves, it was assumed that we were training and forming people who would collaborate in ministry with their congregations and others. By then many books had been written on the subject, a few of which are listed in the bibliography.

However, as noted by Pickard, and cited in the Introduction, people were beginning to ask where all this emphasis on collaborative ministry left the specific ministry of the ordained. There was a new tendency to reinforce the authority of the ordained, by seeing them as leaders, overseers or co-ordinators of the collaborative ministry of all. Collaboration, carefully interpreted, is arguably of the essence of ministry since all the charisms are given and work together for the building up of the one body of Christ, just as the different organs and members 'collaborate' to sustain the life of the human body.

The body metaphor provides a helpful perspective on the working together, or collaboration, of different ministries. The body is not just a 'task' that the organs 'accomplish' – as if, having done their job, the organs could congratulate one another and go home with a sense of satisfaction! The body is a living being, a 'conviviality' of the organs, which cannot have any life of their own separately from the body. And this conviviality is sustained by the constant communication and interchange between the members – through neural, circulatory and lymphatic networks.

In a comparable way, in a healthy congregation collaboration is sustained by good communication which, in turn, relies on conviviality. That is why in this chapter we group these three interdependent 'co-' words together. Out of this circle of communication and conviviality arises the possibility of conceiving and collaborating in tasks and visions, and the collaboration again facilitates good communication and builds greater conviviality.

In the Pauline lists of ministries, there is nothing specifically corresponding to these three concepts, yet it is precisely this working together which builds up the body. And there is one gift – tongues or languages (*glōssa* – 1 Corinthians 12.10, 28, to which v. 10 adds the interpretation of tongues) – which is self-evidently about communication. The gift of speaking in tongues (presumably tongues you have not been taught) is discussed extensively in the first letter to the Corinthians, who seem to have treasured it particularly as part of their worship; but it does not figure much in the other letters, or in the later lists of ministries. It seems to connect with the event described in the focusing passage above from Acts 2. Here it relates to a gift of communication of the gospel beyond the barriers of race and language, undoing the confusion of tongues at the destruction of the tower of Babel (Genesis 11.1–9).

This gift surely relates also to the ability to communicate not only across language barriers, but across the barriers of culture, class and education that so often make it difficult to understand and empathize with one another. The inability to do this lies behind most wars and conflicts. Transcending these barriers with the love of Christ and the wisdom of the Spirit can be one of the distinctive features of Christians who have learnt not to scrabble – and squabble – in the barnyard (see pp. vi–viii).

Pentecost of course enabled a new breadth and energy of communication, and in the same breath – so to speak – created a new conviviality. The disciples seemed to outsiders to be drunk with new wine – which in a non-literal sense of course they were – and soon they were sharing their lives and goods in common too (3.44). In the same breath also the Spirit created collaboration. From being a congregation huddled tightly in one place, afraid and unsure of their role, they became a confident faith-sharing group dispersed throughout the known world but united in the common task of preaching the gospel.

Such is the work of the Holy Spirit. In his classic, *The Go-between God* (new edition, 2004), John V. Taylor describes the work of the Spirit in creation and redemption as 'the builder of relationship, the one who weaves parts together into wholes'. In the cosmos we can see the Spirit at work in the way new forms emerge out of the coming together of parts. In things like bodies and ecosystems, and the Earth itself, wholes emerge through the interdependence of parts – or what the Vietnamese Buddhist monk Thich Nhat Hanh has called 'interbeing' (founding an order of that name in 1966). Taylor sees the Spirit's role in redemption as analogous: the Spirit is the go-between who communicates God's message, and the one who unites individuals in the 'body' of Christ. The 'co-' words express different kinds of 'togetherness' or 'interbeing' generated by the Spirit: life together, knowing together and working together.

Anyone who has attended the Orthodox liturgy will have noted how the role of the deacon is that of a kind of go-between, or conductor (another co-word). He is forever saying to the people things like 'Let us . . . pray; let us . . . attend', drawing people into the act of worship. In Orthodox ecclesiology, just as the priest represents Christ, so the deacon is said to represent the Holy Spirit, whose role is to gather and lead the people together in response to Christ. In turn, this can be thought of as a metaphor for the way members of a church live and work and share together guided by a 'conductor'.

Conducting

John Adair defined the three main functions of a leader as meeting three different levels of need (1997, p. 16):

1 Task need – getting the job done.
2 Team maintenance need – creating and maintaining a cohesive group.
3 Individual need – attending to this and developing individuals' capacities to do their part of the task (cf Nash et al. 2008, p. 12).

Sometimes collaborative ministry is advocated as a means of 'getting the job done' in response to clergy shortage. But, in our experience, collaborative ministry is not much of a time-saver. Getting people trained and confident in tasks, enabling people to work and plan together, resolving the clashes that result when people with different temperaments and agendas are working on the same task, finding replacements for those who find they are unable to continue, and so forth, all take time, and often it would be quicker and more efficient to do all the work yourself. If it is imperative, collaborative ministry is a theological imperative quite as much as a practical one.

What is interesting is that when Adair's triad is moved from a secular to a church context, his three factors begin to interpenetrate. For the ultimate task 'to be done' for the church includes things like:

- the greater glory of God;
- establishing conviviality in Christ and extending it to the whole creation;
- building people into the full stature of Christ.

According to Irenaeus, the first of these aims, 'the greater glory of God', consists in human beings fully alive (and, we might add, a creation fully alive and interdependent, and a world at peace with itself). This means that the second and third factors in Adair's triad, the building up of conviviality in the team, and the development of individual gifts, are not just means of achieving the task in hand, but part of the end itself.

This brings us back to the image suggested by Robert Warren (1995, p. 25) that the ordained minister needs to be more like a conductor rather than a director. The conductor's task is to enable the performance of a piece of music. We both sing in a local community choir, and often find that when we are on our own we either cannot remember our part, or cannot sing it at all. But when we are in the choir, the conductor gives gentle direction and encouragement (if in one of the parts we get some notes wrong she will tell us how good we were on the rhythm, but . . .); and then while actually performing, she, like any good conductor, will prompt us on when to come in, and when to sing more loudly or softly, and so forth. This enables us, and the other choir members, to sing our parts confidently within the whole piece of music.

Adair's three elements – training and encouraging individuals, drawing people together as a team, and producing the end result – are all present in the work of the conductor. But the song is not just the end product of the conductor and performers' collaboration; it *is* their playing together, which is a sublime act of conviviality that sweeps the audience along with it. In the same way, the ordained 'conductor' enables and draws the diverse members of the congregation together into that cosmic conviviality which is the whole creation giving glory to God.

This suggests that conviviality – which we might otherwise call sharing of life or communion – may be the most fundamental of the three 'co-' elements being considered in this chapter. So conviviality, and how it is sustained through visiting and friendship, is the focus of the next section of this chapter. It then goes on to explore the communication skills that sustain conviviality, and then finally, the collaboration that is thus enabled.

Conviviality

Read **Genesis 18.1–16**. God appears to Abraham by the Oaks of Mamre – also known as 'The hospitality of Abraham'.

Imagine this scene from the point of view of Abraham. What conviviality is involved and how does it arise? What is communicated? Is there any collaboration involved? (Note how the scene continues with Abraham's interceding on behalf of the people of Sodom – one of the reflections in Chapter 3.)

The early Orthodox theologians interpreted this scene as a foreshadowing of the Trinity, taking their cue from the way the passage begins by saying that YHWH (singular) appeared, and then goes on to speak of 'three men' as if the two were interchangeable. The interpretation is imaginative – no Jewish reader, of course, would accept it. Nonetheless you may like to study Rublev's well-known icon of the Trinity which is based on this scene – easily downloadable if you do not have it. Reflect on the way the lines suggest a rounded wholeness, in which the three angels blend but are distinct. Some note that the three are gathered around a table whose fourth side is open to you, as if you are invited to share in the deep conviviality of the Trinity. As Abraham you are the host who has invited the Trinity to be your guest, but now the Trinity is inviting you . . .

You do not have to believe that the Christian doctrine of the Trinity is encoded in this passage to find in it and in the icon based on it a source of profound reflection on the conviviality that is at the heart of the Christian God. The God who is one being yet three persons – or three 'interbeings' – has been seen by theologians such as the Protestant Jürgen Moltmann, the Catholic Karl Rahner and the Orthodox John Zizioulas, as a kind of conviviality that grounds the universe. For relationship to exist, there has to be both unity and separation. If there is only unity and no separation, those relating are merged and lost in oneness. If there is only separation and no unity, there is no real relationship; isolation is ultimate. The doctrine of the Trinity suggests that relationship (specifically, love) is ultimate; the universe itself is neither the manifestation of an ultimate divine unity, nor something separate and existing in its own right apart from God, but something essentially in relationship with its ground in God, and consisting of many levels of interrelation.

So when Jesus Christ incarnates God, the primary thing he manifests is conviviality, sharing, or what goes by the Greek name of *koinōnia*. We see the Triune hospitality reflected in his own table fellowship with all kinds of people, and in his feeding of the five thousand, which takes up Old Testament themes of the messianic banquet (Isaiah 25.6–8) and Wisdom's table of welcome (Proverbs 9.1–6). It is reflected above all in the final table meal which he commanded us to continue to celebrate, the Eucharist which Christians believe to be a *koinōnia* in Christ. As noted in the comments on Pentecost, for the earliest Christians this *koinōnia* appears to have been a real and total sharing of life that included the sharing of wealth and possessions.

If this is so, then sharing of life, conviviality, is not a means to an end but part of the essence of the Church. No *koinōnia*, no church. This means not just the celebration of Holy Communion (though it does mean that) but also a togetherness, a friendship, an enjoyment of one another's company that is contagious and spills over to draw others into itself. Many of the events that linger longest in our memories of parish life include events like Safari Suppers (meals in which different courses, and parts of courses, are served at different people's homes, enabling many to be both host and guest in the course of the evening); community fairs; and the Millennium Hope Show (in which we used the new millennium as an excuse to involve local schools and organizations along with the churches to present in drama, dance and art their own vision of hope for the future).

Quite often tasks which seem to be about something else – fairs and other social events, and maybe even jumble sales – whose ostensible aim is to raise funds are valuable also and perhaps mainly for the conviviality they establish in the community, and the way they enable new gifts to shine in the people who work to accomplish them. Similarly, part of the value of community fairs and craft fairs is not the funds that organizations raise so much as the chance to be creators rather than just consumers of good things; to create things themselves and enjoy what others have created. There is something here that goes to the heart of the gospel, and ministers can welcome such events and affirm the opportunities for conviviality they provide, rather than seeing them as distractions from the main business of the Church.

Befriending and visiting

Aelred of Rievaulx (AD 1110–67) regarded friendship as the truest reflection of the companionship that exists in heaven, as the angels share together in the truth and beauty of God. In other forms of love there is a kind of inequality. In passionate love and adoration the beloved is regarded as greater than ourselves, and we feel ourselves to be in need of the beloved. In charitable and compassionate love we give to someone who needs us, and is less fortunate than us. But friendship is preeminently a love between equals. In that sense friendship mirrors most closely the conviviality of the Trinity, where the persons share equally in the one divine nature.

> In friendship there is no pretence, it is holy, voluntary and true. Its adjuncts are honour and charm, truth and joy, sweetness and goodwill, affection and action. The ever-flowing inspiration of the love by which we love our friend is Christ. (Simpson 1999, p. 157, paraphrasing Aelred)

One of the key tasks of the ordained ministry, we suggest, is to encourage friendship among the congregation.

But however good the level of friendship is, people often say that they want clergy to visit. When they say this, they are probably wanting a number of things. In certain cases, like times of crisis, they want the minister in her representative role: nobody else will do, because the person in a dog-collar represents the love of Christ or the Church in a way no other person is quite felt to do. In other cases, like long-term illness or unhappiness, they need the minister as healer of the soul; but in such cases regular visits from another person gifted with the ministry of healing or listening may be accepted and valued. But in the general case, we have come to feel (after a long period of wondering why visiting is felt to be so important) that what people want is the minister as a kind of friend. Not a best friend, or the most intimate friend, but a companion who knows something of their life and what makes them tick, and whose life and goals they also understand a little from the inside. Someone with whom they can be convivial-in-Christ.

From at least George Herbert onward, but more especially in the nineteenth century, visiting became a central part of the minister's role:

> The most regular, careful, and beautiful services, the most eloquent and thoughtful preaching, the most elaborate music, not one or all of these things will supply the lack of that true pastoral relationship which nothing but personal knowledge of your people will give. I am convinced that the old saying, 'A house-going parson makes a church-going people' is true. (Peter Green (1919), *The Town Parson*, London: Longmans, Green & Co., p. 34–5, cited in Billings 2010, p. 121)

However, one senses that lately this ministry of visiting people in their homes has declined. Partly no doubt this is because the clergy-to-people ratio has declined sharply. In one parish, people remarked how much more they were visited in the old days; but in the old days, it turned out, the vicar had four curates and the population was much smaller. Another reason may be that clergy, along with the rest of society, have become more focused on goals and evaluation, so that the time spent just befriending members of their congregation seems hard to quantify or justify. Third, there are obvious dangers of being over-friendly with some members of the congregation – those with whom you have a natural affinity, perhaps – at the expense of others, creating envy. And finally, in an increasingly risk-averse society, visiting of people, especially single people in the privacy of their homes, has become thought of as dangerous, fraught with the pitfalls of inappropriate relationships or accusations of such.

All of these may well be good reasons for reducing the ministry of visiting. But the reduction will leave a gap in conviviality that will need to be filled in some way. There is no reason why the lines of befriending should all converge on the ordained minister, and in larger congregations this would place an impossible burden on him. (It has been suggested that 120 is about the limit to which a 'minister-centred' congregation can grow (Croft 1999, p. 195); it is hard to be friends in any real sense with more people than that.) In some ways the Methodist class system and the more recent burgeoning of house groups has provided a way of developing friendship in a way that is not minister-centred. The groups of three and four involved in mutual soul-guidance mentioned in Chapter 4 (p. 85) may be another way.

Nevertheless collaboration is founded on conviviality, partly because to give the person the right task in collaboration relies on a deep knowledge of that person's gifts and aspirations. So the collaborative minister will need to find ways of getting to know people on the level on which those gifts and aspirations emerge. Extroverts have the advantage here, but introverts have their own forms of conviviality, which may take longer to establish, but which can result in a quiet understanding of people's gifts and longings.

Implicit conviviality: explicit communication

Psalm 19.1–6: creation's silent communication.

Read this psalm through very slowly, allowing a pause between each verse in which you ponder the imagery of the verse.

- What sense do you make – if any – of the paradox of creation proclaiming the glory of God without words?
- What do you think you proclaim apart from using words?
- Recall the words attributed to Francis of Assisi: 'Proclaim the gospel. Use words if necessary.' How do you understand this?

If everything is created by God, then everything manifests and declares God's reality just by being what it is. The paint on the canvas expresses the artist who created it, so that we often instantly recognize a painting as being made by Van Gogh or Rembrandt. Even so the heavens (as described in Psalm 19) and the earth declare God's *kabod* (in Hebrew, meaning weight, influence, glory) or God's *doxa* (in Greek, meaning worship, appearance, repute, glory) simply by being what they are. Conviviality – our life together on this planet – is already communication.

But we humans are one of the few creatures (perhaps the only one) that has speech. We can regulate our breathing through our vocal chords and waggle our lips and tongues to make sounds that express more of what we are. We are capable of rejoicing, reflecting, imagining, dreaming, preaching, creating, presenting, representing, articulating, communicating, narrating, evoking, treasuring, honouring, celebrating, performing, and many other tasks of communication.

But this brings about another possibility. Mute creatures cannot lie. Nor can they pretend to be other than they are. We can do both. We can say things we do not believe to be true. And we can say things with words that belie what our bodies are saying. We can say things with words that reveal something about us that, if we were aware of it, we would not want to be saying.

An instance of this was introduced in this chapter's focusing exercise. The failure to tell people who Mabel was, or, positively, to invite new readers and intercessors, actually communicated to a newcomer that they were not very significant and certainly not invited to offer for those roles. Nothing was said to that effect, and probably the person who made the announcement would, if challenged, immediately deny that such an implication was intended. But actions – and, in this case, silences, failure to say certain things – can speak louder than words.

Stephen Cottrell has an interesting example (2008) of a church which was assiduous and highly organized and well connected with the community in the way it organized its quarterly jumble sales, but had little or no other connection with the community, and no font in the church or noticeboard outside it. People argued, 'We're all baptized already; and we know what time the service starts.' It had not occurred to the good-hearted people who worked so hard collecting and selling jumble what message they seemed to be giving: that the church existed primarily to enable the efficient recycling of clothes, books and bric-a-brac. Leaflets were distributed each quarter about that, but none were ever sent out inviting people to Christmas or Easter services, or to encourage people to bring children for baptism or learn about the Christian faith. By gently pointing this out, and getting committee members to write down what they thought was really essential to the life of the church, and suggesting an 'Open Day' as an alternative to one of the jumble sales, the minister enabled the people to begin to work in a new way.

This is perhaps an extreme example, but in the life of many churches, without regular and mindful reflection on what is done and how, what is communicated by the church's activities may be found to have rather little connection with the gospel we seek to proclaim. The faith of the Church is not, of course, only or even mainly, a matter of spoken and written words. It is primarily manifest in actions. If there is a discrepancy between the words and actions of a group, then to find what is really believed we should look to the actions. The first letter of John (4.20) puts this point very forcefully: 'Those who say, "I love God", and hate their brothers or sisters, are liars; for those who do not love a brother or sister whom they have seen, cannot love God whom they have not seen.'

As the authors of a recent critique of 'Fresh Expressions' argue:

It is usually quite obvious what a group of people hold to be true and significant: you see it in the way they behave . . . To see what matters most for a group or for a person, we need only look at what is ordinary for them: what is regular, habitual and conventional. It is there, in the practical, commonplace features of our everyday lives that our basic, governing convictions are to be found. (Davison and Milbank 2010, p. 14)

For these reasons it is not enough – the argument proceeds – to be seeking 'fresh expressions' to communicate the gospel in new ways. The gospel inhabits the life of the Church implicitly in its forms of conviviality as well as in its explicit communications: it is this that gives faith the dynamic 'momentum' that carries it forward from past to future (Guiver 1990). What we need therefore is not a grasping around in thin air for 'fresh expressions' or ways of expressing a faith with which we are already familiar, but a recovery of authentic Christian conviviality, ways of being together inspired by the living Christ, already present – but imperfectly – in the traditions of the Church, which will themselves express the gospel with or without words.

One of the weaknesses of the critique just quoted is that it assumes that the traditional Church already does this, if not perfectly, at least reasonably well. But what all churches, traditional or 'fresh expression', need to be asking is not, 'How can we, who "have" the gospel, communicate it better to those outside?', but the prior question, 'What does the way we live and worship together *already* communicate, whether we intend it or not, and how does this need to change (or stay the same)?'

The well-known Johari Window was developed by a Joe (Joe Luft) and a Harry (Harry Ingham) – Jo-Hari – to help clarify the kind of discrepancy we are exploring, between explicit and implicit communication. In any relationship people give information about themselves and receive information about others. This model suggests how we can seek to know ourselves and each other better.

The diagram (Figure 2) distinguishes between:

- The **Public Self**: what I know about myself and what I am perfectly willing to communicate to others. The public announcement itself, in the understanding of the person giving it, is a clear case of this.
- The **Blind Self**: things you know or see about me that I do not know about myself. They are my mannerisms or aspects of my

Figure 2: The Johari Window

	Known to self	Not known to self
Known to others	The Public Self	The Blind Self
Not known to others	The Private Self	The Unknown Self

behaviour that I don't know about. I communicate them to you without being aware of doing so. The lack of welcome to new-comers was communicated, without the awareness of the person giving the announcement.

- The **Private Self**: things I know about myself that I do not want or choose to share. I may be afraid that they will affect your opinion of me. Probably most ministers – like all involved in highly public work – have areas of their life in this category. English people are said to have a long-standing feeling that our faith belongs to our private self, which makes it very difficult to share.
- The **Unknown Self**: things about me that neither others nor I know: my motivations, anxieties and subconscious needs, my potential. These may include things I am so ashamed of I disown and cast out of my consciousness. The danger is that things in this category, pushed from the private self into the unknown self, have a way of slipping out into the blind self, disclosing them-selves to others without our knowing it through mannerisms, body language, odd habits and the like.

It is important that the minister knows how to manage things in this fourfold scheme, and can help others to do so. Good communica-tion involves maintaining a proper boundary between public and pri-vate, but bringing as much as possible into them out of the blind and unknown arenas. This means establishing a harmony between what we actually say and what our way of saying it says: between the message and the medium through which it is expressed. The prophets were adept at this, often acting out with their bodies the message they were proclaiming. (See p. 135.) And Jesus is the prime example of one whole life and death which was an acted parable of the love he taught.

Detail matters here. Look carefully, with an outsider's eye, at your noticeboard, your parish magazine, the church building, the way people are greeted at the door, the way people are seated, the way they look, the way announcements are given, the way worship is prepared and conducted. Is there some tension between your greeting, 'Alleluia! Christ is risen!' and the slightly formal and jaded way in which it is said? Or between your noticeboard which proclaims 'Jesus is alive!' and the dog-eared jumble of out-of-date posters? Does the body language of the person who says 'Welcome' at the door really suggest 'We're such a tiny congregation we're absolutely desperate for new people. Thank you so much for coming to join us!' or alternatively, 'We're quite happy as we are, thank you – but you can come if you want to'?

These are caricatures, of course, but attentiveness in such areas is fruitful if communication within a congregation, and between it and the wider world, is to be genuine and without a hidden agenda; and if there is to be congruence between the gospel message proclaimed and what is expressed by the quality of the congregation's life together. It was doubtless this congruence in the Christians after Pentecost between their *kerygma* (proclamation) and their *koinōnia* that drew so many to join them.

Synergy and energy

Read Table 2, which summarizes the occurrence of the word '*synergos*' (in its various declensions) in the New Testament.

- How would you translate *synergos* in these passages?
- In what context do most of the examples arise?
- What sort of person do you deduce a *synergos* is?

The word '*synergos*' means literally 'one who works together'. 'Collaborator' is the straightforward Latin equivalent, though the English word tends to have negative associations of plotting together. Terrorists are 'collaborators', whereas people we approve of tend to be 'allies', 'colleagues' or 'fellow-workers'.

Table 2: Synergoi in the New Testament

Romans 16.3–4	Greet Prisca and Aquila, my *synergous* in Christ Jesus, who risked their necks for my life.
Romans 16.9	Greet Urbanus, our *synergon* in Christ, and my dear friend Stachys.
Romans 16.21	Timothy my *synergos* greets you, as do Lucius and Jason and Sosipater, my compatriots.
1 Corinthinans 3.9–10	For we are *synergoi* belonging to God. You are God's field, God's building. According to the grace of God given to me, like a skilled master builder I laid a foundation, and someone else is building on it. Each builder must choose with care how to build on it.
2 Corinthinans 1.24	Not that we are ruling over your faith, but we are *synergoi* with you for your joy; for by faith you have stood firm.
2 Corinthinans 8.23	As for Titus, he is my companion and fellow *synergos* among you. As for our brothers, they are delegates of the churches, an honour to Christ.
Philippians 2.25	In the meantime I think it necessary to send to you Epaphroditus, my brother, *synergon* and fellow soldier, as well as your messenger and minister to my need,
Philippians 4.3	Yes, I ask you also, my true comrade, help these women who have labored side by side with me in the cause of the gospel, along with Clement and the rest of my *synergōn*, whose names are in the book of life.
Colossians 4.11	. . . and Jesus who is called Justus greets you. These are the are only ones of the circumcision among my *synergoi* for the kingdom of God, and they have been a comfort to me.
1 Thessalonians 3.2	and we sent Timothy, our brother and *synergon* for God in the gospel of Christ, to establish and encourage you in your faith, so that no one would be shaken by these persecutions.
Philemon 1.1	Paul, a prisoner of Christ Jesus, and Timothy our brother, to Philemon our dear friend and *synergō*…
Philemon 1.23–24	Epaphras, my fellow-prisoner in Christ Jesus, sends greetings to you, as do Mark, Aristarchus, Demas, and Luke, my *synergoi*.
3 John 1.5–8	Beloved, you do faithfully whatever you do for the friends, even though they are strangers to you; they have testified to your love before the church. You will do well to send them on in a manner worthy of God; for they began their journey for the sake of Christ, accepting no support from non-believers. Therefore we ought to show hospitality to such men, so that we may be *synergoi* for the truth.

A closely related term is 'synergy' – working together – which is often used to express God's grace working together among us. Eastern Orthodox theology makes much of 'synergy' in this sense, which is closely related to 'energy', the inward working of God's uncreated Holy Spirit in us. The Introduction noted that 'energy' was a term closely linked with charism or ministry. Ministry is primordially the *energy* of the Spirit in us, symbolized by the one Pentecostal fire distributed to each person, which leads us into *synergy* not only with God but with our *synergoi,* our fellow-workers, symbolized in the new wine of conviviality and the new tongues of communication. In this ancient context, ministry involves collaboration as *energy* involves *synergy.*

This suggests that collaboration or synergy is of the essence of ministry. It is not something added to ministry to make it more efficient. Rather, when ministry becomes autocratic or hierarchical, something has been taken away or lost from it. And the synergy of ministries cannot be separated from our synergy with God. Although collaboration is sometimes linked to the idea that we are 'co-creators' with God, human beings can never create in the divine sense of bringing something into being out of nothing. All we can do is mix what already exists together in different ways and pray that God's creator Spirit, en-ergizing and inspiring us, will enable something new to emerge. The first task of the collaborative leader, then, is to encourage people to trust and run with the energy of the Spirit; only then will they begin to trust one another and bring new things to birth together. The minister as pray-er and as guide are the foundation of the work of the minister as collaborator.

For Paul, it appears that the *synergoi* are a special category of people committed to working for the gospel. He does not seem to be talking about every-member ministry. Perhaps this is realistic. It is usually a subset of the people attending church for worship who come with an expectation of working and giving rather than receiving and being nourished. An expectation that all who attend are *synergoi* can lead to ministers feeling disappointed and tentative newcomers – and also busy people whose ministry lies elsewhere than in the Church – feeling undervalued or 'got at'. On the other hand the *synergoi* should be neither a *closed* circle, nor an *elite* circle of 'true Christians'. People can always be welcomed – though not forced – to contribute more to the work of the Church, while at the same time those who do not feel called to 'collaborate' more should not be consciously or subconsciously regarded as second-class Christians, but as manifesting the energy of the Spirit in their own different way.

Conversely it can be acknowledged that there may be people outside the Church altogether in whom the Spirit is at work, who are *synergoi* working for the coming of what Christians call the Kingdom of justice and reconciliation, though they may not use that language. We have found this to be so in many small ways, from a profound synergy among diverse people working (unsuccessfully in the end) to save a local secondary school from closure, through the collaboration involved in events like the Millennium Hope Show (see p. 113), to the remarkable number of people in an unremarkable suburban parish who were willing to save 20p pieces in Smartie tubes to help put a new roof on what to them must have been their rather drab and unremarkable parish church.

Collaboration in reflection, decision and action

For the reasons just explored, it would be a mistake to try to move the whole people through the theologically reflective process of experience, reflection, decision-making and action. It would be more realistic to see collaborative ministry as aiming to ensure that some people are involved through all stages, while all are involved at some. To sustain collaboration at all stages, while retaining lucid lines of accountability, is a big challenge: one we ourselves have certainly not always met. There is in fact a range of ways of running a church, from the totally autocratic to the fully collaborative (cf Nash et al. 2008, p. 13).

It is easy to have collaboration only on the level of action. The minister in charge decides what to do and delegates tasks to the layfolk. This can generate a happy buzz: people genuinely collaborate at a practical level but do not have to spend time on decisions that may be controversial or complex. Nor do they have to shoulder responsibility, because everyone knows that the buck stops with the minister. But this is surely not the ideal to which the Holy Spirit calls.

In recent years most churches have developed more democratic processes of decision-making. It is not always clear which decisions the councils are empowered to make and which ultimately rest with the clergy, and this varies from denomination to denomination, and church to church, and also in some cases, with the approach of the minister in charge. These moves are to be welcomed, but not uncritically. As we see clearly in our national politics, democracy can polarize the decision-making process, and marginalize minorities who get outvoted. We need to remember that God's voice in history often spoke through a minority or a handful or even just one: the lone prophetic voice in the wilderness. Sometimes the role of the minister in such contexts will be to encourage the hearing of the dissident voice, even if he disagrees with it.

Figure 3: Meetings and Decisions

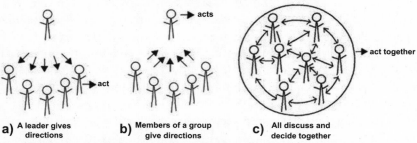

a) A leader gives directions   b) Members of a group give directions   c) All discuss and decide together

[© Catherine Widdicombe (1994, 2000), Lutterworth Press. Reproduced by permission.]

Clearly, democratic structures can help to enable good collaboration, but structures alone are not enough; and even within agreed structures there can be very different ways of proceeding. Figure 3 (From Widdicombe 2000, p. 186) illustrates this very clearly. In a church meeting or sub-committee it may sometimes be appropriate to operate according to diagram (a) in which one person (not necessarily the minister) makes the decisions and assigns tasks to different members to get the job done. In diagram (b) it is the members who, collectively, make the decisions, and one person – again, not necessarily the minister – carries them out on their behalf. Diagram (c) illustrates a process that may quite often happen in a small church community or a sub-committee, where everyone together makes the decisions, and everyone together carries them out.

It is not the place, here, to discuss the ins and outs of different models of ministry teams, committees, sub-committees or informal groupings, away-days, consultations and the like that might be used to enable church decision-making. What is appropriate will, in any case, vary according to the size of the church, its history, location and vision, and from time to time. Whatever the existing or developing structure, the mindful minister, lay or ordained, will seek to ensure that the kind of conviviality, communication and collaboration that this chapter has explored are embodied in the decision-making processes of the church.

The 'how' of decision-making within a meeting also needs to be reviewed and reflected on. *Meetings that Work* (Widdicombe 2000) provides very practical guidelines on various alternatives. It is also always worth having clarity about which agenda items are:

- for giving information: no discussion or decisions needed at this stage. These are simply factual statements of what has happened or is planned to happen.
- **for discussion:** to ponder and reflect on and consider, leading towards a decision at a later meeting. Questions become much

more central to the process, as do value judgements so long as they are not expressed as facts. So statements like 'Last week's hymns were awful' should be challenged and rephrased in terms like 'I personally did not like the hymns we had last Sunday, because . . . and I hope in future we will . . .' Votes are inappropriate and divisive at this stage; it is much more important to try to reach consensus, and allow time for this.

- **for decision.** Here the mode is imperative and clearly actioned: 'So and so to do such and such by such and a date.' So long as good discussion time has been allowed previously for issues people care about, if consensus is not easily reached, it may be appropriate to vote at this stage to carry the meeting forward.

By this clarity the collaborative minister will help people tease out a dense tangle of fact and feeling into something like a collective pastoral cycle, moving from experience and perceived fact through reflection towards goals and thence to possible future actions. Tempting as it often is to short-circuit the process by doing the theological reflection yourself and imposing it on people, the collaborative way demands that we involve the whole people in the whole process. Not everyone, of course, will be equally adept at every stage; there will be those who are good at noticing things, those who are good at analysing situations, those who have a deep practical grasp of scripture and tradition to relate to the issues at stake, those who have a good nose for decisions, and those who are reliable to entrust with future actions. The facilitator of good collaboration will have a sense of who to draw out, and who to hold back, at each stage of the discussion.

The alternatives to mindful collaboration in meetings are:

- Mindless meetings when there maybe a good deal of conviviality and chatter but there is little shape or direction or sense of purpose. Or people may avidly discuss tasks without considering the goals they are meant to achieve, simply because they are the things that have always been done. If they find it easier to discuss tasks than goals, congregations will have a tendency to multiply tasks to saturation point, leaving no room for consideration of other tasks that might achieve the goals better, or tasks that might be dropped because there are better ways of achieving their goals. In one way or another the convivial buzz falls short of collaboration: no work is done.
- **Ego-minded meetings.** In any genuinely collaborative discussion there will be times of tension and opposition. People may experience things differently, understand them in a different light,

relate them to their faith differently, or want to make opposing decisions. But such differences can become contests at which participants are keen to fight their own corner and guard their own egos, creating a failure in conviviality. Catherine Widdicombe (2000, pp. 142–6) outlines a number of positive strategies for responding to conflict in a way which enables greater transparency of issues and feelings and helping opponents better appreciate each other's point of view. She suggests, initially, moving the discussion away from the issue about which people are in conflict to a consideration of whether they want to try to work towards a resolution and how this might be done. If this shift in focus can be achieved through careful listening and with a lightness of touch, it can, in itself, be a kind of conviviality, relieving the tension and encouraging participants to recall their deeper commitment and a desire to work well together.

- **Absent-minded meetings** when one person – usually the chair who is probably the minister – does nearly all the talking and decisions are made by default. The minister will feel happy that he has taken the people through the decision-making process, but the whole process has been in his head, with nobody invited in to participate. It is not necessarily the minister who is 'absent-minded', of course: sub-committees and 'standing committees' may make all the real decisions, and invite only a 'rubber stamp'. Or people may pursue actions for their own reasons, until big differences in overall aims and objectives emerge, which, because they have not been aired and negotiated early on, may lead to explosive ruptures. One way or another there is a failure in communication.

Conclusion

The nuts and bolts of how meetings are conducted and how decisions are made seems a long way from the Pentecostal fire with which this chapter began, and bringing this to mind is a good illustration of the tension that can exist between keeping ourselves open, always, to the movement of the Spirit while also needing to conform to practical and collaborative processes for decision-making. Conviviality and friendship – with God and one another – have been explored as the bedrock of good communication and collaboration; and *synergy* of God's grace working within and among us as necessary for both. The next chapter builds these three essential qualities of working together into the ministry of sharing the Good News through evangelism.

For reflection and discussion

1   In what senses do you think the minister should be, and not be, the **friend** of those to whom she ministers?

2   How far does and how far doesn't your experience of collaborative ministry connect with the experience of the disciples at and after Pentecost? How might it work better?

3   In this chapter much is made of 'conviviality' as the basis of good communication and good collaboration. How far do you agree with this? In your experience, what helps and what hinders the establishment of good conviviality in a church community?

7

The Herald of Good News:
Mindful Evangelism

Here the minister has turned the gifts of organization and communi-cation outward, clearly focused on the task of bringing the gospel to those who do not yet believe. This minister sees the gospel itself – and his doctrinal and moral understanding of it – as given and beyond question. The minister employs a great variety of ways of presenting the gospel to differing groups of people, and can readily become 'all things to all people', quick to see ways of connecting their need with some aspect of the Good News. He can seem laid back and easy going, full of fun, and generally unthreatened by the gifts of others. He is happy to make use of and develop the gifts of ministry in any whom he feels to be soundly rooted in the gospel. At the same time, he and his congregation have clear 'no go' areas of morality and doctrine, which are not seen as worth discussing, as that would only divert the energy and focus away from the task in hand.

The worship of the Church is geared, like everything else, to the preaching of the message. There are plenty of gadgets, from puppets to data-projectors, to bring the message to life; a music group and lively and upbeat choruses in which emotional fervour is sometimes in harmony with, and sometimes displaces, doctrinal content; and a team of pastors and welcomers ready at hand to make newcomers feel they belong, and can find help and advice when needed.

The evangelist – whether named as youth worker, reader or lay preacher – is often a prominent form of lay ministry, especially valu-able when the stronger gifts of the minister lie elsewhere, in pastoral or administrative work.

Focus: a question easily fluffed

You, the local minister, have just caught a group of about five young boys throwing stones at the church windows. Luckily nothing has broken yet. You have walked slowly up to them, trying to look much more calm, assured and authoritative than you probably feel. You know that nothing will incite more stones in the future better than obvious anger or obvious fear – 'fight or flight' reactions will quickly turn the stone-throwing into a game of 'Let's wind up the vicar.' In reasonable tones you explain why you think stone-throwing is not a good idea, how dangerous pieces of glass can be to innocent people, including children, how tiresome it is to clear up, and how much you would like it if they did not throw stones in the future. One of the boys is now looking at you with puzzlement in his eyes, and out of the blue he asks you, with all the directness of children on this estate, 'How come you're a vicar?'

What do you say?

How do you feel?

Would it make a difference to the answer to either of these questions if the person asking were someone from your church, someone you regularly chatted to at the local pub, or a resident of the local care home? Or if you were not the vicar, just an ordinary lay member of a church, and the question was, 'How come you go to church?'

Something approximately like this actually happened to one of us. I had been given what some would call an opening for evangelism. I cannot remember exactly what I said, but I remember the overwhelming feeling that I 'fluffed' the opportunity, and gave very little away in my answer. I have since forgiven myself. The context was tense, and I was having not to let my real feelings be seen, so the question came as a complete surprise, and a proper answer to it would have opened up my deepest feelings. I was geared up to cope with ridicule and derision, and I did not know how seriously to take the question. Would it lead only to mockery or mirth? How in any case could I explain my journey into ministry in a way that these boys would understand, but at the same time would not be a travesty, a terrible simplification of the complex web of aspirations and feelings within me – a bit like being asked, out of the blue, to show someone your beating heart? And I could remember my own feelings about those who, on the street or a doorstep, start unfolding their journey of faith, and how easily the story can become stereotyped and lose all the interest that attaches to the uniqueness of each life.

So there are plenty of factors that prevent us wanting to evangelize, even when an opportunity like this presents itself. Similar factors are probably also at work making people reluctant to allow themselves to be evangelized:

- the feeling of vulnerability to rejection;
- the fear of simplifying something that is complex and subtle;

- a dislike of externalizing what is deeply internal, or publicizing what is deeply private.

There may be other factors you can think of. All of them are understandable. But are they valid?

- Does it actually matter if what we say is rejected?
- Is it not often appropriate to simplify things? When someone asks us how we are, is it appropriate to list all the positive and negative factors in our physical, emotional and spiritual life? Don't we usually just say 'Fine', or 'I'm good, how about you?' Does that make us feel dishonest or crude?
- Is the Good News of Jesus Christ fundamentally a private matter? The preachers of the early Church saw it as *kērygma*, something to be published, proclaimed in public. This was the task of the *kēryx*, the herald, whose feet are beautiful on the mountains.

The herald

Read **Isaiah 52.1–12**.

Focus on the feelings in the first part. First the hope of liberation is outlined in the image of being freed from chains on the neck, to sit on a throne . . .

Next, the feelings of oppression . . . being sold for nothing, like a worthless slave . . . going down to the slavery of Egypt . . . being taken away for nothing and mocked.

And then imagine how you feel when the herald of better tidings comes over the mountains and into view. Imagine this scene as if you were a watchman on the tower. What first convinces you that the news is good? What does the herald proclaim?

Can you recall a time of being overwhelmed or oppressed, and then being told good news? What first made you realize the news was good?

Focus on the feeling of hearing good news after a time of darkness.

Now list three pieces of good news you would want to be able to share with someone who asked out of the blue (like the boy in the focusing exercise).

And list three things you would want to herald and make public.

The passages in 1 Corinthians 12 and Romans 12 (see Table 1 on p. xv) mention prophecy as an important spiritual gift. Though sometimes interpreted as simply an ability to predict the future, prophecy is surely rather to be related to the great Hebrew tradition of speaking truth to power, which is discussed below as one of the central aspects of evangelism. Evangelism as such appears listed as a charism only in Ephesians 4.11. But of course the heralding of the Good News was a central work of the apostles. We also noted in Chapter 3 that evangelism may have been part of the ministry of the deacon, and certainly two of the seven appointed by the apostles – Stephen and Philip – were prominent early evangelists, whether they were deacons or not. Evangelism – meaning literally being a good messenger or 'angel' but clearly relating, like 'herald', to being a messenger of the Good (News) – remained central to the ministry of the Church. Many of the saints celebrated in the churches' calendars are described as 'evangelist', because they first brought the gospel to a new nation. Countless more, not recorded, spread the gospel to neighbours, family and workmates.

These days we seem to be keener than ever to evangelize, but less keen than ever too. The churches of Britain declared the 1990s a 'Decade of Evangelism' and launched a host of initiatives, but the decline in church attendance continued unabated. National and local initiatives urging us to evangelize those around us continue to spawn. The tide of mission that spread the Christian faith across the globe through the colonial period has abated: some say it has reversed, so that the converted nations, where a youthful Christianity is vibrantly alive, are now ready to evangelize us. But there is little evidence that this has happened, or that it would be welcomed if it did. Of course there are churches that evangelize energetically and even aggressively, and experience dramatic growth. But this has not reversed the overall decline, and cynics would say it represents not growth, but a clumping together of Christians into larger churches, leaving others in even steeper decline. This does not augur well for the long-term evangelization of the nation.

The fact is that the evangelist, in the imagination of many of us, is far from that of the nimble herald with his beautiful unencumbered feet leaping across the crags, bursting with good news to share with the general public. In the imagination he is more like a heavily armoured Roman legionary, marching in military fashion to intimidate us into believing with subtle and not so subtle threats. So when we are in conversation and 'off duty' and the matter of faith comes up, we experience a sense of heavy awkwardness, and become anxious to disencumber ourselves of what we think others will think of us and our faith.

What do I do? Well actually . . . I'm a Christian minister [*uttered in a quiet tone that says 'Don't let that worry you'*] . . . Well, we're not all Victorian and straight-laced, you know. We're quite relaxed, come along just as you are . . . You don't want to go to church? That's fine; you don't have to go to church to be a Christian . . . What, you're not Christian? That's fine by me; I know lots of very spiritual people who aren't . . . You're not into spirituality? Well, it's how you live your life that matters. God loves you whether or not . . . You don't believe in God? That's quite understandable, I often wonder myself. . . .

This is a caricature, of course, but we are probably not the only ministers or Christians who can remember saying things a bit like this, not all at once, but with different people on different occasions. We're ever so keen to ditch the image of the heavy militant soldier-evangelist. But we don't get anywhere near being the nimble and beautiful herald of good news. We've got rid of the armour not so we can be vulnerable, open and free, but so we can slip into an unassailable cleft beyond all possible criticism!

Our hope is that, if these words ring bells for you, by the end of this chapter you'll see how evangelism can become a light and beautiful ministry, free from all overt or hidden desires to wield power.

An important question to address is how evangelism can express the heart of God's powerless love for the world. God is not powerless, of course, but his love is, because that is the nature of love. Evangelism can only be an act of love and can only therefore be enjoyed – by both parties – rather than endured, when it is not at all, not even at the subtlest level, an exercise in power or manipulation of any kind.

This key issue needs to be explored further before going on to apply it to various aspects of prophecy and evangelism.

Love and response

The Anglican priest, W. H. Vanstone, roots the whole ministry of the Church – evangelism included – in the love of God shown in the crucifixion. He argues that the cross, rather than enabling God to love his creation unconditionally, expresses the fact that he always has done so. God's love is *limitless* – nothing can exhaust it or prevent it – yet *vulnerable* – God suffers from our rejection in the way the cross reveals – and *precarious*, because God has created the world in such a way that a tragic outcome is possible (1977, p. 57).

It is in the nature of all love, and all creativity, God's included, to take risks. No artist wants to compel people to recognize his creation.

Likewise nobody who performs a truly loving act wants to force the beloved's response. But the artist wants the work itself to be recognized for its own merits. The lover wants the beloved to love him in return, or to cherish the gift he offers in love for what it is and the love it represents. Response is in both cases intensely desired, but not compelled: a great self-implicating risk is involved.

'So it is', Vanstone argues, 'with the creative love of God.' Which is why God offers, for the most part, not dazzling theophanies that compel response, but subtle hints of his presence for those with eyes to see. The cross and resurrection are among the more obvious of such hints.

> The love of God, in waiting upon the response of recognition, waits upon its own celebration. It waits upon the response in which its own nature and quality is understood . . . Recognition of the love of God involves, as it were, the forging of an offering: the offering is the coming-to-be of understanding: only where this understanding has come to be has love conveyed its richest blessing and completed its work in triumph . . . The creativity of God is dependent for the completion and triumph of its work, upon the emergence of a responsive creativity – the creativity of recognition. (p. 96)

An artist or poet may want his work recognized for two reasons: a narcissistic desire to be admired, or a desire to communicate to an audience through the work. Communication cannot happen unless the work is seen or read and enjoyed; but wanting a work that is felt to be worthwhile to be known is different from wanting oneself to be known and admired. In the same way a lover may want a response for two reasons: a narcissistic desire to be loved and admired, or a desire to establish a relationship in which love may come to fruition. In most cases the reasons will be a mixture.

However, God cannot seriously be believed to benefit from our adoration, or need to be needed. But essential to God is mission: God's goodness is not static goodness, but what the writer known as Dionysius the Areopagite in his *Mystical Theology* called an *ecstatic* goodness: a goodness that pours itself out in communication beyond itself, seeking a response, not in order to aggrandize itself (for how could the Infinite become any greater?) but in order to multiply love – and in Mary's term 'magnify' it – through an infinity of loving relationships.

This clarifies the place of the evangelist. His task is not to aggrandize himself or even God, but to facilitate 'the creativity of recognition'. He is called to celebrate the love of God in cross and creation, and so bring it to completion by the power of the Spirit. He will be swept along by a passionate commitment to the passionate love of God, yet this commitment will not want to force a response but to share God's own vulnerability, being open to the tragic possibility of rejection.

Evangelism takes place in many contexts, from the formal setting of preaching in church, indirectly through school assemblies, through church-based and open youth work, door-to-door visiting, and street pastoring, to simply 'gossiping the gospel' among friends or those you encounter in the day-to-day round. In some of these contexts it will not be thought appropriate to proselytize or try to convert people to explicit Christian belief, while in others such belief will be assumed to exist already. But in all cases there will be a seeking for a space where a response to God's love may grow in people's own good time. This space may be opened up through:

1 **witness**: the sharing of personal experience, in a way that invites wondering and pondering rather than alarm or imitation;
2 **apologetics**: argument that seeks to remove mental barriers to the possibility of God, and invites people to think in new frames;
3 **imagination**: the use of story, humour, art, drama and other media to enable people to entertain new imagery that may make sense of their experience;
4 **rhetoric**: the use of language to address the heart and will, liberating passions of appropriate anger, longing, compassion, repentance and hope;
5 **life**: perhaps the most important factor of all is beyond words. People say that Christian faith is 'caught not taught'. A sense that the evangelist embodies in her own life what she is saying, and is committed to a love that flows from beyond her, is the most likely factor to open up a space for response to that love in the hearer.

The next section considers how these elements worked together through the prophets, and then the rest of the chapter examines in turn these five modes of evangelism.

Prophecy as a kind of theological reflection

The five elements just cited are all to be found in the writings of the prophets, where they work together to generate a cycle of theological reflection which is an invitation to respond afresh to God. In this respect – though not in all respects – the prophets provide a good model for the ministry of evangelism. In the 'herald' passage in Isaiah 52 just considered, the five elements can be seen at work in this way:

1 *Witness to experience*

The prophets were travellers in the spiritual world, familiar with dreams and visions (for example 2 Kings 2.6–14; Isaiah 6.1–6; Ezekiel 1.4–3.3) but also with despair and rejection (Elijah on the way to Horeb (1 Kings 19), Jeremiah, Hosea). To all of this they bear witness, despite the risk of being thought crazy or rejected, as they often were. In addition, they often narrate and describe the past and present experience of the Hebrew people, both the times of joy and triumph and the times of suffering and shame. In Isaiah 52 the latter predominate: 'Long ago, my people went down into Egypt to reside there as aliens; the Assyrian, too, has oppressed them without cause . . . Their rulers howl, says the LORD, and continually, all day long, my name is despised' (vv. 4–5).

2 *Apologetics and dialogue*

The prophets often depict God as entering into dialogue with his people and trying to reason with them (for example Isaiah 1.18). Some of their writings represent explorations of the nature of God, arguing for his reality as against the idols of the nations (for example Isaiah 40.12–26). However, such reasoning and dialogue are far rarer in the prophetic than in the Wisdom writings, and there is no clear example in Isaiah 52.

3 *Storytelling, humour and imagination*

Typically the prophets use very powerful imagery to make sense of their experience and that of their people in history. Sometimes this imagery is drawn from traditions like the Exodus and – in Ezekiel especially – the architecture and cult of the Temple, which they and the people would have known. Sometimes they take the form of short narratives, perhaps relating to the prophet's own life – Hosea and his unfaithful wife (Hosea 1.2–9) and teaching his child to walk (11.3–4). Sometimes the parables are drawn from everyday life – Amos' basket of ripe fruit, his plumb-line, Isaiah's vineyard that grew sour grapes. Sometimes the prophets acted out their parables in a weird, uninhibited way, which is the closest they seem to come to a sense of humour: Ezekiel (4 — 5) digs a trench around a brick, lies down for days on one side, eats a barley loaf baked over human dung, cuts off portions of his hair and sets light to some and scatters others to the wind, and forges a chain, all to act out various aspects of the coming fall of Jerusalem. The Isaiah 52 passage abounds in images that are like fragments of stories, inviting us to imagine further and carrying immense emotional weight – in one case, inspiring a well-known hymn:

> Shake yourself from the dust, rise up, O captive Jerusalem; loose the bonds from your neck, O captive daughter Zion! (v. 7)
>
> How beautiful upon the mountains are the feet of the messenger who announces peace, who brings good news, who announces salvation, who says to Zion, 'Your God reigns.' Listen! Your sentinels lift up their voices, together they sing for joy; for in plain sight they see the return of the Lord to Zion. Break forth together into singing . . . (vv. 7–9)

4   Rhetoric, stirring the heart to act

All this intense emotional freight of imagery – sometimes joyful, sometimes peaceful, but most often fearful – had a purpose, which was to move people on from their experiences to appropriate action. In general, this would be action that restored justice among people, and faithful, responsive relationship between the people and God. Our passage concludes with a summons to return from exile as in a new Exodus, in which, as before, God will protect his people before and behind. But this new Exodus will be better, because not undertaken, as the first was, in haste and flight.

> Depart, depart, go out from there! Touch no unclean thing; go out from the midst of it, purify yourselves, you who carry the vessels of the Lord; for you shall not go out in haste, and you shall not go in flight; for the Lord will go before you, and the God of Israel will be your rearguard.

5   Beyond words

We have already mentioned, under (3), the way the prophets lived out their teaching in acted parables.

The movement from experience through rational and imaginative reflection to emotion and appropriate action is, of course, the pastoral cycle involved in theological reflection. As already noted in Chapter 4, the teaching aspect of preaching ideally consists in helping people to reflect on their experience in the light of scripture and tradition, with a view to action. The difference in emphasis was noted between that of the teacher, who can assume and build upon a desire to learn more about, to grow in and be changed by Christian faith; and that of the evangelist, who seeks to arouse and inspire just that desire. Certainly the focus of prophetic preaching is not the marriage of experience and tradition as such, but rather the change of heart and intent, which in the Gospels is called *metanoia*, often translated 'repentance'. Prophetic preaching seeks to open people to want and desire God and his Kingdom of justice. And of course that is the core aim of evangelism too, in all the aspects we now briefly explore.

Witnessing: publicizing personal experience

Read **John 9.1–34**: the man whose blindness Jesus cured.

Imagine yourself as the man born blind. At the beginning you are unable to see. You feel the strange medicine being applied. Imagine what it must be like to see, never having done so before. As a baby first sees the face of the mother who has given it birth, so the first thing you see is the face – never having seen a face before – of the man who has cured you and given you new life.

Then the experience of interrogation. Quite different faces. List the things you are recorded as saying. Say them carefully to yourself. Is there a common theme? A progression?

And finally the casting out or excommunication. While blind you were part of a tightly run community. Now, seeing, you are on your own. But the man you first saw, the man who opened your eyes, seeks you out. You see him again, and . . .

Note the steadfast faithfulness of the man to his own experience. He refuses to go beyond it, and refuses equally to compromise on it, offensive as this truth is to his interrogators. To power he speaks plain truth, and they are offended and disturbed. Only towards the end does he begin to argue a case based on his experience, as a lawyer might argue on the experience of a witness in the box. Most of what he says is in the indicative: straightforward description. He does what a witness is sworn to do: rather than trying to persuade, he just tells the truth, the whole truth, and nothing but the truth. The conclusions are for his hearers to make.

But the conclusions the questioners draw are hostile. The man is cast out, forbidden henceforth to attend the synagogue or to communicate with his family and friends. It is like going from the isolation of blindness to that of deafness and dumbness. So he is a *witness* in a deeper sense, a *martyr*. (The word in the Greek is the same: martyrs are those who bear witness to the truth at whatever cost.)

The prophets were martyrs, convinced of their experienced truth, the Word of God, which they had to proclaim whether or not it met with approval or with any response at all (Ezekiel 2.5, 7). Some of them became martyrs in the stronger sense.

If we follow the example of the prophets and of the man born blind, when we 'witness' to Christ – whether in a sermon, or in a street, or to friends, or to a hostile or cynical crowd – we do not have to argue a case or try to convince our hearers. We are just called to say what we have experienced or found in our life to be true. No more, and no less. We need neither to hide nor to exaggerate. It is as much a false witness to claim we have experienced more of Christ or faith than we are really sure of, as it is to dissemble and disown the experience we have had.

The chief temptation in the witnessing aspect of evangelism is to be 'ego-minded'. We may elaborate our story in order to impress others and convert them; or edit it into a conventional mould in order to please fellow Christians who think all 'truly Christian' life stories should have the same key features; or we may water the story down to what we think our hearers can accept. In all these cases, our ego has come between our actual experience and our narrative. Perhaps this danger was why Jesus told his followers not to plan how they were going to witness to him, but to let the Holy Spirit give them what they needed to say (Luke 12.11–12), allowing his energy to flow more strongly than their needs for affirmation and security.

The factors cited may make us reluctant to tell our story at all. It is, after all, quite a difficult thing to go public on what is, at least in part, very private and personal, and some of it perhaps painful. There are cases when it is not appropriate to witness to Christ by telling our journey of faith. There may be hurts we have yet to resolve, or which involve others, which would not benefit from being aired in public. And those hurts may be essential parts of the story, such that we would be dishonest to tell a version that edited them out. Better, at this stage, not to tell the story at all. The apostles, and notably Peter, took a long time to come to the stage when they could witness to Christ. Not all Christians and perhaps not all ministers are called to be witnesses, and not all are ready yet: but those who are called to do so may need to discover resources of courage and trust and wisdom to enable this to happen, and to discern the right time and occasion and the right approach.

Apologetics and dialogue: opening the mind

Read **Acts 17.16–34**: Paul at Athens.

List the ideas Paul uses that the Athenians would have been familiar with.

At what point does Paul seem to lose most of his audience?

There is nothing else like this address elsewhere in the New Testament. At Athens, cradle of democracy and the cultured capital of Hellenic philosophy, Paul abandons his normally prophetic style and argues with his audience on their own terms, drawing on the ideas with which they would have been at home, and trying to beat the philosophers at their own game. It was the first recorded attempt to 'contextualize' the gospel or express it in the terms of local culture. Unlike the monologue of the herald, we find an attempt to establish dialogue. Paul, unusually, was engaging in apologetics.

He does not seem to have been very successful! There was only a handful of converts, and no church was established at that time in Athens. There is no 'Epistle to the Athenians' – though it would be an interesting project to write one. Yet Paul was arguably just taking one step further, the move he had already insisted on, taking Christianity out of its original framework of Jewish law and observance so that it could be acceptable in other cultures. It is certainly arguable that Christianity spread so remarkably quickly through the pagan world in the post-apostolic period precisely because of its apologetic approach.

In a classic work (1992) David Bosch has analysed the extraordinary growth of the Church as it moved beyond the bounds of Judaism in the early centuries of its life. The terminology that Christians used in explaining their faith was extraordinarily similar to the concepts promoted in pagan religions. Because of these close parallels it was easy for Christians to present their religion as the fulfilment of other religions. Under the influence of Christian scholarship which was increasingly able to hold its own against sophisticated philosophical views, the Church, which was originally held in contempt because it was uncultured, became itself a bearer of culture. Christianity presented itself as an enlightened faith, with other religions regarded as inferior, on socio-cultural rather than theological grounds. The same could be said of the nineteenth century, another great growth period for the Christian faith. This emphasis on intellectual credibility and cultural worth is the essence of the apologetic approach.

Apology in this sense, of course, has nothing to do with 'apologizing' for one's faith, which sounds like the direct opposite from witnessing to it. But many of the early Church's apologists (including Justin and Polycarp) became martyrs. The Greek term 'apologia' means a reasoned, verbal defence of one's views. Perhaps the most famous example is the Apology of Socrates, penned by Plato, in which just before his martyrdom Socrates defends before his accusers the principles on which he has lived. The essence of apology is the defence of one's position against critics by the systematic use of reason. An apology is like one-half of a debate, in which possible criticisms are put, only to be refuted.

Our situation is not unlike that which the early Christian apologists faced. Christianity has many 'cultured despisers' (to use the phrase made famous in Friedrich Schleiermacher's own masterwork of apologetics (1996)). In the twentieth century, pioneered by Karl Barth and the like, there was a tendency to revert to a purely kerygmatic approach that foreswore any attempt to make the faith credible in philosophical or rationalist terms. In our experience there are some Christians who think that the difficulty of believing a proposition makes it *more* rather than less worthy of belief, because of the faith required. 'Fideism' is the technical version of such an approach. Faith was becoming defined as irrational belief, defying all argument and evidence – just the kind of thing the cultured despisers despised. The rational middle ground is ceded, in effect, to the cultured despisers.

However, this strategy, not surprisingly, did little to avert the twentieth-century decline of Christian faith. In places like Africa and parts of Asia, where there was more of an attempt to 'inculturate' the gospel, the story was different (cf Donovan 2003). But we sense a change in the air. The debates about the credibility of faith between the new atheists – such as Richard Dawkins, Sam Harris, Christopher Hitchens – and what we might call the new apologists – including Alister McGrath, Keith Ward, John Warwick Montgomery, John Lennox and a 'revived' C. S. Lewis – have attracted immense public interest. The time, we feel, is right to reassert Christianity, not triumphalistically as a supreme faith that cannot be critiqued on rational or moral grounds, but as a wise and rational faith with a rich culture and at its (often betrayed) roots a life-enhancing morality, ready to enter a mutually transforming dialogue with those of other faiths and atheists on equal terms.

But at grass-roots level we seem, as yet, ill equipped for this. Sermons are probably not the place for full-blown exercises in apologetics, but sermons can contain good arguments, and good awareness of the areas where they might reasonably be criticized. They can be argued with a gentle confidence that inspires hearers with a sense that their faith can hold its own in public places and public debates. In discussion groups focusing on the challenges of science and philosophy, there will be more opportunity to pursue the arguments in the depth they really need. That is the way to build an intelligent Christianity, or a Christian intelligence, that can respond when challenged in the pub or the market place, with articulate responses and further apt questions that can take the debate to a higher level.

There are dangers, of course, in preaching a *purely* rational faith, and getting lost in what interests you, answering questions that are not being asked rather than those that people are raising. All this represents an 'absent-minded' monologue in order to avoid dialogue; something of course the atheistic despisers are not themselves immune from.

True dialogue is not ego-minded. We do not want to coerce others into faith. We want the arguments to do their own convincing, so that we can leave people to consider them while we ourselves become dispensable.

> We should be wary of being seduced by charismatic purveyors [of faith]. For true friends seek not to coerce us, even gently and reasonably, into believing what we are unsure of. These friends are like midwives, who draw forth what is waiting to be born. Their task is not to make themselves indispensable but redundant. (Batchelor 1998, pp. 50–1)

The primary modes of apologetic and dialogue, then, whether in a sermon or a discussion, are the interrogative – the searching Socratic question that sets hearers seeking afresh for answers – and the subjunctive: the 'What if . . .' hypothesis that invites people to think in a new frame.

And in true dialogue – as opposed to debate – we are inviting ourselves, as well as the other, to ask questions and think outside the compartments that define us as opponents. We can only invite others to change their minds if we are willing to do so ourselves; only expect others to listen to us in a way that might transform them, if we are ready to listen to them in a way that might transform us.

Storytelling, humour and imagination: awakening the Spirit

Read Matthew **20.1–16** – the parable of the vineyard.

This is of course a parable, but one that invites you into imagining yourself into it. Imagine it as if you were a labourer who had worked all day in the hot sun. Focus on the giving out of the wages at the end. How do you feel when you're given the wage you agreed on, but find that it is the same as everyone else's? Some arguments are on your lips in the parable, but you may think of others you might put.

Do you find yourself able to think *and feel* outside the frame of your initial expectations?

How might this new way of thinking and feeling affect life in your congregation? In society generally?

Thinking outside the frame usually needs more than intellectual argument. Jesus' parables are not arguments: they are stories and images that invite us to think and feel in a new way. Often they shatter the preconceptions we have always assumed to be fundamental to decent living in society, and create a dialogue in which we feel very strongly the pull of both sides. We may feel outrage: it's *unjust* to give people the same pay regardless of how long they have worked! The people who worked all day have been duped! It's mean! Then we look closer. No deception was involved. No meanness, only a rather reckless generosity. A landlord who behaved like that would soon go out of business. No one would work all day if they could get away with just an hour for the same wage. But of course, the Landlord here is God and the vineyard is God's Kingdom. God will not go out of business. Jesus is suggesting that the Kingdom he wants us to emulate on earth is like that. It might be nice if everyone was treated with equal generosity. But it wouldn't work – and so the inner dialogue goes on . . .

Something happened at a church lunch we heard about, which reminded us of this parable. At the morning service the vicar invited anyone who wanted to, to come along. He made no mention of any ticket or price. Some of the paid-up regulars were angry that it might mean that these late-comers would get away without paying, while everyone else had bought tickets in advance as requested. As it turned out, no ticketless person came. There were lots of empty seats, and a lot of the food that had been prepared had to be given away or thrown away. The event may have made a loss. If people without tickets had come for free it would have made the same loss, but there would have been less waste – and more joy. The vicar had wanted to be indiscriminately generous with the bountiful and excellent food provided. But for some, that would have been profligate and 'unjust'. We can imagine a similar dialogue here, related to that set up by the parable.

To think outside the frame, we need to stimulate the imagination. Our cerebral Christianity needs to be 're-enchanted' (Tomlinson 2008). Storytelling is one way of doing this. It is noticeable how a congregation's attentiveness intensifies as soon as you start telling a story – whether the story of your own life or some imagined parable. But imagery and art can do the same, as can wit and humour (which are, surely, less absent from parables like that of the vineyard than our solemn way of reading them in church often conveys). People will often remember a sermon for its visual aids. And according to Tim Beaudoin (1998), our younger people (who are now, more than a decade on, becoming our middle-aged people) live in an age of 'virtual faith' in which the culture and argument behind Christendom have fallen away, but isolated images – crucifixes, Madonnas, rosaries – still fascinate and draw the imagination, enough to enter the lyrics of our pop music and the images on our cinema screens.

The strength of images and stories is that, unlike arguments, they do not force themselves upon us. They just invite us to contemplate and reflect. As Bill Countryman points out:

> Jesus . . . uses no high-pressure evangelistic methods to persuade people to conform to his teaching. He utters the word, lets it fall where it may, and respects the freedom to refuse as well as to consent. He gives no creeds, no do's-and-don'ts of the usual religious sort. Much of what he says is riddling; it leaves the hearer to sort out its true import. His parables conceal his meaning but thereby open up in the listener an opportunity for surprise and new understanding. 'Let the one who has ears to hear, hear!' (1999, pp. 52–3)

The language of stories is neither indicative description nor imperative command. It is subjunctive (the 'What if . . .' of imagination: just suppose reality were like that parable . . .) and optative (inviting hope: wouldn't it be wonderful if it were . . .?).

There is a danger here, of course. A purely virtual faith based on imagery and parable alone might lead us to a mindless, fairytale faith, incapable of reflective critique. Visual aids and drama can also encourage ego-mindedness in a preacher who is a 'performer' and who may get carried away by his own performance. People can enjoy these things as entertainment without making any serious connection to life, and remember visual aids while forgetting the point they were used to make (see p. 71).

But there is a delicate balance to be struck here. Parables and images are invitations to explore thinking and feeling in new ways. If we reduce them to entertainment, this process is closed off. People go away thinking how clever or funny the preacher was, and that is that. But if we nail down the 'meaning' of a parable or image too hard, the thinking is all done for us and the invitation is lost. If the preacher declares, 'What Jesus means in this parable is that everyone should have the same wage', then either we agree or disagree, but we don't go on wondering. Hence the disappointment we sometimes feel at the interpretation given to the parable of the sower, or the allegorical explanations many of the early theologians give to the other parables, explaining just what each item in the story means. Once we know that the thorns mean temptations, and so forth, we stop wondering. The art of the preacher (or youth leader or street evangelist) who uses stories and images and riddles and jokes, is to say *just enough* to invite people to change their ways of thought and feeling (*metanoia*), without saying *so much* as to foreclose this change.

Rhetoric: stirring the heart

> Read **Luke 11.37–54**: Jesus' '*ouai*'s to the Pharisees and lawyers.
>
> Jesus uses the word '*ouai*' six times in this passage. This extraordinary word, consisting entirely of vowels, conveys more feeling than concept. It is often translated 'woe' or 'Alas' or 'How terrible' but is perhaps best rendered by the interjections we find mainly in comics: 'Ugh!' and 'Aargh' and the German '*Achtung*!' or 'Watch out!'
>
> Note what immediately follows each *ouai*: three for the Pharisees and three for the lawyers or teachers of the law.
>
> Ponder each image for the feelings it evokes.
>
> Finally, how would you feel at the end of this diatribe if you were the Pharisee who had invited Jesus for a meal?

There is no dialogue here! And though there is imagery a-plenty, it is not designed to invite a subtle pondering. Whether the passage is original to Jesus or reflects later Christian hostility to rabbinic Judaism is hard to say. But some of the imagery has the kind of enigmatic power we associate with Jesus. *Precisely* why the Pharisees are like unmarked graves is hard to see, but it conveys brilliantly the feeling we have with people with whom we have to tread carefully lest we trample on some unspoken taboo. The idea of locking the door to knowledge so that neither you nor others can enter (perhaps throwing away the key?) is likewise telling. And the element of repetition based on that desperate expletive *ouai* enables image to pile upon image with devastating power. (The rhythm is broken up at some points with longer passages, leading us to wonder if behind this passage is a much terser, more rhythmic and more enigmatic series of phrases.)

We see at work the dimension of *rhetoric* – a word which derives from *rheo* meaning 'flow' and conveys the use of a flow of language to move people to strong emotion. If change of heart and mind is to occur, and response to God is to be awoken, we need to do more than witness, argue and entertain with stories. Those elements need to move toward action. What moves us to act is emotion and desire. In rhetoric, the sermon or address moves us from the optative voice – the language of hope and aspiration, including (as in this passage) hopes and wishes *not* to be a certain way – to the imperative: the language of command, what we must do. Unlike imagery, which relates mainly to the visual imagination, rhetoric relates primarily to the rhythm and sound of language.

Rhetoric is dangerous. In some ways it has become discredited through its use by demagogues like Lenin and Hitler to stir people to violence and fanaticism. R. S. Thomas' preacher who caught fire (Chapter 2) – his language blazing, perhaps, with an emotion that others caught – is seldom seen these days. The solemn and stirring rhetoric of Lloyd George or Churchill, and even Enoch Powell, has given way to the seductive pleasantry and so-say common-sense of Thatcher, Blair and Cameron. Tele-evangelists, swept in the same broad current, now entertain us as much as they assail our consciences. In the world of 'virtual faith' it may seem wiser to suggest than to stir.

Now certainly rhetoric can be ego-minded in the extreme. It is all too easy to harness people's worst feelings – bitterness, envy, arrogance and resentment – in the service of a cause we believe in. That is what Hitler and Lenin did so well; but the preacher who heaps hellfire on all those *others* who are sinners is surely essentially doing the same? Evangelists need continually to examine themselves for any demagogic tendencies, however subtle.

But if evangelism is about eliciting a response among human beings (who are not robots who automatically do the rational thing) there must be some gentler, power-free way of engaging people's feelings. There must be a way of opening up those better feelings of charity, generosity, humility and hope, and helping them to transform and redeem the more negative feelings. This is not an easy task. But preachers and evangelists need to remember something that is obvious but sometimes forgotten or underused: that the sermon set out on the preacher's page, for all its topical relevance, profound arguments and stunning images, is not yet a sermon. A sermon is something heard, something conveyed in sound; a movement on the wind, which exists only once and then is gone – but can live on in the way it moves people, as Jesus and the prophets knew so well. Those rhythms and cadences matter, and can have surprising power for good or ill.

Use words if necessary . . .

Early on in the chapter you probably noted that the fact that the herald brought good news would have been evident before he got within ear-shot. The lightness in the way he ran – the 'beauty' in his feet, the way he raised his arms – such 'body language' would already have conveyed that the news was good. In the same way, when the secretary comes to summon you to the boss's office, her body language will probably already give you a pretty good idea of whether you are in for commendation or reprimand, promotion or redundancy. The result of an operation will often be communicated by the look of the surgeon's face before he starts to speak.

In the same way, with authentic evangelism a large part of the Good News will be conveyed in our body language. This is not something we can manufacture. A strained effort at a smile is even more off-putting in someone sharing the Good News than the doleful countenance of someone who obviously finds sharing the gospel an unpleasant duty. The body language will only tell good news if our bodies and emotions believe it to be true.

'Preach the gospel always; use words if necessary.' These words, often quoted, are ascribed to Francis of Assisi. There is truth in them. They remind us of the indispensable part that our bodies and our lives play in conveying the gospel – or failing to. As noted with the Johari Window (pp. 118–19), if there is a contradiction between what our bodies say and what our words say, it is the former that will be believed. Nevertheless the quotation can be misleading, in two ways.

To grasp the first, imagine how you would feel if the secretary just bounced into your room and smiled and gave you a thumbs-up and a wink – and then went away without saying anything. Or if the surgeon came to your bedside and threw his arms wide with a big smile, and then went away. You would know that the news was good but you would still want to know what it was. You would want the kind of detail which only a verbal conversation with the boss or the surgeon could provide. In the same way, the body language of Christians may convey that they are onto something good, but if the Good News is to be known and shared, some words are indeed necessary.

And second, the notion of proclaiming the Good News in our lives, valid as it is in itself, can lead to one of two misunderstandings. It may lead Christians to feel they are obliged to lead self-consciously holier-than-thou lives, or self-consciously happier-than-thou lives. That leads people to think Christianity is not for ordinary, sinful and suffering people like them, or to feel that the Good News is about an end to sin and hurt. But the Good News is quite different. It is that though we will continue to sin, we are forgiven and can begin afresh; and though we will go on getting hurt, the hurt need not damage us and overcome us, but can be redeemed and made good in Christ. The demeanour that conveys that kind of good news is quite different from a consciousness of our own sanctity or invulnerability. It is a body language that conveys a humility and sense of being forgiven and able to forgive others, an openness to one another and to the whole range and depth of human feeling, as well as our liberation from a lot of the material and mental baggage many people fret about. It is a body language that conveys that we are fully human, and fully alive and in a deeper, richer way – daunting yet alluring. This is the Good News which the herald, leaping over the mountains, longs to share! Its substance is the subject of the next chapter: the ministry of liberating subversion.

Conclusion

This chapter considered the evangelistic ministry of the herald. Following Vanstone, the primary task here was identified as eliciting the free response of being to the love of God; evangelism therefore means sharing in the vulnerability of God who will not force a response. Various aspects of evangelism were considered: prophecy, as a mode of theological reflection; witnessing or speaking in public of experience that can seem very private; apologetics and dialogue, as engaging reflectively with those of other faiths and no faith to advance the rational claims of Christianity; story-telling, humour and other appeals to the imagination; and rhetoric, focusing on the sonic and rhythmic power of words to stir the heart to action. But preaching of the Good News needs to go hand in hand with living it and enabling others to do so: the eschatological task of the liberator.

For further reflection

1 How did you first hear the Good News of the gospel, and how did you respond to it?

2 What have been your best and worst experiences of trying to share that Good News with others outside the church community?

3 Which of the five listed approaches of the prophets might be most readily adapted for use in your own context; and how might this best be achieved?

4 How else might you and others with whom you minister be able to recapture the energy and joy of the herald bearing Good News?

8

The Liberator: Mindful Subversion

This minister has the same overt, expansive thrust to take the gospel beyond the walls of the church as the evangelist, but based on a rather different understanding of the gospel. The emphasis is not so much on individual conversion as the social transformation, and the welcoming of a Kingdom of justice that is good news for the poor. Unconventional, sensitive, intelligent but a little gauche, slightly out of place in the tough setting where she ministers, but possessed of more resilience than meets the eye, she has a deep impatience with what the Church and the world of the rich regard as 'success'. Yet her ministry finds its focus in the Eucharist which is seen as an egalitarian meal in which all, however poor and beleaguered, find their Christ-like nature reaffirmed.

Around this focus almost anything can happen, as children, young people, and various marginalized groups take their turn to contribute, in a style that is rough and ready, to a fragile and uneven beauty overall. If the evangelist seeks to help others find Christ, the heart of the liberator's ministry is a search to find Christ in others: Christ already present at the forgotten edges of society, and in and among the various faith and non-faith groups that minister alongside the little church community in this God-forsaken yet God-rich part of the world.

It is significant, perhaps, that among the many lay ministries that have long existed or been recently developed in the Church, there is none that really corresponds to the liberator. The work just described goes on in many a church, but we have as yet nobody really responsible for it. The ministry to the fringes is in many ways a ministry of the fringes, even though we see in it many aspects of Jesus' ministry.

Focus: a regeneration project

Your vast church building towers over a bleak 1960s fringe estate. Built in the same period, of experimental materials, it is now dilapidated and much vandalized, with a leaky roof that would cost more to repair than the tiny congregation can afford. This congregation has dwindled to a 'righteous remnant'. A small group of local people, who have never known power in any other walk of life, exercise total power over the church council, giving people who think differently from them such a rough time that new people are seldom prepared to stand for election. But just lately a highly articulate and educated head teacher has joined the church and been elected to the PCC. She lives outside the parish, but comes to your church because she has high ideals about 'liberating' the people of the estate. She is full of enthusiasm but tends to patronize the 'old guard' who resent her middle-class eloquence.

She has been involved in discussions with the city council, and a plan is being considered to demolish the old building and replace it with a new, all-purpose community centre. Urban regeneration funding might be available for the new building, which would include, along with a drugs rehabilitation centre and indoor sports facilities and meeting areas, a beautiful but much smaller worship area, which the church would hold on a long-term lease but not own. The church would be part of a hub of new activity, and these plans could liberate the church as well as many others on the estate. But several factors displease the 'old guard': the loss of ownership of the church; the ceding of power over the building to a management committee on which the church would be represented, but in the minority; and the presence near the church of several threatening groups, including drug users undergoing rehabilitation, and, possibly, groups representing sexual and other radical minorities which some church members feel are at odds with Christian values; and the very youngsters who had been vandalizing the church.

What position do you take? Do you choose to serve the wider community, who are largely indifferent to the Christian faith, at the price of uncertainty for the faithful members who have supported the Church through thick and thin? Or do you choose to keep the church's independence, so that it can chart its own course in the long-term future, even though survival in the medium term will be a hard struggle? Do you choose to follow the majority in your church, or to 'liberate' the wider majority on the estate as a whole (whether or not they have expressed a desire to be liberated . . .)?

Such scenarios are not rare in inner-city and outer estates. Churches often have to make a choice between trying to go on being the Church as it always has – but shrinking, or becoming something much freer and also more vulnerable; between primarily serving the spiritual needs of its members, or serving those of the wider community also; between preserving autonomy or choosing a collaborative situation in which Christians are in a minority.

A majority of the ministries described in this book so far – representing, serving, teaching, planning and collaborating – could be seen as ministries to individuals and groups aiming primarily to build up the church so that it can minister to the 'wider world'. The last two ministries – evangelizing, and the one considered now, which we call liberation – are more directly ministries to the world. But the first, evangelism, is about announcing the Kingdom to the world; this last, liberation, is about transforming the world itself to be more like God's Kingdom. Both ministries, or course, involve the Church (as is clear from our example above) but the aim in this case is not to strengthen the Church as such. Indeed, as we shall see, to achieve the wider aim, the Church and its ministers may in some senses have to become weaker.

The glory of God is a human fully alive

The Introduction to this book begins with the story of a golden eagle who grew up among barnyard chickens believing he was one of them, and never discovering or living out his true nature. But in God's eyes, are we not all 'golden eagles' who persist in behaving like barnyard chickens because that is what we think we are? The task of all ministry is to awaken people to their true glory in Christ. That task will include evangelism: telling people of the 'golden eagle' Christ whose nature we are called to share. But the other part will be the more arduous task of teaching those who believe they are only chickens to fly like the eagles they truly are. It is this that we call 'liberation'. We might have used more traditional terms like 'salvation' and 'sanctification'. But those words have a very church-bound ring, and suggest a process that mainly happens to individuals, soul by soul. Liberation has the advantage of being common currency, not just church-speak; and of suggesting a process that is both individual and corporate – social and political.

Those who have always thought of themselves as barnyard chickens will require a lot of encouragement to believe they can fly and learn to do it. That is the individual dimension of the ministry of liberation, the dimension that includes things like enabling, initiating, anointing,

giving permission, training, challenging, strengthening, nurturing, edi-
fying, enlivening, enriching, releasing, opening, realizing abundance,
enjoying . . . Such things are doubtless to be included as aspects of
the charism described in Romans 10.8 with the verb *parakaleō*, to exhort, cheer, encourage, console or excite – from which we get the noun
paraclētē, the Comforter or Holy Spirit.

But the chickens (who are really eagles) will be up against the whole
basis of chicken society, the social structures and 'pecking orders' that
depend on chickens not flying, and that instil deep in corporate chicken
life that flying is out of the question. Chickens that believe they can fly
and try to teach others to do likewise will be seen as subversive dissi-
dents or irresponsible fools. And this is the corporate dimension of the
ministry of liberation, which is counter-cultural.

Both individual and corporate dimensions of liberation are premised
on Irenaeus' understanding that 'the glory of God is a human being fully
alive' (see the section on conducting in Chapter 5), and on Jesus' declaration in John 10.20 (see the Good Shepherd in Chapter 3) that he came to
bring life in all its fullness – to enable us to flourish fully as the humans
we are. Many of the ministries described in the other chapters relate to the
individual dimension. In this chapter we focus mainly on the corporate
dimension, which is about overcoming the many discouraging voices we
have internalized from an early age; learning – to change the metaphor –
not to dance to society's limiting music, but to God's grander symphony.

This dimension of corporate struggle has no designated charism, but
is implied in many writings: 'Our struggle is not against enemies of
blood and flesh, but against the rulers, against the authorities, against
the cosmic powers of this present darkness, against the spiritual forces
of evil in the heavenly places' (Ephesians 6.12). The writer here takes
up a theme expressed more fully throughout the apocalyptic writings,
which depicts in heavily symbolic terms a cosmic conflict between the
forces of light and darkness, in which the individual believer is swept
up. These forces are larger than individual humans, and the uncanny
and powerful images we find in apocalyptic writings like Daniel and the
book of Revelation are codes for political and historical empires like
that of Babylon, Greece and Rome.

We do not have to accept the cosmic dualism of these works to accept that in the struggle to be fully the human beings we are created
and called to be, we have to struggle against something bigger than
our own nature, against voices and forces that come to us from wider
society telling us to be narrow and safe, rather than expansive and
vulnerable. Modern theologians like Walter Wink have brought these
dense and obscure writings to life by interpreting the dark evils they

symbolize in terms of *The Powers that Be* (2000) – social and political forces that need to be named, unmasked and confronted. Meanwhile other liberation theologians have cast light on the gospel through use of a latter-day apocalyptic framework, that of Marxism, criticizing the mainstream churches for their captivity to power, and finding hope in small 'base communities' of the poor, the marginalized and oppressed.

> 'To what will I compare this generation? It is like children sitting in the marketplaces and calling to one another, "We played the flute for you, and you did not dance; we wailed, and you did not mourn." For John came neither eating nor drinking, and they say, "He has a demon"; the Son of Man came eating and drinking, and they say, "Look, a glutton and a drunkard, a friend of tax collectors and sinners!" Yet wisdom is vindicated by her deeds.' (Matthew 11.16–19)

Jesus here describes the social voices that tried to make John the Baptist and Jesus himself follow a set script. John's asceticism and Jesus' liberty were likewise threatening because their behaviour was not like that of a safe, respectable holy man. The people are likened to children playing tunes and expecting their leaders to dance and mourn like puppets held on their strings. Observe any major political leader today, and you will note how closely they dance to the required tunes. When there is a military victory, the same words and phrases and the same body language repeat themselves time and again; and likewise, when there is some tragedy. It is as if the same bodily demeanour is being fetched out of the wardrobe and put on, and the same tape replayed. But John and Jesus refused to dance to familiar tunes. Both were disturbing; both were in the end disposed of.

Three ways of dancing to another tune

> Read **Matthew 4.1–11:** the temptation of Jesus.
>
> Do not try too hard to imagine Satan. Focus on the three temptations.
>
> Probably you have not succumbed to these temptations literally, but do they stand for anything you have felt drawn or impelled to?

In a famous passage, Fyodor Dostoyevsky's character Ivan Karamazov created a remarkable re-working of this story. Jesus – the story goes – has returned to earth in sixteenth-century Spain, where in his name his followers, the Inquisition, are rounding up other followers, the heretics, to commit them to the flames. The Grand Inquisitor has no hesitation in having Jesus arrested so that he can interrogate him. He accuses Jesus of having misled people into craving a spurious freedom. In rejecting Satan's three temptations, Jesus rejected the things people need in order to be happy: a good supply of material things (symbolized by turning stone into nourishing bread), a church that can dazzle them with its spiritual power (symbolized by jumping off the top of the Temple and remaining unscathed) and a tight hierarchy in which everyone obeys those set over them and commands those under them (symbolized by Satan's invitation to worship him, and be worshipped and obeyed by all the peoples on earth). Thankfully, the Inquisitor explains, the Roman Catholic Church has accepted all three of Satan's offers, taking away people's spiritual and political freedom in return for happiness and material well-being. Now Jesus has returned, threatening to disrupt the Church's plans and offer a delusory freedom. In reply, Jesus breaks his total silence by kissing the Inquisitor. The Inquisitor releases him but tells him never to return.

As a scathing critique specifically of the Catholic Church, Dostoyevsky's tale is no doubt unfair. But the parable ranges wider than its author intended. As a prediction of the rationale that Communism would adopt in the Soviet Union it is remarkably apposite; but then arguably the aspirations of the modern secular Capitalist welfare state are not dissimilar. But its relevance here is as a parable of three ways in which the minister of any church might fail to lay hold of and offer to others the freedom that Christ offers: three ways in which the Church's minister may dance to the tune of the world . . . and the Inquisitor.

1 **Turning stones to bread**: he may be tempted to be the omni-competent provider of all that people think they need, making them happy and content.
2 **Jumping from the Temple tower**: he may be tempted to displays of moral rectitude, craving the kind of respect people give to those who 'do the holiness thing' on their behalf.
3 **Worshipping the rulers of this world**: he may play the world's power games, metaphorically licking boots in order that his boots may in turn be licked.

The temptation story in the Gospels depicts Jesus, pondering the future shape of his ministry, as being vulnerable to all three of these temptations, but forswearing them in order that people might be liberated. Our contention is that if the minister is mindful of these temptations in herself, and yet acts against them, she will be free, and capable of leading others to freedom. Let us see how this is so in the case of each of the three temptations.

1 Free not to provide what is wanted

> Read **Luke 10.38–42**: Jesus with Mary and Martha.
>
> Imagine the story from the point of view of Martha. Focus on your feelings.
>
> Elaborate your feelings into an argued case for yourself, Martha, against Mary and Jesus' support for her.
>
> How do you imagine Jesus would have responded to your case?
>
> Is there any time in your ministry when something similar has happened? What were your feelings then?
>
> On balance, does your ministry feel more like being Martha or more like being Mary?

Commenting on the many of Jesus' parables that are, like the one just referred to, set in a domestic context, feminist poet Nicola Slee notes how often

> . . . the unexpected erupts, the absurd is postulated. The patch tears the cloth, the wine bursts the skins . . . the lamp is put under the bed, the master serves the meal to his servants, the friend calls at midnight . . . The parables suggest that within the context of the domestic the unexpected, the wholly gratuitous and unlooked for, erupts – but in so doing, the very world of the everyday is irretrievably shattered, irreversibly transformed . . . To discover the presence of God within the confines of the mundane and domestic is radically and explosively to transform these realities – and this may be as uncomfortable as it is unexpected. (1990, pp. 41–2)

God's Kingdom – as a well-known poem of R. S. Thomas (1995, p. 233) suggests – is a world of ordinary and everyday things but with 'quite different things going on' in and among them.

The liberating task of the minister could be described as living in the ordinary world in such a way that quite different things can go on, and the unexpected can erupt, in the way in which it does in the parables of Jesus. And the way it erupts in the story just considered is particularly relevant.

Martha dances to the patriarchal tune. As a Middle-Eastern woman, her task is to prepare the meal and stand in the background waiting on the men as they have their lofty discussions. Her role is that of the provider and carer. But Mary has transgressed. She is there among the men, unashamedly sitting at the Teacher's feet. If they were reclining around a table, this would not have implied the submissive inequality it suggests to us, but rather a bold intimacy – it would mean she was reclining next to Jesus himself. She is listening to him along with the men, and doubtless taking her part in the discussions that follow. Martha's protest is understandable on two counts: she is left to do all the hard work, and Mary has offended against a universally accepted taboo. She is refusing to dance to the common tune.

In ministry we often succumb to the temptation to be Marthas. We dance to the tune of other people's wants in order to please them. Like waiters, we do our best to meet people's desires. We think we are being good servants – though, as argued in Chapter 3, this slave-like ministry is not the true ministry of the deacon. We are busy all the time turning stones to bread for the people to eat. But as well as feeling good on one level, at another we feel drained. We have little time to sit at table with Jesus, absorbing the nourishment of his teaching. We complain we are too busy to say our prayers.

To be liberators, we can discover the ministry of saying 'No' to people's desires and expectations. We can stop dancing to others' tunes, and start playing a different tune for others to dance to. We need to know, as R. S. Thomas' poem goes on to say, that entry to the Kingdom is free only to those who have overcome their 'desire' and offer themselves with their 'need only' and 'faith, green as a leaf'. So to open the door of the Kingdom it becomes necessary to refuse desire and respond to need. This requires mindfulness of the difference between need and desire in ourselves also.

Though Jesus did not turn stones to bread, he did spend a lot of time meeting people's needs with healing. But he knew the difference between need and desire: he told the religious leaders, not what they wanted, but what they needed to hear. That requires a remarkable ability not to dance to the prevailing tune. And he knew when it was time to move to a quieter space, or move on elsewhere (for example Mark 1.35–39) when the press of people's expectations was getting too great, and perhaps a dependency was setting in.

Perhaps the most mysterious part of the episode of Mary and Martha is what Jesus says at the end: 'There is need of only one thing. Mary has chosen the better part, which will not be taken away from her.' Traditionally Martha was seen as symbolizing the active life of service, and Mary the contemplative life of adoration: so perhaps Jesus is saying that only the latter continues after death. But the meaning may be more mundane, yet more profound. Service of others ought to be leading to its own redundancy. The time is coming (which parents sometimes dread) when those cared for will be grown up enough to meet their own needs. Caring ministers ought to be planning for their own redundancy. But learning alongside others the ways of God and his Kingdom in the everyday is something we do more and more; the more we understand, the more we know we do not yet understand. This part – the part of a 'male' disciple which Mary has presumed to take – will never be taken away (hard as we might think the Church has tried!).

2   *Free to be wrong*

Read **Luke 19.1–10**: Jesus and Zacchaeus.

Read the story from the point of view of Jesus.

Imagine the kind of person you find most intolerable, whose way of life fills you with loathing. Now imagine that this kind of person is in a group you are speaking to. He is clearly eager to hear what you have to say, but is short and finds it hard to find a place near the front of the group where he can see. So he has found a prominent place near the back. Now you can see him.

What can you plausibly imagine yourself doing?

- Ignore him?
- Harangue him?
- Invite yourself to a meal with him?
- Other?

What factors do this passage and the Martha and Mary passage have in common?

Once again, Jesus has broken out of the frame. Zacchaeus was not only a despised outcast, but bad, and justly despised. Only a greedy, unprincipled, self-serving man would collaborate with the Romans against his own community, extorting money from them and sometimes threatening them for his own profit. He would have excited the same disgust in his society as drug barons do in ours. This short, offensive man would have been shunned and jostled as he tried to move through the crowd. But he wants to see Jesus, and consequently has shamelessly climbed a tree where everyone can see him.

Any respectable teacher would have either denounced him or shunned him. But Jesus addresses him directly, and invites himself to a meal with him. No mention of sin, or forgiveness! It's like a bishop or a cabinet minister inviting himself to a meal with a drugs baron, without any apparent agenda except to be sociable. Muck spreads: the shamefulness of the drugs baron – or the tax collector – would spread to the person who socialized with him, and discredit him also.

But Jesus does not mind that. From the time when he refused to impress people with a leap from the Temple, letting the angels miraculously save him, to the time when he refused to 'leap' from the cross and let the angels save him and show him to be more than an execrable criminal, Jesus consistently refused to do the thing that would impress, the thing that would enhance or preserve or restore his respectability. Quite the reverse: he seemed to make a bee-line for the unrespectable and notorious. Either he did not understand what it was to be pure and holy, or he had a completely different – shattering and liberating – understanding of how holiness worked.

Spreading the contagion of holiness

As noted in Chapter 2, at the core of Hebrew law or torah lies the 'holiness code' in Leviticus. And at the heart of this code we hear the command, 'Be holy as I am holy' (Leviticus 11.44, repeated at 11.45, 19.2, 20.26, 21.8). The very next sentence in 11.44 gives the tenor: 'You shall not defile yourselves with any swarming creature that moves on the earth.' Holiness was essentially about being pure and not defiled by the impure. Of course, the code also included matters of charity towards foreigners and justice for widows and orphans, and much that we still treasure as the foundation of morality. But by far the greater part of the code concerns the protection of holiness. God's presence, centred for this text on the 'holy of holies' in the Temple at Jerusalem, had to be protected from the unholy people and things that might pollute it. In other, perhaps more 'primitive' traditions, it was the impure people who had to be protected from the holiness of God, which might break out and consume them like a fire. But the upshot was the same. Laws had to be in place to keep the holy and the profane apart and protect them from each other. The task of the priests was above all to police this border and deal with situations where the boundaries had been transgressed. Though the later rabbis and Pharisees were based on the synagogue rather than the Temple, and did not offer sacrifice, they retained the priestly concern with policing the boundaries of the holy, and kept themselves away from contact with profane things or people – which, of course, is why the priest in the parable of the good Samaritan walks by on the other side when he sees what looks like a dead body.

But the one the Christian priest represents was neither a priest, nor in any conventional sense a rabbi. He was known – and condemned – for his flagrant transgression of the boundaries. He and his disciples ate with dirty hands; and they associated with lawless, sinful people. This was not just some carelessness that might be forgiven; it seemed to be policy. Jesus healed people on the day nobody was supposed to work – the Sabbath – even in cases that could clearly have waited another day and been carried out without offence. And Jesus did not just come across sinners, he invited them to his feasts and himself to theirs, so that there was absolutely no chance of avoiding their moral contagion.

So, had Jesus abandoned any sense of the ancient call to divine holiness? No, but he was working with a different model of holiness. On the old model, when holiness and corruption met, it was as if the corruption would win. So the holy had to avoid impurity. But on Jesus' model it was if when this happened the holiness had the power to convert and transform the impure, as fire purifies gold of all its dross. So the holy – Jesus – was attracted to the impure like a magnet. Jesus reiterated the Levitical command when he commanded, 'Be perfect, for your Father in heaven is perfect' (Matthew 5.48). The key word here is *teleios*: complete, finished, having reached your goal. But this was set at the heart of Jesus' own holiness code, which was more about loving your enemy than resisting the evil one or maintaining ritual purity.

Jesus' precept was illustrated not by a further command against contaminating yourself with swarming creatures, but by the saying that God 'makes his sun rise on the evil and on the good, and sends rain on the righteous and on the unrighteous'. We are to be perfect not in shunning the bad but in shining equally on the good and the bad. The priests of the Temple kept the fire of God burning in the holy of holies, but Jesus said he came 'to cast fire upon the earth'.

But in time, somehow, the old model of holiness came back. The holy of holies was restored in the 'sanctuary' of the churches, where only the priests and their attendants could go. And the priest was once again 'set apart' to police the boundaries of the holy. The freedom and courage of Jesus' approach to the holy were replaced by caution, hierarchical bondage and the Grand Inquisitor.

And yet the Church never quite gave up on Jesus' approach. Michael Dwinell remarks:

> Holy spaces throughout the world, from culture to culture – temples, churches, ashrams, shrines – are adorned and guarded by carved statues, monsters, griffins, gargoyles, lions, dragons. The more horrific the representations of the monster, the better. The more ugly

and frightening the beast, the more likely it is to appear guarding the entry to the holy space. How are we to understand why the approaches to holy spaces are guarded by what appear to be the most unholy, the most demonic, the most grotesque? (1993, p. 153)

Dwinell suggests that these monsters serve to hold together (symbolize, meaning 'throw together') the holy and the profane, and goes on to remark that the priest (like Christ, we note) is called to be this kind of monster, spreading the contagion of holiness:

> Priest is, therefore, *symbolos*, a monster. Priest is one who 'tells it like it is'. Priest is one who does not trivialize or sentimentalize; priest is not cynical. Priest is one who bears witness to how bad things really are when they are bad, and how glorious things really are when they are glorious; how dead people are when they die; and how freshly alive people are when they are born. Priest says, 'Let us look again, and again, and again', that 'things are always more than they first appear. Let us always look under the surface to search for the hidden mystery even though it makes us most uncomfortable.' . . . Priest points to the reality that all space, inner and outer, is holy space . . . As the monstrosity of priest approaches, the boundaries expand and the levels increase, and the mystery deepens, and life is again vibrating with holiness. (pp. 154–5)

Spirit versus Satan

Dwinell remarks that the devil does the opposite of this; he is *diabolos*, the one who 'throws apart' the sacred and the profane. Certainly we have seen how Satan, preferring magic to mystery, would like Jesus to have taken position at the high point of the Temple precincts, to show his powers and ensure that people would see him as a worker of wonders and utterly unlike them.

In this, however, the Holy Spirit is completely different from Satan. Here we have learnt from the arguments of James Alison (1998). The Holy Spirit is referred to in the ancient litany as 'Advocate and Guide', and John 16.13 describes the Spirit as 'leading into all truth'. The word translates *parakletos*, literally the one who says 'please' (the '*parakalo*' familiar to this day in Greek) or makes a plea on behalf of someone. It can name (as noted above) the bringer of affirmation and reassurance, and is sometimes translated 'comforter' and (less accurately) 'counsellor'. In trials the *parakletos* was the lawyer who presented the case for the defence before the judge. He was opposed by the 'accuser' – in Hebrew the 'Satan' – who presented the case for the prosecution.

Now it is highly significant that the roles of judge and defender are ascribed to the Trinity (Christ and Holy Spirit respectively) but the role of accuser is ascribed to a non-divine, even anti-divine, figure. The case for the prosecution against us is ascribed to the Satan whom tradition identifies with the devil – *diabolos*, the slanderer. Both the sense of accountability, as before a judgement seat, and the sense of being justified, supported, defended, are ascribed to the divine, but the experience of being accused and found guilty or wanting or condemned is ascribed to what is least divine, to a purely human or even evil tendency to slander and backbiting.

Walter Wink relates the Satan to an inner accuser that is forever belittling and discouraging us – whispering in our ears as it were, that we are nothing more than barnyard chickens:

> Where does this life-quenching power come from? Why does it desire murder (the devil is 'a murderer from the beginning', John 8:44)? Why does it seek to suck us down into feelings of worthlessness and despair ('Beliar', one of Satan's names, is a corruption of Belial, 'worthless', 2 Cor. 6:15)? . . . I am familiar with the voice of that 'slanderer'. It is the voice that whispers to us, just when we most need to marshal all our abilities in order to perform an important task, 'You're no good, and you never will be any good.' 'You're not smart enough, you'll never succeed in this job.' 'You deserved this, you had it coming, this is what you get.' 'You're ugly, fat (or skinny), and unlovable.' . . . It wants to persuade us that we ought to die – not in order to overcome the illusions of the ego or to liberate us from perfectionism, but simply to exterminate us. (1986, p. 27)

Against such strong inner accusing voices the pastor needs to go deeper than simply being the 'enabler' described in Chapter 6, who encourages and skills people in new tasks. He needs to enable at the level of being rather than doing, addressing people's hearts with the energy of the Advocate who is the Creator Spirit, the One who liberates, gives new life and enables beings to be.

Typically an advocate for the defence interviews the defendant and works out the best possible account to present, both of the defendant's character and of what the evidence suggests she has done. The 'advocate' seeks to present the defendant in what we significantly term 'a good light', and the Holy Spirit seeks to present the truth about each person 'in a good light'. The pastor likewise sees his people and presents them to themselves and one another 'in a good light' so as to be able to guide them all to the ultimate 'good light' of God. This is far from easy. Such is the strength of the accusing voices that we have sometimes found that people feel 'got at' in sermons where we have been striving only to encourage. But of course, just as (we hope) the Holy Spirit can speak through sermons, so can the Accuser.

Divisions in the community generally arise through the literally 'satanic' and 'diabolical' tendency to darken this good light with slander, mutual accusation and struggles for power. Each person feels they have to accuse the other in order to remove blame from him- or herself. Reconciliation often comes when a third party is able to make both parties feel supported and affirmed, so that making concessions and even admitting a degree of mistakenness no longer means 'losing face'.

But, as we see in Jesus' case, being the reconciler can be costly: the reconciler may become the target of both sides' accusations. Accepting this is the most radical and sacrificial dimension of the liberator's gift of liberation.

3   Free to be powerless

Read **John 18.33—19.6**: behold the human.

Imagine Pilate in this scene, seated on his throne, asking questions about truth and power.

Then focus on Jesus in his clownish 'mock king' garments, standing there weakened by his torture. Reflect on the answers he gives.

Consider what each of them says in their conversation about truth and kingly power.

Think of yourself in your ministry in terms of these two figures, Jesus and Pilate. In what ways are you like Jesus, directed by truth and justice which you cannot forsake at any cost? In what ways are you like Pilate, colluding with false and unjust views out of fear, or just a desire to get on with others and not make a fuss, and washing your hands of issues you feel powerless, despite your many strengths and abilities, to do anything about?

W. H. Vanstone notes that up to the time of his handing over (see Chapter 1, pp. 4–5) Jesus is supremely active, always taking the initiative, the subject of most of the verbs, but in Mark's Gospel 'from this point on, Jesus is the grammatical subject of just nine verbs . . . Now he is no longer there as the active and initiating subject of what is done;

he is there as the recipient, the object, of what is done' (1982, p. 20). Yet this passivity has a strange power. Pilate invites us to 'behold the human being' (*ecce homo*) (John 19.5) – and indeed it is possible to see in this tortured, mocked figure, clownish in his false-king's array, both the pathos of the human condition and the dignity of those who have only truth to speak to power, yet say it nonetheless.

Hieronymus Bosch vividly depicts this powerful vulnerability. Consider for example his painting of Christ mocked by the soldiers, or before Pilate (probably painted by a follower of Bosch) or carrying the cross – images readily available on the internet. The faces surrounding Jesus are 'satanic' – either brutally accusatory or viciously sanctimonious – in a way that dehumanizes them, renders them animal caricatures of themselves. In their active aggression they are curiously passive, swept along by a tide of victimizing desire. Jesus, by contrast, is curiously powerful in his gentle passivity. His eyes closed or fixed on the distance in meditative sorrow, he seems to hold a central place that is unaffected by the swirling currents of emotion around him. He seems to be the only real human being in the picture.

A mindful minister would not cultivate being a martyr. If he deliberately puts himself in this position, he is not truly passive in Vanstone's sense, for he has actively engineered the situation. Nevertheless the minister is called to encounter the overt and subtle manipulations of power armed only with courage and truth.

> When we look at priest in his traditional role as parish clergy, we see someone armed with a book, a bottle of water, a cruet of oil, a chalice of wine, and a plate of bits of bread. These, especially the wine as spilt blood and the bread as broken body, are the weapons and tools that he brings with him to every possible human gathering: to celebrations of birth and marriage, to the grief of death and burial, and to all the other major events of our life cycles. Spilt blood, broken body, signs, symbols, and facts of failure, suffering, powerlessness, disease, and death are the only things powerless enough to transform our power-constipated lives. (Dwinell 1993, pp. 45–6)

So the minister exercises the liberating power of no-power.

But the minister has a choice here because there are two kinds of Church he can belong to, as described by liberation theologian Leonardo Boff.

> One is oriented to the church as grand institution, with all its services institutionally organized and oriented to the needs of the church

universal, the dioceses, and the parishes. This model of the church generally finds its sociological and cultural centre in society's affluent sectors, where it enjoys social power and constitutes the church's exclusive interlocutor with the powers of society. The other is centred in the network of the basic communities, deep within the popular sectors and the poor masses, on the margin of power and influence over the media, living the horizontal relationships of co-responsibility and a communion of brothers and sisters more deeply. (1986, pp. 7–8)

In Latin America when Boff wrote, these two Churches were diametrically opposed. There was a very cultic and nationalistic hierarchy supportive of and supported by the right-wing military juntas; and there were small groups of Christians allying themselves with the Marxist left in struggles for freedom. In our situation the two Churches are less polarized and more fused. There are a number of denominations – one the officially established Church, the others quite influential at a national level – closely allied to a liberal democracy; and largely within this Church, often at its fringes, there are many small groups dedicated to a less violent – indeed often explicitly pacifist – struggle on behalf of the oppressed. The situation is subtle; nevertheless we believe that the minister, and indeed any Christian, still often faces a choice between a power and influence that ensnares and a truth and integrity that may be costly, but liberates.

We have considered Jesus before Pilate, but it is worth glancing at one of his predecessors, Moses: a Jew with an Egyptian name and up-bringing, a murderer, a shepherd isolated from his people in the wilderness, with perhaps a speech defect or an uneducated weak power of language. Even among his own marginalized people he was a strange outsider. Even when he met with success, he never became king. And he never entered the promised land of freedom. Nevertheless Moses exemplifies the essentials of the liberator:

- He had an encounter with the liberating truth at the heart of being, and remained ever after faithful to it.
- With only Aaron as a companion, he repeatedly spoke truth to the mighty power of Pharaoh, and demanded justice.
- When the people were discouraged, he spoke words of encouragement to prod them to travel ever onwards into the unknown. He held out the hope of freedom when others despaired.
- He sustained his own contemplative vision, meeting with God in the tent and on the mountain, conversing as a friend, face to face.

- Though not a king, he brought the law and was prepared to make judgements when there were disputes among the people (a role that Jesus, we note, eschewed).

Fools and creative failures

Moses died without having succeeded in the whole of the task to which he was called. In the earliest accounts, Jesus dies despairing of God's faithfulness, in what any detached commentator would regard as failure and disgrace. Only in retrospect – a retrospect echoed in the final words that John puts on Jesus' lips, *tetelestai*, it is accomplished – can we see in Jesus' and Moses' apparent failures a deep creativity and accomplishment.

To be a priest in Western Europe today, as congregations go on declining overall and the voices opposed to Christianity grow stronger, is to be committed to more of what people count as failure than what people count as success. But as Rabbi Lionel Blue is reported to have said, 'Your successes will make you clever, but only your failures will make you wise.' And Paul, of course, insists on the strength of the weakness and 'foolishness' of God, and those who bring his message:

> Jews demand signs and Greeks desire wisdom, but we proclaim Christ crucified, a stumbling block to Jews and foolishness to Gentiles, but to those who are the called, both Jews and Greeks, Christ the power of God and the wisdom of God. For God's foolishness is wiser than human wisdom, and God's weakness is stronger than human strength. (1 Corinthians 1.22–25)

Paintings of the French artist Henri Rouault such as *The Holy Face* (1933) and *Christ and the Apostles* (1937–8) (easily searchable on the internet) pick up this foolishness of God, manifest in a Christ who is clown-like and yet serene, vulnerable yet somehow strong.

Failure resisted and resented can, of course, make fools of us. But failure acknowledged as part of life's rich pattern may make us wise, and creative in the future. Mark Townsend, writing out of his own experience of failure as an Anglican priest in *The Gospel of Falling Down* (2007, p. 78), relates an anonymous Chinese parable about a man who carried two pots. One was cracked and leaked, and felt useless, but in its well-watered path grew flowers its owner cherished.

The power of flawed, vulnerable people to convey truth in a world distracted by power was once institutionalized in the fool – until in the eighteenth century with the worship of rationality we began institutionalizing such people instead in asylums and the like. The shaman, mentioned in Chapter 4, may be his predecessor in his crazy wisdom-inducing antics.

> A good shaman has great power at image-making. He is an utterly convincing performer, a superb storyteller who makes present for a people their vision or myth of the world. The shaman's dress, his masks, his instruments are used with trickery and irony to turn the world of his clients upside-down, to crack their common-sense presuppositions imposed by the structures. In this sense the shaman is a personified parable, who leads us out . . . to the very edge of the abyss. In fact, in the mythology of some seafaring tribes, he goes down into the fathomless ocean to talk to the spirits . . . Shamans are creatively weird, not just crazy, as it used to be common to think. (Holmes 1978, p. 79)

The minister who would be wise can learn a lot from such creative weirdness. From ancient Egypt onward, it seems, kings had employed misfits and scapegoats who were the focus of mirth, and the role of 'fool' became semi-official in the medieval court (Welsford 1935). The fool was the one person who could freely criticize the king. A laughable figure in the eyes of the world, he stood no chance of taking real power, but for that very reason he often became the king's confidant. He combined something of the prophet with something of the wise man and something of the vulnerability of Christ.

There is a strong tradition also of holy fools in Russia – able to challenge and rebuke even feared tsars like Ivan the Terrible; but probably the most familiar fool to us is the fictional one in *King Lear*. He is full of biting witticisms that expose the foolishness of the king, but most crucially he stays by the king when he becomes dispossessed in the storm, vulnerable and mad. Friendship through thick and thin, seeking no 'gain' in the relationship, following no 'form': this is the kind of foolish faithfulness required of the minister today. It may place her at the margins of a society dutifully straining to achieve goals, to enhance lifestyles and gain success, but it places her at the heart of the universe in which God's wisdom delights.

The power of no power

This chapter has focused on *not* doing: on the three temptations to avoid. We hope it has not suggested a quietistic passivity, but rather, something of what the Taoists call 'the power of no power'. Jesus' ministry seems to have begun not with an 'action plan' but with a sojourn in the wilderness where he said a firm 'No' to certain courses of action. But out of that sojourn he was catapulted to where the action was. As he encountered the violence of those in power, he neither reacted with violence nor simply crumpled as a victim. What he did was rather like what we see in the Taoist-inspired martial arts-like ju-jitsu, which are inspired by an ethos that could be called 'active pacifism'. Such techniques work by deflecting the energy of the violent away from the potential victim and against the violent themselves, though with the minimum force necessary to keep the victim safe. We see a similar active pacifism, or power of no power, at work in the life of non-violent liberators like Mahatma Gandhi, and Jesus himself. We suggest it is at the heart of the ministry of liberation.

When faced with the injustices and delusions that pervade a lot of contemporary society, the liberator can fail in the usual three ways:

1 He can be an **'absent-minded'** 'armchair liberator' who has a very clear ideal of justice and truth, but very little of the subtle practical prudence of the 'serpent'. He is all 'dove' (Matthew 10.16), all 'innocent' as he leaps from the top of the Temple, or into struggle with cynical powers, sure that the angels will protect him and his people as they follow him. In our example, he is the one who would have handed the Church over to the community no strings attached, and failed to notice that on the plan the church premises were only the size of a telephone booth!

2 He can be **ego-minded**, bristling with anger at the oppression of the poor, but prepared to bully on their behalf: the subversive who on gaining power becomes the dictator. Confusing the cause of the people with his own ego, once he has power he uses it to quell the enemies of his ego. He is the one who does dark deals with the Prince of Power in order to rule the earth, or a part of it. In our example, he would have railed at the congregation for their indifference to the estate around them, but in the new centre he would still have had to fight a cause, driving out many for whom it was designed.

3 He can be **mindless**: the activist who has always, like Martha, to be active, and responds to injustices not with appropriate challenge, but with desperate action to plaster over the wounds. He resists asking the big question: why, when some have so much bread, others have so little. Instead, he desperately tries to remedy the situation by handing out what little bread he has. In

our example he would have felt terribly torn trying to please all the parties, and probably come to some unworkable compromise that pleased nobody!

However, if the minister can hold together the analytical clarity of (1) – but grounded in practical common sense; the anger and motivation of (2) – but free from ego-investment; and the compassion of (3) – but balanced with social critique and understanding, he will have the kind of mindful energy that sets people free.

Conclusion

This chapter focused on the minister as a subversive liberator, who enables people to 'dance to another tune'. Following Dostoyevsky, the three temptations of Christ were seen as suggesting three temptations the minister needs to resist in order to be free. She needs to be free not to provide what is demanded; free not to be respectable in worldly terms, free not to protect holiness but let it spread contagiously, liberating people from their slavery to accusations; and free to be powerless, foolish, and creative in failure. Such freedoms are deeply vulnerable, yet powerfully subversive of the world order.

For reflection and discussion

1   What connections can you find in your own ministry with the analogy about teaching those who think they are chickens to fly like the eagles that God created them to be?

2   Which of the temptations in ministry, as outlined on page 154, can you recognize as something you have struggled or need to struggle to resist?

3   What struck you about the treatment of the Martha and Mary story on p. 155 or/and the Zacchaeus story on page 157?

4   Identify, if you can, one or two features of the life of a church with which you are familiar where the emphasis has been too much on 'policing the borders' to preserve its own holiness rather than spreading it contagiously.

5   When have you felt the need to speak the truth to power, no matter the consequences?

Conclusion: Mindful Integration

The eight chapters have explored eight 'ministries' and how they can be practised mindfully and reflectively. But mindful ministry requires not only that each ministry is practised mindfully, but that there is a mindfulness in the way they come together. There needs to be an integrity and wholeness both in the way the different ministries are exercised by people in the Church, and in the way the minister holds them together in his own ministry and his own person. This concluding chapter seeks to suggest how the various mindful ministries may come together in mindful ministry.

As has been pointed out at a number of points in this book, although the eight ministries have been differentiated so that they can be described and reflected on, they blend into and support one another. And, of course, they come together in the minister, in ways of which the minister needs to be mindful. This chapter suggests how the ministries work together in the central act of Christian worship and how, together, they serve the coming of the Kingdom adumbrated in the Beatitudes. It concludes with a summary, based on the Beatitudes, of each of the ministries, affirming how each contributes to the coming of the Kingdom in which, at last, the 'barnyard chickens' with whom we began, will each find their true identify in Christ.

The ministries in one another

There is a kind of organic progression in the order in which the book has described the ministries. The earlier ones have to do with roots, the things from which a church draws its life; the middle ones are more like shoots and leaves, which structure and sustain a church; and the later ones are like flowers, fruits and seeds, which pass on and disperse that life. Just as not all plants produce these things in the same proportion – some have shallow roots and big fruits, others the reverse – so the 'roots' and 'fruits' of each ministry will vary in proportion.

As already noted, the ministries are not separate, but flow into one another and help define each other. In the language of the Trinity they are 'perichoretic': look inside any ministry and you will see the others at work. One way to put this is that if we look at any ministry as a verb, the seven others are its qualifying adverbs. For example, if we take 'serving' as the verb, we can discern ways in which it is offered:

- **Representatively** – as representing the service of Christ.
- **Prayerfully** – as rooted in intercession and leading to thanksgiving.
- **Through teaching** – as nurture and care of the soul.
- **Overseeingly** – bearing in mind the effect on the whole Church.
- **Collaboratively** – in conjunction with other carers within and beyond the church community.
- **Evangelistically** – as a proclamation of the Kingdom in which wholeness is found.
- **Liberatingly** – as setting people free.

In the same kind of way, prayer can be offered representatively, through teaching and oversight, collaboratively, or in ways that are evangelistic or liberating. You may like to consider how each of the other six ministries are qualified in a similar way by all of the others. These qualifications can help in examining your own ministry. For example, in reflecting on a ministry of service, it is helpful to consider whether that service was offered mindfully in the ways described by the qualifiers: was my ministry of service carried out representatively, prayerfully, and so forth . . .

The ministries in the minister

We have suggested that the ordained minister is the one who holds all the ministries together in the unity of her person. But what does this mean? And how can it be achieved mindfully?

Among other things it requires awareness of the strengths and limitations of your own personality. This will mean, first, being aware of when you are playing 'at home' on the basis of your natural inclinations and gifts; and, second, when you need to play 'away' on the alien ground that is less comfortable, but where you can learn and develop new skills. Third, there are likely to be some aspects of ministry which will be better served by other church members who have the inclinations and skills needed, but may need to be empowered for certain tasks they can do better than a formally accredited minister.

We invite you to consider, of the eight ministries described in this book:

1 Which is the form of ministry that you feel corresponds best with your own natural skills, strengths and inclinations?

2 Which corresponds least – which do you find most difficult?

3 Which is the kind of ministry your congregation most values, or expects of you?

4 Which kind of ministry is most needed in your situation: not only among church members but more widely in your parish or area?

5 Note where the correspondences lie, and reflect on whether the differences matter, and if so, what might be done about them.

Some will find personality typing helpful here. Broadly speaking, the widely used Myers-Briggs Type Indicator (MBTI) may tell which ministry will accord with our natural bent and approach to the world, while the Enneagram may help us become aware of the ministry to which we are most strongly drawn, and which will feel closest to our self-understanding as ministers. These may or may not be the same.

There are summaries of the MBTI and the Enneagram in our *Study-guide to Theological Reflection* (2008, pp. 135–42) and a meditation using the Enneagram at www.holydust.org/Reflection/Enneagram.aspx. There is also, of course, a vast literature on both typologies, to which we need to add little here. Table 3 (p. 172) makes some suggestions about which MBTI and Enneagram types correspond to which ministries. But the table represents, not the conclusion of research, but a hypothesis for you to consider in your own case, if you feel so drawn.

Self-understanding and mindfulness in ministry are not dependent on the use of these tools, which for some are very helpful, and for others are anathema. More important are the practices of mindfulness outlined in the Introduction, which help to increase awareness of the Holy One who is Christ himself, so that we, and those to whom we minister, may be drawn to him and the fullness of life which he offers all humankind. Such mindfulness, together with appropriate self-care (see p. xxii), will also help us to recognize the strings – from inside us and from external demands – which can so easily pull us in the wrong direction. This, in time, makes it possible to shape an integrated ministry that uses strengths and weaknesses in a mindful way, so that they no longer 'use us'.

Table 3: Suggested Links of Ministry to Personality

Ministry	Core Activity	Focus	MBTI Type	Enneagram Ideal
1 Apostle	Representing	Faithfully representing Christ to world and world to God in Christ	Introvert Sensing ISFJ ISTJ	6 Loyalist
2 Holy One	Praying	Life focused on God – living on the borders of the Holy	Introvert Intuiting INFJ INTJ	1 Perfectionist
3 Pastor	Serving	Serving people's needs, seeking out the lost, healing people in spirit	Introvert Feeling ISFP INFP	2 Helper
4 Teacher	Nurture	Teaching, nurturing faith, guiding to Christ and birthing Christ in people	Introvert Thinking ISTP INTP	5 Sage
5 Leader	Overviewing	Managing the whole and ensuring that the Church is advancing God's Kingdom	Extravert Thinking ESTJ ENTJ	3 Achiever
6 Go-betweeen	Collaboration, communication and conviviality	Befriending, ensuring transparent communication, enabling collaboration	Extravert Feeling ESFJ ENFJ	9 Peacemaker
7 Herald	Evangelizing	Proclaiming the Good News, eliciting response in experience, reason, imagination and will	Extravert Sensing ESFP ESTP	8 Warrior
8 Liberator	Subverting	Celebrating freedom of the Kingdom in word, life and art, subverting convention	Extravert Intuiting ENFP ENTP	7 Dreamer or 4 Artist

The ministries in the Eucharist

It is above all in the central act of worship, the Eucharist, that we see all the ministries of all the priestly people of God playing together in concert. In particular parts of the Eucharist different ministries come to the fore, making the Eucharist a good focus for deepening mindfulness in the ministries. The following is a simplified suggestion.

- The **gathering**, when we confess our sins, involves the **ministry of the guide** leading us towards the place of refreshment, via the ministry of absolution.
- In the readings and creed, people are apostles **representing** the inheritance of scripture to the world.
- In the **sermon** the preacher is **herald**, proclaiming the Good News to the world today.
- In the **prayers** people are **serving** the world and bringing it to God for healing and wholeness.
- In the **peace and offertory** they are 'holy ones' consecrating themselves as temples of the presence of Christ.
- In the **eucharistic prayer** and the **breaking of bread**, as well as representing Christ they are **stewards administering** his gifts.
- In the **Holy Communion**, people are bound together in **conviviality** within Christ the true vine.
- In the **blessing** and **dismissal** people are **liberated** and **empowered** to manifest the Kingdom in the world.

That said, the Eucharist is not like a recipe in which we do first this, and then that, and we end up making something good. To return to an analogy we have used a lot, it is more like a symphony in which, though now one instrument and now another comes to the fore, all the instruments are playing together. Throughout the Eucharist we represent Christ and pray. The whole liturgy is an act of service, and contains power to heal and guide and teach. Throughout it the people are stewards of the mysteries of God, held together in conviviality and *koinōnia*. And the whole thing is a proclamation of the death of Christ until he comes (1 Corinthian 11.26), empowering and liberating people in their mission to the world as a whole; to which we now finally turn.

The ministries in the Kingdom of God

Read **Isaiah 11 1–10**: the Messianic Kingdom.

Reflect on this image of the Kingdom.

Who leads it?

What does not happen in it?

Who and what are included in it?

Here we see a kingdom of lions and lambs at peace. Elsewhere we learn that the whole earth is full of God's *kabod* (Isaiah 6.3) – a word which means weight and repute and glory. The world is heavy with God like a pregnant mother. Psalms 19 and 148 are among many that describe the whole creation as giving glory to God. The beings that God created could be likened to the strokes of paint created by an artist: each reveals its creator, not by being itself alone, but by being part of the great whole.

Following clues in the Pauline writings, early theologians like Origen and Gregory of Nyssa speak of the *apokatastasis*, the restoration of all creation to its pristine state through Christ. The word (which is incidentally the theme of a beautifully piercing song by John Taverner) literally means up–down–standing, and suggests the turning of an upside-down world the right way up again. It may be linked with Irenaeus' concept of recapitulation, based on passages like Colossians 1.15–20, whereby Christ retraces the steps of Adam, putting right every step he took wrong, so that the creation is put to rights, reconciled to Christ as its guiding head. The image suggested by these understandings is that of a painting we see upside down, which looks to us like a meaningless jumble of paint. Then Christ the artist takes the painting, sets it the right way up, and we see a wonderful order, a veritable symphony of paint in which each part contributes to the glory of the whole, forming, moreover, a self-portrait of the artist himself.

We live in a human world in which parts of the cosmic painting compete to organize the painting around themselves. Plans are made, bits are moved, in a vain effort to organize everything around some powerful person or ideology. But Christ moves nothing; he leaves the painting as it is, exercising the power of no power. Instead he shifts the perspective so that we see a whole which transcends the parts, and cannot be idolatrously centred on any part. Rather, all the parts make their contribution equally within the whole. In that perspective, we begin to see that we are not just barnyard chickens; rather, we are borne aloft on the eagle-wings of the divine glory (cf Exodus 19.4; Deuteronomy 32.11; Isaiah 40.31).

Many modern narratives (Nietzschean, Darwinian . . .) tell us that the struggle for power between parts is all there is: the survival of the fittest, the triumph of some master-race or master-ideology. Such stories exhort us to fight our own corner, as a people, or as a species, because things can never be otherwise. But the ministries we have considered are not about conforming us to a master-narrative called Christianity, which is superior to all others. They are about shifting people's perspectives away from all such seductive narratives, even those that have been put together in Christ's name. They are about standing the upside-down power-crazed hope-less world the right way up again, so that in its pristine glory it will show forth God; and people 'justified' (aligned rightly) in the Christlike whole.

A beatitudinal summary

The Beatitudes summarize the values with which Jesus turned the world the right way up. In the simpler Lucan version (6.20–26) they are starkly counter-cultural: poverty, hunger, sorrow and persecution are blessed, while what the world values – riches, fulfilment, happiness, reputation – are the subject of Jesus *ouai*, watch out! The more familiar version in Matthew (5.1–12) softens the blow a little, but remains the blueprint of a Kingdom where things are done quite differently.

We believe that the ministries described in this book all serve this counter-cultural Kingdom of God. Ultimately that is the most important thing the minister needs to be mindful of and reflective about.

So we conclude the book by summarizing the ministries in a series of eight 'beatitudes'. Each takes up key ideas of the chapters, and concludes with a suggestion of how this particular ministry blesses the whole Church.

> Blessed are you, **faithful apostle,** flawed icon of Christ and critical friend of tradition; through you will arise true glorification of God.

> Blessed are you, **prayerful one,** who turns aside to see the fire, and lives where heaven meets earth: through you, people will hear the silent music of God.

> Blessed are you, **discerning servant,** good shepherd and healer of souls: through your companionship in joy and sorrow the love of God will flower.

Blessed are you, **wise teacher**, mining old truth and giving birth to new; through your guidance jaded lives become glorious journeys into God.

Blessed are you, **skilful leader**, steward of mysteries, making the visions real: you draw our diverse work into the creative plan of Wisdom.

Blessed are you, the **Spirit's go-between**, enabling life, talk and work to happen among us: through you our synergy takes on the energy of God.

Blessed are you, **evangelist**, honest witness, debater, storyteller, wordsmith; through you experience, reason, imagination and passion all herald the Good News.

Blessed are you, **liberating subversive**, refusing to deliver on demand; contagious in goodness, scandalous creative fool: you teach us to dance to Freedom's tune.

Bibliography

John Adair (1997), *Leadership Skills*, London: Institute of Personnel Development.

——(2001), *The Leadership of Jesus and its Legacy Today*, Norwich: Canterbury Press.

James Alison (1998), *The Joy of Being Wrong: Original Sin through Easter Eyes*, New York: Crossroad.

——(2001), *Faith beyond Resentment*, London: Darton, Longman and Todd.

Peter Allan et al. (1993), *The Fire and the Clay: The Priest in Today's Church*, London: SPCK.

Anglican–Roman Catholic International Commission ('ARCIC') (1978), *The Three Agreed Statements: Eucharistic Doctrine, Ministry and Ordination, Authority in the Church*, London: SPCK/CTS.

Archbishops' Council of the Church of England (2011), *Criteria for Selection for the Ordained Ministry in the Church of England*, London: Ministry Division of Archbishops' Council.

Stephen Batchelor (1998) *Buddhism without Beliefs: A Contemporary Guide to Awakening*, London: Bloomsbury.

Tim Beaudoin (1998), *Virtual Faith: The Irreverent Spiritual Quest of Generation X*, New York: Jossey-Bass.

David Benner (1998), *Care of Souls: Revisioning Christian Nurture and Counsel*, Carlisle: Paternoster.

Jerome W. Berryman (2002), *Godly Play Vol. 1: How to Lead Godly Play Lessons*, Living the Good News.

Alan Billings (2010), *Making God Possible: The Task of Ordained Ministry Present and Future*, London: SPCK.

Wendy Billington (2010), *Growing a Caring Church: Practical Guidelines for Pastoral Care*, Abingdon: Bible Reading Fellowship.

Chris Blakeley and Sue Howard (2010), *The Inner Life of a Christian Leader*, Cambridge: Grove Books.

Leonardo Boff (1986), *Ecclesiogenesis: The Base Communities Reinvent the Church*, Maryknoll, NY: Orbis.

David Bosch (1992), *Transforming Mission: Paradigm Shifts in Theology of Mission*, New York: Orbis.

Rita A. Brink OSB (1996), *Playing and Praying with Children: Guided Meditations for Children*, New York: Paulist Press.

Rosalind Brown and Christopher Cocksworth (2002), *Being a Priest Today: Exploring Priestly Identity*, Norwich: Canterbury Press.

Walter Brueggemann (1993), *Biblical Perspectives on Evangelism*, Nashville: Abingdon.

Helen Cameron (2010), *Resourcing Mission: Practical Theology for Changing Churches*, London: SCM.

Helen Cameron, Deborah Bhatti, Catherine Duce, James Sweeney and Clare Watkins (2010), *Talking about God in Practice: Theological Action Research and Practical Theology*, London: SCM.

Alistair Campbell (1981), *Rediscovering Pastoral Care*, London: Darton, Longman and Todd.

Jackson W. Carroll (2006), *God's Potters: Pastoral Leadership and the Shaping of Congregations*, Grand Rapids, MI and Cambridge: Eerdmans.

Elias Chacour with M. E. Jensen (2001), *We Belong to the Land*, South Bend, IN: University of Notre Dame Press.

Paul Chilcote and Laceye Warner (eds) (2008), *The Study of Evangelism: Exploring a Missional Practice of the Church*, Grand Rapids: Eerdmans.

Church House Publishing (1995), *Stages on the Way: Towards an Integrated Approach to Christian Initiation*, London: Church House.

Stephen Cottrell (2006), *From the Abundance of the Heart: Catholic Evangelism for All Christians*, London: Darton, Longman and Todd.

——(2008), *Hit the Ground Kneeling: Seeing Leadership Differently*, London: Church House Publishing.

L. William Countryman (1999), *Living on the Border of the Holy: Renewing the Priesthood of All*, Harrisburg, PA: Morehouse.

John Cowan (2004), *Taking Jesus Seriously: Buddhist Meditation for Christians*, Collegeville: Liturgical Press.

Steven Croft (1999), *Ministry in Three Dimensions: Ordination and Leadership in the Local Church*, London: Darton, Longman and Todd.

——(2005), *Evangelism in a Spiritual Age: Communicating Faith in a Changing Culture*, London: Church House Publishing.

Andrew Davison and Alison Milbank (2010), *For the Parish: A Critique of Fresh Expressions*, London: SCM.

Anthony de Mello (1982), *The Song of the Bird*, Gujarat, India: Gujarat Sahitya Prakash, Anand.

Carrie Doehring (2006), *The Practice of Pastoral Care: A Postmodern Approach*, Louisville, KY: Westminster John Knox Press.

Vincent Donovan (2003), *Christianity Rediscovered: An Epistle from the Masai*, New York: Orbis.

Michael Dwinell (1993), *Being Priest to One Another*, Ligouri, MO: Triumph Books.

James Fowler (1987), *Faith Development and Pastoral Care*, Philadelphia: Fortress.

Monica Furlong (1965), *With Love to the Church*, London: Hodder and Stoughton.

Graham Greene (1991), *The Power and the Glory*, Harmondsworth: Penguin.

Robert K. Greenleaf (2003), *Servant Leader Within: A Transformative Path*, Mahwah, NJ: Paulist Press.

Robin Greenwood (1994), *Transforming Priesthood: A New Theology of Mission and Ministry*, London: SPCK.

—(2002), *Transforming Church: Liberating Structures for Ministry*, London: SPCK.

—(2009), *Parish Priests for the Sake of the Kingdom*, London: SPCK.

Malcolm Grundy (2007), *What's New in Church Leadership: Creative Responses to the Changing Pattern of Church Life*, Norwich: Canterbury Press.

Margaret Guenther (1992), *Holy Listening: The Art of Spiritual Direction*, London: Darton, Longman and Todd.

George Guiver (1990), *Faith in Momentum*, London: SPCK.

—(2001), *Priests in a People's Church*, London: SPCK.

Anthony Hanson (1961, 1975), *The Pioneer Ministry*, London: SPCK.

Stanley Hauerwas (1989), *Resident Aliens: A Provocative Christian Assessment of Culture and Ministry for People who Know that Something is Wrong*, Nashville: Abingdon.

David Hay and Rebecca Nye (2006), *The Spirit of the Child*, London: Jessica Kingsley.

David Heywood (2011), *Reimagining Ministry*, London: SCM.

Seward Hiltner (1959), *The Christian Pastor*, New York: Abingdon.

John Holdsworth (2003), *Communication and the Gospel*, London: Darton, Longman and Todd.

Steve Hollinghurst (2010), *Mission-shaped Evangelism: The Gospel in Contemporary Culture*, Norwich: Canterbury Press.

Urban T. Holmes (1978), *The Priest in Community: Exploring the Roots of Ministry*, New York: Seabury Press.

Rodney J. Hunter (ed.) (1990), *Dictionary of Pastoral Care and Counseling*, Nashville: Abingdon.

Eric James (ed.) (1979), *Stewards of the Mysteries of God*, London: Darton, Longman and Todd.

E. Kadloubovsky and G. E. H. Palmer (eds) (1954), *Early Fathers from the Philokalia*, London: Faber.

Martin Laird (2011), *Sunlit Absence: Silence, Awareness and Contemplation*, New York: Oxford University Press.

N. Lash and J. Rhymer (eds) (1970), *The Christian Priesthood*, London: Darton, Longman and Todd and Denton, NJ: Dimension Books.

Kenneth Leech (2001), *Soul Friend: Spiritual Direction in the Modern World*, Harrisburg, PA: Morehouse.

Kate Lichfield (2006), *Tend My Flock: Sustaining Good Practice in Pastoral Care*, Norwich: Canterbury Press.

Philip Luscombe and Esther Shreeve (eds) (2002), *What is a Minister?*, Peterborough: Epworth.

Ashley Martin and Andy Kelso (1986), *Scene One*, Eastbourne: Kingsway.

Ian McEwan (2002), *Atonement*, London: Vintage.

R. C. Moberly (1897, 1969), *Ministerial Priesthood*, London: SPCK.

Christopher Moody (1992), *Eccentric Ministry: Pastoral Care and Leadership in the Parish*, London: Darton, Longman and Todd.

J. H. L. Morrell (1958), *The Heart of a Priest*, London: SPCK.

Sally Nash, Jo Pimlott and Paul Nash (2008), *Skills for Collaborative Ministry*, London: SPCK.

John Nelson (ed.) (2008), *How to Become a Creative Church Leader: A MODEM Handbook*, Norwich: Canterbury Press.

Christie Cozad Neuger (ed.) (1996), *The Arts of Ministry: Feminist-Womanist Approaches*, Louisville: Westminster John Knox Press.

Patricia O'Connell Killen and John de Beer (1994), *The Art of Theological Reflection*, New York: Crossroad.

Rudolf Otto (1958), *The Idea of the Holy*, Oxford and New York: Oxford University Press.

Stephen Pattison (2000), *A Critique of Pastoral Care*, Third Edition, London: SCM.

Neil Pembroke (2010), *Pastoral Care in Worship: Liturgy and Psychology in Dialogue*, London: T&T Clark.

Eugene Peterson (1993), *The Contemplative Pastor: Returning to the Art of Spiritual Direction*, Grand Rapids: Eerdmans.

Stephen Pickard (2009), *Theological Foundations for Collaborative Ministry*, Farnham: Ashgate.

Sue Pickering (2008), *Spiritual Direction: A Practical Introduction*, Norwich: Canterbury Press.

John Pridmore (2008), *The Inner City of God: The Diary of an East End Parson*, Norwich: Canterbury Press.

John Pritchard (2007), *The Life and Work of a Priest*, London: SPCK.

Michael Ramsey (1936), *The Gospel and the Catholic Church*, London: SPCK.

——(2008), *The Christian Priest Today*, London: SPCK.

Alastair Redfern (1999), *Ministry and Priesthood*, London: Darton, Longman and Todd.

Ann Richards (2009), *Through the Eyes of a Child: New Insights in Theology from a Child's Perspective*, London: Church House Publishing.

David Robertson (2007), *Collaborative Ministry*, Oxford: Bible Reading Fellowship.

John Robinson et al. (eds) (1963), *Layman's Church*, London: Lutterworth Press.

Alan Roxburgh, M. Scott Boren and Mark Priddy (2009), *Introducing the Missional Church: What It Is, Why It Matters, How to Become One*, Grand Rapids: Baker Books.

Michael Sadgrove (2008), *Wisdom and Ministry: The Call to Leadership*, London: SPCK.

Sara Savage and Eolene Boyd-Macmillan (2007), *The Human Face of Church: A Social Psychology and Pastoral Theology Resource for Pioneer and Traditional Ministry*, Norwich: Canterbury Press.

Edward Schillebeeckx (1963), *Christ the Sacrament of Encounter with God*, London: Sheed and Ward.

Friedrich Schleiermacher (1996), *On Religion: Speeches to Its Cultured Despisers*, Cambridge: Cambridge University Press.

Ray Simpson (1999), *Soul Friendship: Celtic Insights into Spiritual Mentoring*, London: Hodder and Stoughton.

Nicola Slee (1990), 'Parables and Women's Experience', in Ann Loades (ed.) (1990), *Feminist Theology: A Reader*, Louisville: Westminster/John Knox Press.

James Bryan Smith and Lynda Graybeal (1999), *Spiritual Formation Workbook*, London: Fount.

Donald P. Smith (1996), *Empowering Ministry: Ways to Grow in Effectiveness*, Louisville: Westminster John Knox Press.

John V. Taylor (2004), *The Go-between God: Holy Spirit and the Christian Mission*, London: SCM.

R. S. Thomas (1995), *Collected Poems 1945–1990*, London: Phoenix.

Judith Thompson with Stephen Pattison and Ross Thompson (2008), *Studyguide to Theological Reflection*, London: SCM.

Ross Thompson (2009), *Spirituality in Season: Growing through the Christian Year*, Norwich: Canterbury Press.

——(2010), *Buddhist Christianity: A Passionate Openness*, Winchester: O Books.

——(2011), *Wounded Wisdom: A Buddhist and Christian Response to Evil, Hurt and Harm*, Winchester: O Books.

Dave Tomlinson (2008), *Re-Enchanting Christianity: Faith in an Emerging Culture*, Norwich: Canterbury Press.

Mark Townsend (2007), *The Gospel of Falling Down: The Beauty of Failure in an Age of Success*, Winchester and Washington: O Books.

Mary Travis (2008), 'Supporting Clergy in Postmodern Ministry', *Practical Theology* 1.1, pp. 95–130.

Carla van Raay (2006), *God's Callgirl*, London: Ebury.

W. H. Vanstone (1977; revised edn. 2007), *Love's Endeavour, Love's Expense*, London: Darton, Longman and Todd.

——(1982), *The Stature of Waiting*, London: Darton, Longman and Todd.

Simon Walker (2010), *The Undefended Leader* (Trilogy), Carlisle: Piquant.

Roger Walton (2009), *The Reflective Disciple*, London: Epworth.

Robin Ward (2011), *On Christian Priesthood*, London: Continuum.

Robert Warren (1995), *Building Missionary Congregations*, London: Church House Publishing.

Simone Weil (1959), *Waiting on God*, London: Fontana.

Enid Welsford (1935, 1970), *The Fool: His Social and Literary History*, London: Faber.

James Whitehead and Evelyn Eaton Whitehead (1995), *Method in Ministry: Theological Reflection and Christian Ministry*, Oxford: Sheed and Ward.

Catherine Widdicombe (1994, 2000), *Meetings that Work: A Practical Guide to Teamworking in Groups*, Cambridge: Lutterworth Press.

Elie Wiesel (1995), *The Trial of God*, New York: Schocken.

Rowan Williams (1979), *The Wound of Knowledge*, London: Darton, Longman and Todd.

——(1994), *Open to Judgement*, London: Darton, Longman and Todd.

——(2000), *Lost Icons*, London and New York: Continuum.

——(2003), *Silence and Honey Cakes: Wisdom of the Desert*, Oxford: Lion Hudson.

Walter Wink (1986), *Unmasking the Powers: The Invisible Forces that Determine Human Existence*, Philadelphia: Fortress Press.

——(2000), *The Powers that Be: Theology for a New Millennium*, New York: Bantam Doubleday Dell.

——(2001), *The Human Being: Jesus and the Enigma of the Son of the Man*, Minneapolis: Augsburg Fortress.

World Council of Churches (1982), *Baptism, Eucharist and Ministry*, Geneva: World Council of Churches.

Index of Biblical References

Index